Teaching Passionately

Related Titles of Interest

Current Issues and Trends in Education
Jenny Aldridge and Renitta Goldman
ISBN: 0-321-07978-7

*Impact Teaching: Ideas and Strategies for Teachers
to Maximize Student Learning*
Richard Howell Allen
ISBN: 0-205-33414-8

The Way Schools Work: A Sociological Analysis of Education, **Third Edition**
Kathleen Bennett de Marrais and Margaret LeCompte
ISBN: 0-8013-1956-0

New Teacher's Performance-Based Guide to Culturally Diverse Classrooms
Timothy R. Blair
ISBN: 0-205-38206-1

*How to Develop a Professional Portfolio: A Manual
for Teachers,* **Third Edition**
Dorothy M. Campbell, Pamela Bondi Cignetti, Beverly J. Melenyzer,
Diane H. Nettles, and Richard M. Wyman
ISBN: 0-205-39341-1

*Researching Teaching: Exploring Teacher Development
through Reflexive Inquiry*
Ardra L. Cole and J. Gary Knowles
ISBN 0-205-18076-0

Developing a Professional Teaching Portfolio: A Guide for Educators
Patricia Costantino and Marie De Lorenzo
ISBN: 0-205-32955-1

Moral Education: A Teacher-Centered Approach
Joan F. Goodman and Howard Lesnick
ISBN: 0-321-09359-3

The Moral Stake in Education: Contested Premises and Practices
Joan F. Goodman and Howard Lesnick
ISBN: 0-321-02340-4

Philosophical and Ideological Voices in Education
Gerald L. Gutek
ISBN: 0-205-36018-1

Historical Documents in American Education
Tony W. Johnson and Ronald Reed
ISBN: 0-801-33314-8

The Digital Teaching Portfolio Handbook: A How-To Guide for Educators
Clare R. Kilbane and Natalie B. Milman
ISBN: 0-205-34345-7

Your First Year of Teaching and Beyond, **Fourth Edition**
Ellen L. Kronowitz
ISBN: 0-205-38156-1

Life in Schools: An Introduction to Critical Pedagogy in the Foundations of Education, **Fourth Edition**
Peter McLaren
ISBN: 0-205-35118-2

Handbook for the Beginning Teacher
Courtney W. Moffatt and Thomas L. Moffatt
ISBN: 0-205-34372-4

How to Get a Teaching Job
Courtney W. Moffatt and Thomas L. Moffatt
ISBN: 0-205-29924-5

Teaching in America, **Third Edition**
George S. Morrison
ISBN: 0-205-34470-4

Teaching and Schooling in America: Pre- and Post-September 11
Allan Ornstein
ISBN: 0-205-36711-9

Strategies for Successful Student Teaching: A Comprehensive Guide, **Second Edition**
Carol Marra Pelletier
ISBN: 0-205-39682-8

Teaching, Learning, and Schooling: A 21st Century Perspective
Eugene F. Provenzo, Jr.
ISBN: 0-205-28970-3

Philosophical Documents in Education, **Second Edition**
Ronald Reed and Tony W. Johnson
ISBN: 0-8013-3316-4

Ask the Teacher: A Practitioner's Guide to Teaching and Learning in the Diverse Classroom
Mark Ryan
ISBN: 0-205-37076-4

American Schools, American Teachers: Issues and Perspectives
David Schuman
ISBN: 0-321-05399-0

Teaching Convictions: Critical Ethical Issues and Education
Patrick Slattery and Dana Rapp
ISBN: 0-321-05401-6

Teaching to the Standards of Effective Practice:
A Guide to Becoming a Successful Teacher
Robert Wandberg and John Rohwer
ISBN: 0-205-34407-0

Philosophic Conflicts in American Education, 1893–2000
Joseph Watras
ISBN: 0-205-38621-0

For further information on these and other related titles, contact:

College Division
ALLYN AND BACON, INC.
75 Arlington Street, Suite 300
Boston, MA 02116
www.ablongman.com

Teaching Passionately

What's Love Got to Do with It?

Joan Wink

California State University, Stanislaus

Dawn Wink

PEARSON

Boston ■ New York ■ San Francisco
Mexico City ■ Montreal ■ Toronto ■ London ■ Madrid ■ Munich ■ Paris
Hong Kong ■ Singapore ■ Tokyo ■ Cape Town ■ Sydney

Executive Editor and Publisher: *Stephen D. Dragin*
Senior Editorial Assistant: *Barbara Strickland*
Marketing Manager: *Tara Whorf*
Editorial-Production Service: *Omegatype Typography, Inc.*
Manufacturing Buyer: *Andrew Turso*
Composition Buyer: *Linda Cox*
Cover Administrator: *Kristina Mose-Libon*
Electronic Composition: *Omegatype Typography, Inc.*

Library of Congress Cataloging-in-Publication Data

Wink, Joan.
    Teaching passionately : what's love got to do with it? / Joan Wink, Dawn Wink.
      p. cm.
    Includes bibliographical references and index.
    ISBN 0-205-38933-3
    1. Teaching. 2. Teachers—Professional relationships. 3. Critical pedagogy. I. Wink, Dawn. II. Title.

LB1025.3.W56 2004
371.012—dc22

                                        2003062343

Printed in the United States of America

10 9 8 7 6 5 4 3 2 1   08 07 06 05 04 03

To Dean, from the two women who love you most.

CONTENTS

LIST OF FIGURES

PREFACE

What's love got to do with it? The purpose of this book is to provide clear, clean, and concise pictures of passionate pedagogy in a broad range of contexts and to lead the readers to reflect on their own personal pedagogy. Diverse examples of pedagogy in action will be taken from multiple contexts.

The focus will be on our personal and professional principles and their inherent links to pedagogy, policy, and politics. Discussions will be grounded in the belief that each person has principles, beliefs, and assumptions that inform actions. These principles are often unexamined. Our goal is to challenge the readers to reflect on their own personal beliefs and how those beliefs can be turned into passionate pedagogy. Much has been written about the place of love and passion in life. We will extend that to the place of love and passion in teaching and learning.

Our Readers

This book is written specifically for preservice teachers who are learning to teach, for inservice teachers who are discovering that there is much to be learned while teaching, and for librarians who link us all with literacy. We envision this book as a supplementary text in a broad range of teacher education classes, but particularly for foundations, social foundations, and curriculum and instruction classes.

In addition, we hope this book will find its way to the coffee tables in the homes of teachers' families and friends. Life teaches us lessons that can be applied in schools, and dialectically speaking, schools teach us lessons that can be applied in life. We will show that passion has the power to link the knowledge of schools and the knowledge of life.

We invite all to the table for this discussion. *Teaching Passionately* will appeal to parents, taxpayers, voters, policy makers, and educators. Those who share our passion for a critical and caring pedagogy in a pluralistic setting will be our readers.

The Organization of the Book

The organization of this book reflects some of our own pedagogical passions. The first, introductory, chapter is followed by eight chapters, each of which could stand alone for a quiet read. However, our goal is also to link each chapter to the theme of the book.

Chapter 1, Teaching Passionately—The Spiral of Literacy, links passionate pedagogy to living and learning.

Chapter 2, Teaching Passionately—Learning, Living, and Loving, provides a glimpse into the past, present, and future pedagogical perspectives of the authors.

Chapter 3, Teaching Passionately—Theoretically, is a wide lens looking at the last century of educational thought from various perspectives.

Chapter 4, Teaching Passionately—Collaboratively, reveals the advantages of collaboration, whether it be in rural or urban education.

Chapter 5, Teaching Passionately—Parentally, paints pictures of parents and their powerful place in pedagogy.

Chapter 6, Teaching Passionately—Bilingually, reflects our belief that being bilingual/multilingual is not bad; actually, it is very good.

Chapter 7, Teaching Passionately—Spiritually, expands our pedagogical thinking even more. Yes, we will do it with passion. This is not a chapter about the separation of church and state; rather, this is a chapter about a variety of ethnic, cultural, and spiritual traditions and how they affect or have the power to affect teaching and learning.

Chapter 8, Teaching Passionately—Politically, continues to take us even farther from what we might have traditionally learned in teacher preparation programs.

Chapter 9, Teaching Passionately with Action, draws on aspects of all previous pedagogies and invites readers to create their own plan for practical passion.

Distinguishing Features

The first chapter and each of the remaining chapters are divided into patterns of discussion. The same headings are repeated in each chapter. We encourage the readers to use these predictable headings as cognitive coat hooks. Use them to link the topics discussed across or between chapters.

The Voice of Schools is the first section of each chapter. This reflects what we have come to think of as mainstream knowledge of schools. Although this is a conventional approach to assumed knowledge that teachers need, we tell the stories from our own perspectives.

The Voice of Life follows. This reflects what we have come to think of as mainstream knowledge of life, which can be used to enhance teaching and learning within schools and the community.

Praxis: Let the Magic Begin is a section with activities and methods.

The Literacy Link reflects our passion for reading. Whether you are a pre-K teacher, a high school math teacher, or an assistant professor struggling for tenure, we are all linked through literacy.

What Can Be Learned from This? links each chapter to a broader perspective on learning, living, and loving.

Line drawings/metaphors provide an opportunity to rest, reflect, and reason. Metaphors and visual graphics help us make meaning *from* a different perspective and *of* a differing perspective. The prevailing metaphor used throughout is a spiral.

Acknowledgments

It is often said that writing is a solitary process, and often it is; however, many contributed to the creation of this book.

To Denise, invaluable techno-goddess, whose warmth, humor, and wisdom are a part of every page.

To Tove Skutnabb-Kangas, Alma Flor Ada, Steve Krashen, and Jim Cummins, whose lives and work continue to inform and inspire us.

To the many teachers, students, colleagues, and friends, whose companionship and courage motivate us.

To Chris Kerfoot, Le Putney, Pat Graham, Susan Sandretto, Fay Shin, Jennifer Wolfe, Sarah Doyle, Sheryl Luttringer, Pamela Keyes, and colleagues at Monte Vista Montessori school, whose wise thoughts regarding the text and references are an integral part of this book.

To our virtual friends and colleagues, wherever you may be, we thank you for reading, writing, thinking, and sharing every day.

To Mari Gutierrez, Dee Hawksworth-Lutzow, and Carrie Diehl, whose assistance shaped the annotated bibliography. To the Grad Group for your support and love.

To the Allyn and Bacon reviewers—Lois M. Christensen, University of Alabama at Birmingham, and Karen L. Graves, Denison University—whose astute words enlightened this book for the better.

To Steve Dragin, our speedy and spunky editor, whose support never flagged throughout the writing of this book and an errant friendly e-mail.

To our family for their love and laughter. It takes a ranch.

Teaching Passionately

1 Teaching Passionately— The Spiral of Literacy

What matters is passion.
HILLMAN, 1996, p. 160

In this book we will talk about love, learning, and language. We will ask you to think about what you love, and we will ask you to think of ways that you could use that passion to enrich teaching and learning. We will ask you to ponder your own pedagogy.

What's love got to do with it? As we seek to find answers to this central question, we will use visuals to expand our thinking. We have chosen a spiral to capture the idea that at any one time, our understandings are similar to a dot on a continuum of professional growth. The purpose of the spiral is twofold. First, a spiral provides something solid to grasp, as we reflect; and, second, the spiral demonstrates the continuum of learning and developing. For example, think of literacy: How did you learn to read?

Joan asked herself this question and captured a few of the highlights of development on her own continuum of learning to read (see Figure 1.1).

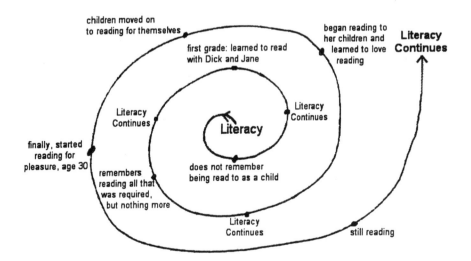

FIGURE 1.1 Joan's Spiral of Literacy

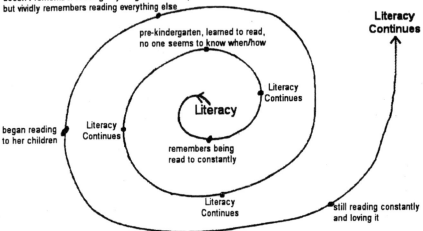

FIGURE 1.2   **Dawn's Spiral of Literacy**

"But, Mom, that's not right," said Dawn when she saw Joan's spiral of literacy development. Dawn quickly grabbed a pen and drew her own spiral of literacy development (see Figure 1.2).

Joan and Dawn's spirals of literacy development are each unique. We learn to read in our own way, just as we each develop and learn in our distinctive way. Drawing these literacy spirals made Joan and Dawn reflect more on their own literacy. These stories tell much about the perspectives of authors and where this book will take the readers.

How I Learned to Read: Joan Reflects

I learned to read by way of phonics in the first grade. First, I learned the individual letters and their sounds. From letters and sounds, I moved to individual words, from words to sentences, to paragraphs, to pages, to stories. I learned to read by building up the parts, bottom to top. Reading specialists would say I was a parts-to-whole reader. Some would say that phonics gets the credit. I slowly and carefully put the puzzle together piece by piece. In school I read every assignment, every chapter, every set of comprehension questions at the end of chapters, every spelling list, and every grammar assignment. I read everything I was told to read; I got good grades and graduated at the top of my high school class. One problem: I hated to read. I read only the exact number of pages assigned; I never took a book home to read for pleasure. I went to college and continued the same pattern. I spent every free moment in the library, got good grades, graduated with honors in literature, and yet I still hated to read.

When my children were babies, I started to read to them. The baby books said I should, so I did. With our first child, Dawn, something started to change: I loved the big black-and-white checkered book *The Real Mother Goose.* I thought *Winnie the Pooh* had been written just for me. By the time we got to *Charlotte's Web,* I was hooked on books. I used to secretly read *The Secret Garden* even when Dawn was asleep. With our son, Bo, I broadened my literary base. I probably have read *The Three Little Pigs* several thousand times, and I still huff and puff with vigor. *Pecos Bill* was the highlight of Bo's preschool years at home. From there he moved on to BMX magazines, and we both became authorities on racing bikes. After BMX magazines, he moved on to motorcycle books. From there, he jumped right into Stephen King and left me far in the dust. It was at this point in my life that I had to find my own books to read. I was probably about 30 years old.

Dawn and Bo learned to read the opposite way that I did. Reading specialists would say that they were whole-to-part readers. They looked at the picture of the whole puzzle first and then put the pieces together. Do they love to read? Yes. Do they read for pleasure? Yes.

When I first started to notice all of this, it seemed like a contradiction. How could my kids possibly learn to read if they didn't do the same thing I had done? Didn't I need to teach them the sounds, the letters, the words first? However, it was clear to me that they were not interested in the *parts.* They wanted the *whole* story again and again and again. Since that time, I have been very interested in the various ways that children learn to read and read to learn. This is what triggered my interest in holistic and critical teaching and learning. It seems that many kids who were read to as little children learn to read and love to read. Homes with books and ideas and love seem to produce kids who love to read (Wink, 2000).

Now, Dawn's story continues where Joan's ended, as Dawn reflects back on her own experiences from her own perspective.

How I Learned to Read: Dawn Reflects

I don't remember reading too much in school. I'm sure I did, but what I do remember is every *Nancy Drew,* the *Black Stallion* series, the *Chronicles of Narnia,* and the *Wizard of Oz* series. I don't ever remember a time that reading has not been central in my life.

In kindergarten I came home crying because the librarian said I couldn't check out *The Secret Garden* because it was too hard for kindergarteners. This same librarian had a rule that you could only check out one book at a time. So, one day I checked out my one book and shoved three others that I wanted to read inside my T-shirt and headed for the door. Of course, I was discovered. I probably weighed 50 pounds at the time and had 15 pounds of books under my little shirt. "Dawn, you are stealing books!" I still remember this large, buxom librarian bearing down on me. It bewildered me that she thought I was stealing. How could she not know that I would just read them and bring them back? One book for the next week would never do. She did not know this and gave me detention for a week, which meant Mom and Bo had detention as well, as we lived an hour out of town and they had to wait for me to drive home (Wink, 2000).

This centrality of reading born from Mom reading to me from an early age continues to this day in my own house. My three young children and I spend hours a day reading aloud together. At the moment, we have read the entire *Harry Potter* series aloud two times. While none of my children are reading independently yet, being read to is far and away their favorite activity. Mom's legacy of reading continues.

Stop reading right now. Take a bit of time to reflect on your own literacy development and to capture it on the following spiral (Figure 1.3).

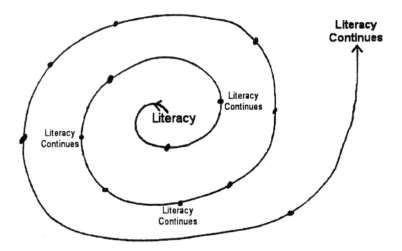

FIGURE 1.3   Your Spiral of Literacy

Throughout this book, we will ask you to reflect. Before going any further, please take a moment and capture your reflections in the space provided in Figure 1.4. What have you learned by taking the time to think about your own spiral of literacy?

Our literacy development, like our learning continuum, is unique for each of us. Our pedagogical path has many twists and turns along its surprising route. Our goal is to return passion, love, and joy to our teaching and learning wherever the path has led or may lead us. Please think of the spiral of learning as you read and reflect on this book. The spiral can be used with students of any age as they ponder their own pedagogy.

A second visual we want you to think of as you read is adapted from the cultural eye (Meeks & Austin, 2003), which is used to demonstrate the importance of perspective. We each have our own. When we saw the cultural eye, we immediately thought of the cultural, historical, political, spiritual, physical, emotional, and experiential background we each bring to any context. However, for us the most vital perspective, the spiritual perspective, is often left out of the dialogue about pedagogy. If you are Christian, Muslim, Jewish, Buddist, or agnostic, it matters. It matters in schools, too, although usually we do not acknowledge it. This is to ignore a core component of life. "Authentic spiritual practice is not a naive experience. It does not lead us away from reality but allows us to accept the real more fully" (hooks, 1994, pp. 119–120). In this book we will also ask you to think about your

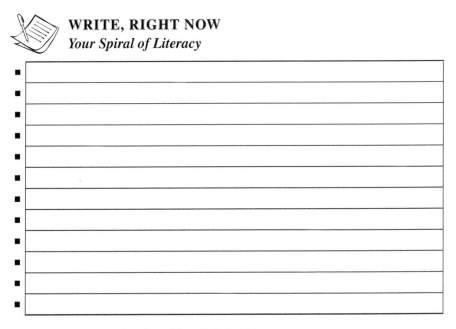

FIGURE 1.4   **Write, Right Now: Your Spiral of Literacy**

FIGURE 1.5   The Spiritual Eye

spiritual perspective, which affects your total vision of all that is *real*. The *spiritual eye* is available for you to grasp onto while you grapple with your own spirituality through this book (Figure 1.5).

The spiral of passionate pedagogy and the spiritual eye have much to contribute as we each work toward self and social transformation.

2 Teaching Passionately— Learning, Living, and Loving

Education is radically about love.

PAULO FREIRE

"What is your passion?" a graduate student asked on the first night of class. Silence fell upon the room. This spontaneous question triggered for us a rethinking of our own pedagogy. It is often said that inquiry leads to discovery—this was the case for us. This is a book of how reflection and transformation can lead to passionate pedagogy.

We reasoned that if the students in class were courageous enough to ask about passion on the first night of the graduate class; if Paulo Freire could speak to the primacy of love in learning; if Plato could take on love in learning in *The Symposium,* then we, too, could write honestly about our belief in the power of passion in pedagogy. A few years ago, no one could have told us that we would eventually write about love, passion, and joy in the context of teaching and learning. We did not learn this in undergraduate school, in our teacher preparation classes, or in graduate classes. Teaching and learning with students taught this to us; life taught this to us.

We come from a pedagogical tradition, which teaches us that we learn with our minds. We have always assumed that learning is a cognitive process, and only a cognitive process. However, who among us has never learned something with their hearts? In this book we will explore our traditional pedagogical assumptions and expand on them.

We are reminded of an experience about which a veteran teacher (Draper, 2001) tells. After teaching for 30 years, this instructor, Ms. Draper, was reduced to silence and awe by the following question from a 12-year-old.

"What is your joy?" she asked.

"What do you mean?" the instructor asked as she stalled for time to catch her breath.

"Just what I said. What is your joy?" the student asked again. Finally, Ms. Draper took a breath and answered her honestly.

"That's a powerful question you're asking, and one that can't be answered quickly or easily. I think philosophers have been trying to figure that one out for centuries. But, for me, I think I find my joy in the fact that I am blessed enough to live my dreams. I get to write, travel, and talk to students and teachers, and that is what makes me happy. That's what gives me joy" (Draper, 2001, pp. 77–78).

In this book, we will look to philosophers, we will look to teachers, and we will look to students as we attempt to bring joy, passion, and yes, even love, to teaching and learning.

What does the face of love look like in a classroom? It turns out that it is highly diverse. The face of love in a classroom can be a deep and abiding respect for people and for learning; it can demonstrate safety. It can radiate a freedom to think, to grow, to question. The face of love for learning can be quiet, thoughtful, and reflective. Love can also be lively and fun. Love in the classroom is as diverse and complex as the learners and their needs and the perspectives, experiences, and philosophies of the instructor. Love can connect the teacher and students and curriculum.

The climate for learning cannot be separated from a climate in which care, concern, and love are central.

By "love" I do not mean a mawkish or sentimental demonstration of concern for students. Rather, we are suggesting that love is at the core of good teaching because it is predicated on high standards, rigorous demands, and respect for students, their identities, and their families (Nieto, 1999, p. 100).

Love is the legacy that lasts. The love in learning that gives us hope is akin to the concept of Noddings's care, which is not necessarily about softness and sentimentality but rather is about a deep sense of commitment for the care of students (Noddings, 1995, pp. 675–676). Cummins (2001) was right: "Human relations are at the heart of schooling" (p. 1). In this book we will explore those human relations and the power we have to make them the best that they can be. We will seek to improve our understanding of those human connections and their relationship to teaching and learning.

> Good teachers possess a capacity for connectedness. They are able to weave a complex web of connections among themselves, their subjects, and their students so that students can learn to weave a world for themselves. The methods used by these weavers vary widely: lectures, Socratic dialogues, laboratory experiments, collaborative problem solving, creative chaos. The connections made by good teachers are held not in their methods but in their hearts—meaning *heart* in its ancient sense, as the place where intellect and emotion and spirit and will converge in the human self. (Palmer, 1998, p. 11)

In the following examples, which are actual stories from classroom teachers, we see the lasting effect a teacher makes by creating positive human connections in the classroom. In this following example, Pam talks about a professor who affected her.

> The most profound experience I had with love in a classroom was when I was a student in a teacher education methods class. Mr. Spencer was a quiet teacher who respected and accepted each of us. He created a caring classroom, and we connected. We laughed. We cried. We learned. We loved the class.

Another teacher, Lisa, reflected on the power of human connections and passion. She tells of how she came to love science because of one teacher.

> Physics: That was my experience with a loving classroom. I don't even remember why I signed up for that class. It wasn't required, and I didn't know the teacher. I had no expectations. However, soon I was drawn into the subject matter, because of the way that the teacher engaged us. He was unmistakably passionate about physics. For example, if we were talking about momentum, he might all of a sudden throw a ball across the room. He loved teaching; it was contagious. Soon I loved learning physics. I never forgot how I felt in that class—nor did I forget physics.

In this book, we will ask you to think about your own passion and ways that you can bring it into your classroom to improve your learning.

"What is your passion?" the teacher educator asked the group.

"I love horseback riding," a student told the group of teachers.

"What can you do to bring that passion into your teaching?"

"Obviously, I can't bring the horse into the class, but I use my love of horseback riding as a reminder that each student in the class has his or her own unique passion. I try to demonstrate that each person's passion requires a lot of time, work, and dedication. It is okay to face challenges. Horseback riding helps me stay grounded, and that helps my teaching," she told the group.

"What is your passion?" the teacher educator asked the group again.

"I love the sunsets on the desert, but I'm always staying late in the classroom and don't get to watch them," a first-year teacher shared.

"Watch the sunsets," the assembled group of veteran teachers told her. "You will be a better teacher."

"What is your passion?" the question came again.

"I love art. When I am drawing, I forget the world and my cares. I am completely in the art, but with all of the mandated curriculum, I have quit doing it," he shared with his colleagues.

"How can you bring your love of art back to your classroom to enrich your teaching and learning with the students?"

"I can use art to link language, math, and science and hopefully instill my love of learning in the students," he told the group.

> *Only if you learn what gives you true joy will you be able*
> *to help [the] students find what gives them joy.*
>
> LESLIE YOUNG *(a teacher, cited in Smith & Hudelson, 2002)*

As you read this book, we will ask you to reflect on your own passion and what you can do to bring it into your teaching and learning. What is it that you love, and how can you share that in the classroom? Your own passion has the power to transform learning for students, even though you may never know about it.

We begin. Like many of you, we have discovered that learning to teach takes a very long time. It is very complex, changeable, demanding, and thrilling. Teaching is filled with simultaneous and contradictory feelings. It is exhilarating and yet it is exhausting. It can be infuriating and yet it is fun. It will fill your heart, and it will break your heart. It is a down-in-the-trenches reality, surrounded by daily moments of magic. When we began our first teaching jobs (Joan in 1966 and Dawn in 1991), we thought we knew how to teach. Since then, we have discovered that we've learned a lot about teaching, as we taught and as we lived.

This book is about learning to teach, and it is about teaching to learn. This is a book about the passion we feel, professionally and personally, about pedagogy. This book is about bringing passion to your educational setting and guiding that energy to invigorate teaching and learning.

Pedagogy is the interactive, subtle, and not so subtle process that informs teaching and learning. The United States comes from a shared national history of pedagogy, which often separates the *knowledge of schools* from the *knowledge of life* and which often separates who we are as *professionals* from who we are as *people*. Many are now reconsidering some of these long-held assumptions. We plan to rethink and rewrite our own histories as we suggest that love and passion are integral parts of complex pedagogical processes. Love and passion are a part of who we are as *professionals* in addition to who we are as *people*. "Unlike many professions, teaching is always done at the dangerous intersections of personal and public life" (Palmer, 1998, p. 17).

What in the world is pedagogy? Pedagogy is the union of teaching and learning. Pedagogy is the interaction of teaching and learning; it is that point where it all comes together. It seems that many are confused about pedagogy. If you are a teacher, or if you are a student, you are a pedagogue. What was it? Pedagogy used to be thought of as only the teacher who was teaching. Presently, the meaning has evolved to include the implications of the interaction processes between the teacher and the student. Pedagogy now includes not only the people in the room but also the entire complex culture of the classroom.

What might it be in the future? Our goal is to expand the complex meanings of pedagogy to include passion for teaching and learning. Many books have been written on pedagogy. Our goal is to write a book about the place of love in teaching and learning. Nieto (1999) credits a teacher in one of her classes for capturing the value of love in the process of learning.

> I read in a book on the writing process that the first thing a teacher has to do is fall in love with the students . . . and she cannot do that until she knows them. I have always spent time at the beginning of the year getting to know the children: talking to them, listening to them as they play, as they talk to their friends, as they try to tell me who they are. But, this year, I took it very seriously. In addition to my usual ways to find out who was sitting in front of me, I asked the parents to tell me who their children were: what they loved, what they hated, what they were afraid of, what made them angry . . . and what

the parents wanted for them, what their goals were, their hopes, their concerns. Some wrote long letters, others called me on the phone, and others came and talked before and after school. So I'm getting to know them—and love them—a lot more quickly than other years. I should have done this years ago. (p. 100)

Throughout this book we will use real stories and imagined metaphors to bring passionate pedagogy to life. We hope to help pedagogues internalize the meaning of pedagogy. We will confront the mysteries of pedagogy and make them more meaningful. As literacy is central to learning and teaching, many of the stories are grounded in literacy communities in action.

Think of a spiral that has been painted on a canvas. We will use the metaphor of a spiral throughout the chapters of this book, as we seek to weave our understandings with yours. We encourage you to find your center in the spiral of our experiences and understandings. Metaphors are a way that humans create meaning by using one element of experience to understand another (Morgan, 1998, p. 4). We will use the metaphor of a spiral to connect Joan's experiences with Dawn's experiences and with your experiences. We strongly encourage you to doodle in this book (see Figure 2.1).

Metaphors have been critiqued as having the potential to make the complex not simple, but simplistic. For example, Edelsky, Altwerger, and Flores (1991) warn of the

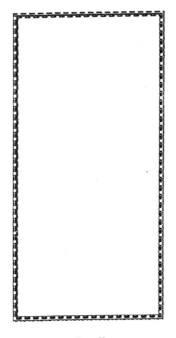

FIGURE 2.1   Doodle

tendency to use metaphors, thereby reducing students and their needs to machines or packages. We concur with their critical thoughts and are determined to use our metaphors to link ideas across the chapters. We do resist metaphors that lead us down a path of *either/or,* as in the way educational literature has been plagued by the pendulum (Wolfe & Poynor, 2001). Often metaphors facilitate meaning making for those who have a bias for visual learning, like Joan, for example. Yes, she reads and writes text, but she sees via pictures of understandings in her head. Therefore, we will use metaphors with our expectation that simple will not slip into simplistic.

> *Everything should be made as simple as possible, but not simpler.*
>
> ALBERT EINSTEIN

The Voice of Schools

In each of the following chapters, this section, The Voice of Schools, will focus on pedagogy in a variety of contexts. Some of this pedagogy will be historically grounded and, even, assumed. In addition, we want to also offer portraits of pedagogy with new perspectives.

The traditional voice of schools often views schools as being separate from a student's life outside the classroom. Teachers and students step into school as if to separate themselves from the rest of their lives. Students often have to leave their personal histories, experiences, hopes, and even dreams behind. In a sense, students have often had to unpack their historical backpack as they entered the schoolhouse door. The traditional voice of schools has taught us: Teachers teach, students learn. The truth of this statement is obvious, but in this book we will ask you to go beyond that to find new truths for the new century. Often we, who have spent considerable time in schools, have a whole set of understandings that the public does not know about or understand. This knowledge seems to spiral through the years and reshape itself, reflecting new needs of new days. At other times, school knowledge slowly fossilizes itself and fails to evolve. Sometimes this is good, and sometimes it is not. However, The Voice of Schools in each chapter seeks to portray those perspectives that reflect the knowledge of schools. Palmer (1998) has been a steadfast voice calling for us to focus on the whole of who we are as complete human beings in the classroom, and to do so with heart.

Professor Beto: Passionate Pedagogy

Professor Beto certainly was a traditional professor in a classic sense. He was this and more. He brought his love of literature and music into the graduate classes and, thus, transformed these subjects into passionate pedagogy. He did not unpack his backpack; nor did the students in his classes. Being a student in his classes transformed Joan's life and learning; the story follows.

I had just finished a master's degree in Spanish from a major U.S. university. It was an extremely demanding and rewarding process for me. I took half of my classes, my comprehensive tests, and my oral exams at the satellite campus in Mexico. I did this on purpose, as learning in Spanish was far more rigorous for me than learning in English. At the end of the program, I was exhausted and proud. Then the director of the program called me in to explain that the Mexican campus provided only a *terminal* degree. A terminal degree is just that: the end. The message was all too clear: the M.A. was to be my educational finish line; I was not to make a run for a doctoral program. I now understood that I was caught in an academic battle grounded in turf fights and perceived academic walls, but at the time I felt completely deflated and even incompetent, although at that point in my life I had teaching credentials from a couple of states, several years of teaching behind me, and more years parenting my own teenage children. In spite of this, I felt less.

The purpose of this story is to demonstrate how the spiral of passionate pedagogy still can transform a life, even when there are roadblocks and challenges. During this M.A. program in Spanish, I had been watching one particular instructor, Professor Beto. I didn't know who he was, or what he taught, or even which department he was in, but I noticed that the adult graduate students who entered his classes left with passion. It's true. I used to sit on benches outside one of his classes and pretend that I was studying or drinking coffee, but the truth is that I was watching Professor Beto and his students. I wanted to be in those classes. But you have to remember that I had that *terminal degree* now on my record.

After a couple of years of this, I simply threw caution to the wind and enrolled in a class. I feared that the computer in the registrar's office might whistle and hiss that I was *terminal,* but it didn't. I entered the class and sat in the far corner of the room, as close to the door as possible. I was the only Anglo in a large room filled with Latinos. I can assure you that they were passionately learning the art of storytelling and the role of music in pedagogy. At the end of the class, as I was quickly and quietly heading for the door, Professor Beto stopped me and introduced me to two other women students who had been sitting in the front of the class. After class, Gloria and Belén asked me to go for coffee with them. The next week in class, I was in front of the class seated safely between my two new colleagues and friends, Gloria and Belén. Thus began my second M.A., and eventually my Ph.D., my other *terminal* degree.

In retrospect, Professor Beto completely transformed my own teaching because he brought his passion for language, learning, and literacy to class. He connected me with his love of learning and teaching, which has since been a spiral weaving through my personal and professional life. The fact that we did it all in two languages did not hurt me; actually, it helped. Did Professor Beto ever know he had done this for me? Probably not. In education, as teachers we often do not see the consequences or the legacy of our teaching. We never know the magical moment when we might be creating a memory. We may never know how we made a difference, with whom, or when. In addition, we often cannot pay back what was given to us; we can only pass it on. The potential to change lives for the better (or for the worse) is always there. It is an awesome responsibility that we, as teachers, must never forget. We do know that we have the power to control the human interactions each day in our classes, and positive human interactions can leave a lasting legacy.

We can never do great things, only small things with great love.

MOTHER TERESA

The Voice of Life

In each of the following chapters, this section, The Voice of Life, will focus on life outside of schools and how that knowledge is linked by the very footprints of students who spend part of their lives in schools and part of their lives at home. Once again we draw inspiration from Nel Noddings, who as a mother was quick to speak about the connections between home and school when she called on teachers to see themselves as parents who are raising a huge heterogeneous family (Noddings, 1992). Our goal is to demonstrate that the knowledge of life has much to offer the knowledge of schools, and vice versa. Who we are as people cannot be separated from who we are as professionals. "We teach who we are" (Palmer, 1998, p. 2).

For Dawn the personal and the professional parts of her life did not come together until she followed her own passion. Only then did her knowledge of schools and of life join together in surprising ways. Dawn felt compelled to stay in education as a teacher, but it was her passion for writing that sustained her. In what follows, Dawn tells her story of using her passion for writing to unify who she was as a person and as a professional.

Life is a spiral.
You keep visiting the same stuff over and over again,
but each time you see it from a different perspective.

JENNIFER LOUDEN

We hiked to the top of the desert valley and were greeted by petroglyphs etched in the cliffs (see Figure 2.2). My three children, husband, and I stared at the carved images of rattlesnakes, people, and animals that stood in muted silence. We, too, stared in silence. I thought of the Native Americans who thousands of

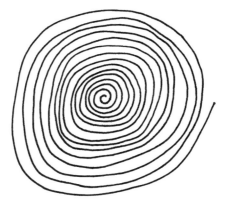

FIGURE 2.2   Spiral Petroglyph

years ago had carved those images and created this day for us, although they never could have known the legacy they were creating.

As we explored, I realized that the predominant images carved into the stone were spirals, perfectly symmetrical spirals, two feet in diameter, with a one-inch space in between the curves as they wound round and round each other. Again and again, spirals dotted the cliffs overlooking the valley below, and again and again I wondered what they might symbolize. I am no expert on the symbolism of cliff petroglyphs. However, it did strike me that over the course of the past few months, I have been doodling more and more spirals in my journals and notebooks. I didn't know why. I had never studied the multiple mythologies of the symbolism of the spiral, but the density of that spiral on the rocks suddenly and simultaneously reached back to the past and forward to the future for me. I just felt the urge to draw them, and so I did. Then I read the preceding quote by Jennifer Louden about seeing things again, only from a different perspective each time (see Figure 2.3).

"Why do I have to learn the same lessons again and again? Why don't I get it the first time around?" I thought to myself. Then I realized that life is a series of encountering similar situations over and over and having to relearn the same lesson.

My educational career has been a spiral, looping through elementary and higher education teaching. Like many teachers' kids, I did not want to be a teacher. Ironically, it has been the center of my professional life. As most first-year teachers discover, teaching is not easy—particularly the first year. I taught during the day and took teacher education classes four nights per week. I was a reluctant and exhausted participant. The spiral seemed to be trying to teach me too much, too fast.

I survived my first year of teaching because of my family and a supportive principal. Mom says that her most lasting memory of her first year of teaching is

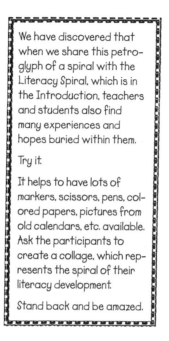

We have discovered that when we share this petroglyph of a spiral with the Literacy Spiral, which is in the Introduction, teachers and students also find many experiences and hopes buried within them.

Try it.

It helps to have lots of markers, scissors, pens, colored papers, pictures from old calendars, etc. available. Ask the participants to create a collage, which represents the spiral of their literacy development.

Stand back and be amazed.

FIGURE 2.3   Spiral Literacy Activity

aspirin. Mine is going to bed so exhausted I don't remember my head touching the pillow. At the end of her first year, Mom swore she would never teach again. So did I. That was more than 30 years ago for her and 11 for me, and we have both been teaching and learning ever since.

My most enduring memory of those years is the Mexican migrant children and their families, who worked the agricultural fields in the area. Weekly, I visited each of the families' homes *a tomar un cafecito* (to share a cup of coffee): These are memories I still cherish to this day. If I thought at that time that my spiral of life was twisting and turning about two loops ahead of me, it was not until a few years later that it shifted into high gear and almost spun me out of control. I married and had three babies in three-and-a-half years. It was the *voice of life* that opened the door to my passion for the hidden connections between spirituality and education. I struggled with the seemingly contradictory and simultaneous directions of my life. I struggled until one afternoon.

I attended an educational conference with Mom. For the previous couple of years I had stepped back from education to focus on my study of spirituality and writing. While Mom was presenting and attending sessions, I sat in the hallway and finished reading another book on spirituality. "What good is all of this information for me in education? What do I do with it?" I asked myself. Simultaneous and contradictory feelings are always a hint that change is coming. I should have known. I stood and walked to a large auditorium where Tove Skutnabb-Kangas, an international champion of human and linguistic rights (March 20, 2002) was speaking to thousands, although it felt like she was speaking only to me.

> Today I have an even more urgent personal reason to continue the struggle. If you look on the screen behind me, you will see my grandson, Uki Erik, born in January 2002. His parents have, it seems, decided to trust in our power to change the world. As you can see in the picture, he is peeping into the world, with just one eye half-open, as if checking whether it is a place that he dares to enter. What can I say to him? What can we say to all the children that are born now? You decide. Will you please help me ensure that Uki Erik can open the other eye too, trusting that it will be worth it? Please, let's make the world safe for little Uki Erik.

Tove embodies that unique and exquisite combination of a person who speaks honestly and powerfully about global inequities and her fear for our planet's health. And for all of her honest, forthright, and fiercely political rhetoric, she simply radiates love. I realized in that instant that the time had come to follow my passion. I did not have to pursue either spirituality OR education. I could use my love of *writing* about spirituality IN education, as I contribute my share of *righting* the world for my family and friends, my children's children, and the children to come afterward. However, it was only after I had the confidence to step back from education for a while and follow my passion for writing that I discovered how these diverse passions enrich one another.

In this book, we hope that the spirals pull and tug you, also, for a few new loops. We anticipate that you will find pages that affirm; in addition, we hope you will find pages that bring you simultaneous and contradictory feelings. Remember, this is good. Change is coming.

Praxis: Let the Magic Begin

In this section of each chapter, we explore praxis, which is the union of theory and practice. It is that magic moment when learning is lively because the methods are not only student centered but also theoretically grounded in social justice.

As we begin this first section on methods, we do so with a bit of trepidation, which causes us to offer this cautionary and seemingly contradictory observation on methods. Depending on the moment, we love them and/or we hate them. Methods are about *how;* theory is about *why.* We admit that we are always fascinated by the *why* of life.

> *[S]he who has a why to live can bear with almost any how.*
> *FRIEDRICH NIETZSCHE*

Joan came to theory through methods, and Dawn came to methods through theory. It was only after years of experimenting with every method imaginable, that Joan came to understand that methods in isolation can look good, feel good, and even sound good; however, unless methods are tightly linked to the lives of the students, they ignore reality—the reality of the students' world.

Dawn, on the other hand, grew up with theory at the kitchen counter, and it was only after teaching that she came to appreciate the power of methods. Likewise, as you teach and learn, this will not be the only time you experience simultaneous and contradictory feelings. Schools are filled with contradictions, as is life.

As teachers, we suspect that the vast majority of us have at one time or another borrowed a method after hearing how wonderful it was—only to have it fail (often dramatically) when we tried it with students in our own classroom. One possible explanation: This method was not linked to the lives of these students. Freire (1987) warned us quite clearly about importing and exporting methods with no regard for the sociocultural context.

Macedo (1997) captures our own love/hate relationship with methods when he proposes an antimethod pedagogy, which refuses the rigidity of models and methodological paradigms. His notion of antipedagogy calls us to an informed dialogue, grounded in praxis, which values student experiences and calls for voice and action within education. Drawing on the Freirian legacy, antimethods pedagogy is teaching and learning that never reduces dialogue and problem posing to mere method.

Bartolomé (2000) informs our understanding of methods when she writes that effective strategies need to be grounded in the sociocultural context of the students and must have fundamental pedagogical features that cut *across* strategies because they are, above all, student centered. She warns teachers of the dangers of reducing complex educational issues to simple methods without critical reflection of the entire context. In this book, we will share methods, but we hope the methods never become (Bartolomé, 1994) "the methods fetish."

Throughout this book, we will share theoretically grounded methods. We believe that methods will take us down a long road, help us enjoy the journey, and maybe even help get us to a destination faster. However, what is the destination? Do we want students who can memorize and tell us what we just told them? Or do we want students who can collaborate, think critically, and solve problems for their own future? Theory works like a compass in that it provides direction. Theory helps us focus on where we are going. Theory guides us. (See Figure 2.4.)

However, we also know that any classroom teacher who daily teaches and learns with 150 secondary students appreciates good methods; any teacher who daily faces 20 wiggling 5-year-olds appreciates good methods. Or let us be more clear: If we are going into a public school to teach tomorrow, we want a few methods, handy in our heads, so that we can enhance the learning of students.

Our goal is that each method we share be firmly grounded in theory. Think of it this way: Theory is the rudder of your ship. Even though invisible, it guides your future direction. It keeps you upright, even in a storm. Not only will theory inform your methods (and methods inform your theory), but also we recognize that each

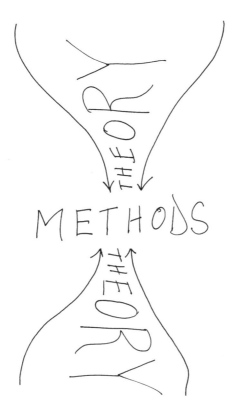

**FIGURE 2.4   Methods Are Horizontal.
Theory Is Vertical.**

method is only as good as the teacher's own knowledge and passionate commitment to pedagogy.

An Example: Big Books and Theory Building

In the following example, we consider how methods become theoretically grounded. In this particular case, the methods preceded the theoretical framework. With a colleague, Fernando, we worked with preservice teachers in various school and family settings, as students of many ages wrote their own stories and created their own books.[1] Most of these student-generated stories were eventually bound in the shape of big books and are still in use in various settings.

However, the truth is that many big books were created before we ever thought of connecting this particular method to a theory. We only knew that it was working, and it triggered a lot of enthusiasm for writing and reading. It was working with small children, teenagers, and university students. We made new friends; we had fun; we loved learning about each other. The project evolved in many directions, and at times we were barely able to stay ahead of the stories, the illustrations, the glue, and the laminating processes. In retrospect, we see the entire process as grounded theory (Mertens, 1998) in which the theory is not stated at the beginning of a project; rather it develops after the data are collected, and, in this particular case, after about 30 big books were made and circulated throughout the community.

Finally and fortunately, after a couple of years, we stopped and looked at each other and said, "Okay, let's theory-build with the big books activity." Suddenly, we had felt a need to generate and articulate a theoretical framework. How to begin? We sat in an office, without speaking, and we simply reflected on what happened when we made big books in communities. Eventually, we started to talk to each other. As we talked, we scribbled on a yellow legal pad as we articulated our mutual ideas.

First, it was so clear to us that positive human connections were established among all involved: the student authors, the university preservice teachers, the school communities, and the families. As the oral histories were captured in the big books, the university students, who were now student teachers, noted also that reluctant readers in September became eager readers at the end of the semester. The credential candidates did not want to rotate during their student teaching experience to other classrooms because they had connected with students. They had created their own community. Even when the semester was over, many university students chose to continue their reading time with the younger students informally after school. During this process, the younger students began to demonstrate a strong sense of self and pride in their language and ability to create stories and illustrations.

Second, it was clear to us that students were generating their own ideas and their own words. Students were writing their own worlds (Freire & Macedo, 1987). Students were working in their own communities for self and social transformation. Families were a valued part of the process; the knowledge from home was brought into the schools and applied in the curriculum.

After our yellow legal pad was a blur of scribbled notes, we stopped again. This time, we simply asked ourselves: Why? Why do we do what we do? In what follows are the answers that we generated:

> to bring in the students' voices
>
> to become transformative teachers and learners
>
> to base our curriculum on the students' lived experiences
>
> to demonstrate a sense of care and respect for students
>
> to generate authentic literacy
>
> to create partnerships between bilingual credential candidates and public school students
>
> to turn promise into practice
>
> to create a process whereby students can negotiate their own identities
>
> to *do* critical pedagogy

At this point, we stopped again. We looked at our list; we thought; we talked. Eventually, we chose to focus our continuing work under the theoretical framework of our final two answers: negotiating identities (Cummins, 2001) and *doing* critical pedagogy (Wink, 2000). We chose these two as we are often asked *how* students negotiate identity, and *how* you do critical pedagogy. For us, it just seemed a good fit.

However, our work was not done: the first question (what?) eventually triggered the second question (why?). Why do we do what we do? Never an easy question. However, it turns out that what we do matters. When Cummins (2001) writes that human relationships are at the heart of schooling, he is saying that the connections that we establish with students are central to their development. These human interactions can have very positive or negative effects on the students. Furthermore, it is through active language use within the human relationships and interactions that students negotiate their own identities. Critical pedagogy calls us to validate students' lived experiences as we read the word and the world (Freire & Macedo, 1987).

This student-authoring project created a process whereby the university students and children in the classroom and community were able to positively negotiate their own identities. The project was the impetus for the development of a positive sense of self and pride in their language. The project brought in the voice of students, based on their own lives. However, even with the various pedagogical paths, which evolved from this one project, all were and are still theoretically grounded by the original framework. Throughout this book, each chapter will have a section, Praxis: Let the Magic Begin, in which we will continue to not only refer to this example of theory building, but also add to it.

Big Books: One Way

Authentic, student-generated literacy can be created in multiple ways with students and families. No *one* perfect way exists; rather there are many meaningful ways. We chose to use the words *big books* because, in our own experience, the books that teachers, students, and families create together often are written and illustrated on large pieces of paper. Of course, they can also be small books, which will be demonstrated in a later chapter.

If you would like to do this in your own context, we offer first the most basic, generic, simplified instructions we can articulate. We have reduced what can be a very complex process to the following simple process. If you have never done this, you might want to copy these pages, highlight the four processes, and stick them in your book bag for later use in your own class. Later we will add more details and steps to the process (Wink & Putney, 2000).

First, teacher and students find something interesting to discuss. This can be based on a story, on anything interesting that happens in class or in the world, on a question planned by the teacher, or by a spontaneous question that suddenly emerges and captures students.

Second, teachers write the language of the students on the chalkboard.

Third, teachers transfer this story to a large piece of paper so that all students in the room can see the book.

Fourth, teachers ask students to copy the story from the chalkboard to their own paper so they can read at home with their families. In Chapter Three, we will expand on this process.

In the previous section we shared our ambivalence about methods, which sometimes fail because they do not connect to the lives of students. One way to avoid this is to think in terms of praxis more than practice. Praxis is the union of theory and practice. Praxis is the art of theoretically grounding all our practices within the classroom.

The Literacy Link

In each chapter to follow, The Literacy Link will include activities and methods that reflect our passionate interest in reading. Reading is the ability to make meaning from written text (Cambourne & Turbill, 1999). The bottom line is: All teachers are reading teachers. Literacy cuts across all curricula in schools and links our learning and our living. Whether you are a pre-K teacher, a high school math teacher, or an assistant professor struggling for tenure, we are all linked through literacy. Hopefully, as teachers, we are voracious and passionate readers outside of the classroom as well.

A word about literacy: We are told of the literacy crisis daily in the news media, although the data do not support this misconception. "What is striking about reading achievement scores in the United States over the past twenty-five years is not how they've declined, but just how *stable* they have been . . . [r]eading achievement has either stayed even or increased slightly over the past three decades" (McQuillan, 1998, p. 2).

Literacy is often perceived to be decoding or reading, as in sounding out, the word on the page, with or without comprehension. Literacy is often narrowly perceived to be something one has or doesn't have, and schools "give" it to you. In addition, if students don't "get" it, schools are to blame. We subscribe to a far broader definition of reading and are continually drawn back to literacy as reading the word and the world (Freire & Macedo, 1987). In this approach to reading students, indeed, decode or sound out the word on the page; they understand not only the word but also the sociocultural and political context of their world. They read the world. This approach to literacy implies that ". . . we understand how and why knowledge and power are constructed and by whom and for whom" (Wink, 2000, p. 56).

The public often sees schools as solely responsible for the nation's literacy. Schools, of course, bear a major share of that responsibility; however, they are only one of the many social forces that generate literacy. Literacy practices are available throughout society, inside and outside of schools. Some students have greater access to those practices than others. For example, Joan's four grandkids have lots of opportunities for multiple experiences with a broad range of literacy practices. However, some students do not have those same opportunities; the playing field is not level. Literacy is not only about skills and abilities but also about cultural practices and socioeconomic opportunities. When we begin to broaden the definition of literacy to include cultural practices and societal forces, we have to ask new questions, which lead to deeper inquiry and to new learning. In this book, we will look at literacy practices from multiple angles. We begin, in what follows, with one of our favorites.

Literacy Is Dangerous

Moffett (1989) was a relatively early contributor in North America to this broader definition of literacy, when he wrote:

> Literacy is dangerous and has always been so regarded. It naturally breaks down barriers of time, space, and culture. It threatens one's original identity by broadening it through vicarious experiencing and the incorporation of somebody else's hearth and ethos. So we feel profoundly ambiguous about literacy. Looking at it as a means of transmitting our culture to our children, we make it a priority in education, but recognizing the threat of its backfiring we make it so tiresome and personally unrewarding that youngsters won't want to do it on their own, which is of course when it becomes dangerous. . . . The net effect of this ambivalence is to give literacy with one hand and take it back with the other, in keeping with our contradictory wish for youngsters to learn to think but only about what we already have in mind for them. (p. 85)

As we begin this first section on literacy, we do not want to talk about students reading or students not reading. Instead, we begin with *you* and *your* reading. Use the mirror to reflect back into your own lived experiences with literacy. At this point, we want you to hold up an imaginary mirror and take time to reflect on your own reading experiences (see Figure 2.5).

Stop reading. Put your feet up. Lean back. Reflect on the following questions. This will look like you are not doing anything. It is okay to take time to think while teaching and learning. With each question, we encourage you to stay right with it for as long as it takes. Think. Write your reflections for each question in your journal (see Figure 2.6).

Questions for your consideration: How did you learn to read? What teacher had a positive effect on your own literacy development? Did you have any negative influences on your own literacy development? What do you read daily? What do you read for pleasure? What is the best book you have read in the last year? What can be learned from your own literacy experiences that will enhance the literacy development of the students in your classes?

Many teachers go into teaching with a driving passion in their content area. This is good. Content is vital. However, once in schools teachers soon come to understand that literacy is central to content and literacy development is a very long continuum. We are all teaching reading and content somewhere along that continuum: Full professors and beginning teachers have this in common. In addition, the way to begin to think about this is, once again, to get out your mirror and reflect. Readers beget readers. Passionate readers beget passionate readers. Love begets love. Love of books begets love of books.

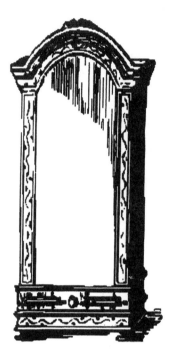

FIGURE 2.5   A Mirror

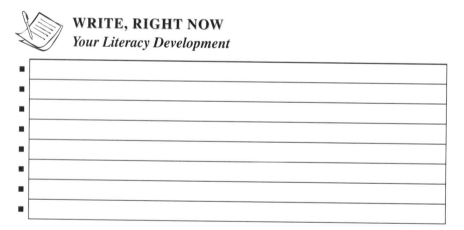

WRITE, RIGHT NOW
Your Literacy Development

FIGURE 2.6   Write, Right Now: Your Literacy Development

Morrison, Jacobs, and Swinyard (1999) conducted a national probability sample of 1,874 elementary school teachers to determine the relationship between their personal reading habits and their use of strategies to promote literacy in the classroom. They found that teachers who read more used more literature-based and whole language–

inspired practices in their classrooms (e.g., reading aloud, taking students to the library, sustained silent reading (SSR) time, book talks, use of trade books).

McQuillan and Au (2001) in their study confirmed that the amount of free reading done is associated with higher levels of literacy. The study also finds new evidence for the importance of the school library; high schoolers who had more planned trips to the school library did more free reading. McQuillan and Au found that those who reported more free reading achieved higher scores in reading comprehension, a result that remained significant when parental education was statistically controlled. This is an important result. Since parental education is strongly associated with SES (socioeconomic status), it suggests that SES per se is not the cause of the differences in reading ability; rather it is the amount of reading done (see also McQuillan, 1998).

Because the amount of reading done is related to access to books (see later, as well as other studies, e.g., Krashen, 1993; McQuillan, 1998), this suggests that there is something one can do about the impact of poverty on literacy development: Provide children with interesting books. Access to books is important for all children but crucial for poor children, who have the most problems learning to read and who often have little to read at home (Krashen, in personal communication, August 23, 2002).

Anna Quindlen (1998) writes of the effect that books have had on her entire life.

> In books I have traveled, not only to other worlds, but into my own. I learned who I was and who I wanted to be, what I might aspire to, and what I might dare to dream about my world and myself. More powerfully and persuasively than from the "shalt nots" of the Ten Commandments, I learned the difference between good and evil, right and wrong. One of my favorite childhood books, *A Wrinkle in Time,* described that evil, that wrong, existing in a different dimension from everyone else I knew. There was waking, and there was sleeping. And then there were books, a kind of parallel universe in which anything might happen and frequently did, a universe in which I might be a newcomer but was never really a stranger. My real, true world. My perfect island. (p. 6)

The reason Quindlen (1998) could travel to these others worlds, to learn of good and evil and find her own real, true world was precisely because she had access to books. However, many children do not have access to find their own perfect island.

Access. Access to books is the bottom line of the current concerns about literacy rates. This is where our role, as teachers, is part of a greater solution. Each of us alone will not be able make sure that books are lying around in every home, but we do have six hours five days a week to make a difference. It is not only that we are all reading teachers but also that we are morally mandated to read in the class; to arrange library cards for all students; to form books clubs; to read with kids; to read for ourselves; or, as the *Teacher from Taft* will teach us in Chapter Four, to love books. Public libraries hold the potential to be powerful partners (Johns, 2002/2003) for teachers, families, and schools.

Life travels upwards in spirals
Those who take pains to seach the shadows
Of the past below us, then, can better judge the
Tiny arc up which they climb.
More surely guess the dim
Curves of the future above them.

(Author Unknown)

FIGURE 2.7   Life Travels in Spirals

WHAT CAN BE LEARNED FROM THIS?

Books matter. The passion of a teacher matters. In the remaining chapters of this book, our goal is to bring to light important pedagogical principles found in surprising places. As we seek to paint powerful pictures of pedagogy in diverse contexts, we hope to lead readers to reflect on what can be learned.

In the next chapter, the spiral of learning continues as we look at the major assumptions of educational thought that have evolved throughout the past century. We will look at how these ideas have affected classroom practice. Please join us in Chapter Three as the spiral of learning continues (see Figure 2.7). Can you paradigm?[2]

CHAPTER NOTES

1. We appreciate the collaboration with Fernando Peña, who originated many of the big book activities.

2. We appreciate Juan Flores's comment "Can you paradigm?"

3 Teaching Passionately— Theoretically

A meaningful connection to the past demands, above all, active engagement. It demands imagination and empathy, so that we can fathom worlds unlike our own, contexts far from those we know, ways of thinking and feeling that are alien to us. We must enter past worlds with curiosity and respect.

GERDA LERNER, Why History Matters

In this chapter we will ask you to reflect on the past to rescue the future. Our goal is to paint a broad picture of the various perspectives or paradigms that have affected teaching and learning in the twentieth century. A paradigm is a particular perspective. We will articulate the various schools of thought, their leaders, and their legacies. We will write about their competing and their complementary ideas. Our goal is to share the dominant ideas that have affected our experiences in schools over generations. We think of this as a "moral arc of history" (Intrator, 2002, p. 264), in which we will share our perspective.

If you are a preservice teacher just beginning a teacher preparation program, this chapter will provide a glimpse of the theoretical underpinnings of your program. If you are an inservice teacher reviewing for a comprehensive test, this chapter will serve to capture the big picture of your learning. If you are a policy maker or interested family member of an educator, this chapter is meant to capture the world of schools.

Think of it this way: In schools, much is visible. How well a school is maintained, student work on the walls, and even the overall atmosphere are visible and palpable. More is invisible below the surface, however. The visible is a manifestation of the invisible: the theories, opinions, and true driving forces behind schools. Sometimes our assumptions and opinions about teaching and learning are centered only on the visible. In this chapter, we hope to see also what is below the surface.

Our wish is that your own reflections on the dominating educational assumptions will lead you to rethink and re-own your conclusions, just as we have done. In this chapter we tell the story of schools from the perspective of our own experiences. This is a story about significant ideas, past, present, and future. Eventually, the ideas lead to action. Theory becomes practice. Reflective action is not easy. We honor the teachers and students who *walk the walk*.

The Voice of Schools

In the Introduction, we wrote that pedagogy was the interaction between teaching and learning. In what follows we will look more closely at differing paradigms and have chosen to separate this discussion into three somewhat conventional categories: transmission, generative, and transformation. These three concepts are often referred to with other language, which we will also mention. However, for our purposes, transmission, generative, and transformative will be the overarching concepts guiding our discussion of pedagogy. Using the metaphor of an iceberg[1] we write about what is visible and what is below the surface (see Figure 3.1).

In addition, we look at pedagogy from others' perspectives. We focus on the effect of history on perspectives and, thus, on pedagogy. For example, do you have the very same educational ideas you had five years ago? Ten years ago? Twenty years ago? If not, why not? One reason that we change our perspectives is that the world changes and changes us in the process. Other reasons we sometimes change our perspectives on pedagogy are that our life experiences (e.g., the people we meet, the conversations we have, the books we read) influence our ways of knowing and seeing. Quoting a classroom teacher, "I suddenly realized that you can't see what you don't know" (Smith & Hudelson, 2001, p. 29). Time touches us all and often enables us to see and know more. The influence of history will lead us to think about then and now and tomorrow (see Figure 3.2).

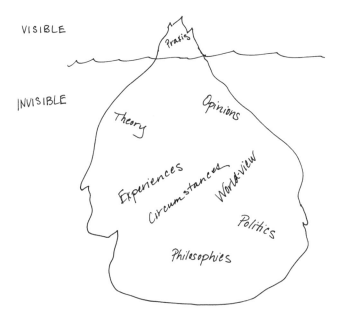

FIGURE 3.1   Iceberg

> What we used to think pedagogy was.
> Why we thought that.
> What we think pedagogy is.
> Why we think that.
> What we think pedagogy will be.
> Why we think that.

FIGURE 3.2 Pondering Pedagogy

We will end this chapter with a discussion of why it is always so easy to slip back into transmission pedagogy. (See Figure 3.3.)

The educational literature is alive with perspectives on pedagogy. As you read our perspectives, please think of them as cognitive coat hooks on which to hang your emerging understandings. Or if you are a more veteran teacher with many years of classroom experience on which you have constructed your own perspectives, we do this only as a reminder. Or, perhaps, it is time for you also to rethink some assumptions. Time does this to each of us.

Transmission

The transmission model of teaching and learning is in the tradition of behaviorism, positivism, rationalism, or empiricism. Historically, Bacon, Locke, Comte, and Kant influenced this pedagogical perspective. In the twentieth century Taylor, Skinner, Bobbitt, Pavlov, Watson, and Thorndike brought this concept into schools. The practice of scientific management in the late 1800s and early 1900s, which worked so efficiently in factories, soon spread to schools and still carries the legacy of its roots. Many refer to it as the factory model of schools.

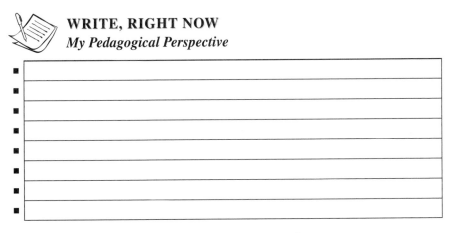

WRITE, RIGHT NOW
My Pedagogical Perspective

FIGURE 3.3 Write, Right Now: My Pedagogical Perspective

This school of thought is often associated with skills, rewards, memorization, discrete-point tests, grades, time-on-tasks, error correction, programmed instruction, and reinforcement. It is "based on the belief that human behavior is determined by forces in the environment that are beyond our control, rather than by the exercise of free will" (McNergney & Herbert, 2001, p. 139). From this perspective, knowledge is a fixed entity; you know it or you don't. Extrinsic motivation is valued. Transmission pedagogy reflects "the behaviorist belief that knowledge exists outside of people and independently of them, and that the major goal of a good education is to instill in students an accepted body of information and skills previously established by others" (Scheurman, 1998, p. 31).

Many believe transmission pedagogy to be the conventional or traditional approach to teaching and learning. The public often perceives it to be the status quo; *the-way-it-was-always-done.* In writing a book, we are told never to say *all* people, because the minute we assume *all,* we will meet the exception. However, we cannot resist the temptation to write that *all* people reading this page will have had experience with this approach to teaching and learning because it was a dominant force throughout most of the last century and continues to gather momentum as we write. The legacy of this approach to teaching and learning is alive and well and gaining strength. The more visible aspects of this pedagogical perspective are the *back-to-basics* movement: tests, high standards, controlled curriculum. The deprofessionalization of education, which questions teachers' expertise and seeks to implement outside control on the classroom, is grounded in transmission, but much of that is below the surface. We will go there in Chapter Eight, Teaching Passionately—Politically.

When Joan began teaching, this was the only way she knew; thus, she firmly believed in it. When Dawn began teaching, she had experienced this and other approaches. As will be seen in the true story of one professor that follows, for many this was the sum total of their pedagogical experiences and, thus, was thought to be the *norm.* No, this is not the way it was always done, but a lot of it was done during the twentieth century, and probably most readers of this book had a lot of it done to them and have done it or will do it to others. This is why it is sometimes assumed to be the *right way.*

One Experience: Professor JS.   For example, Professor JS (Spencer, 2001–2002) reflects on the initial years of his 30 years of teaching history.

> When I came out of graduate school to begin my college teaching career, I was told to go into the classroom and teach . . . I knew nothing of the literature that would introduce me to the subtleties of the teaching-learning process. . . . Teaching is telling and knowledge is acquisition of facts according to time-tested pedagogy. If students could demonstrate sufficient recall of facts, this showed understanding and effective teaching had taken place. . . . The traditional teaching paradigm was simply not concerned with how students learn. (pp. 93–94)

After teaching in the transmission model for 10 years (teachers talk/students listen), Professor JS acknowledged that the students in his classes did well on tests. However, he slowly became aware that their understanding might not be as deep as he wanted. So, the professor set out to fix the problem. He devoted the next 10 years of his professorate to this objective.

> I used all the plays to enhance learning that I had learned by obedient observation of my own instructors. I talked louder and slower, I had students work more problems on the board, I assigned more homework problems, I prepared a study guide, I demonstrated how to solve problems, and I set up recitation sections. (p. 94)

Twenty years gone. Professor JS used up all of the pedagogical tricks he knew. We remind you that his bag of tricks was mighty small, as all he knew was what he had experienced as a passive student. So, he took the next logical professional tactic—blame the students. "Nothing worked, so it couldn't be my fault" (Spencer, 2001–2002, p. 94).

> I had noticed that instructors rarely fault themselves but tend rather to find deficiencies in student background, motivation or ability. More experienced teachers assured me that students were much better in years gone by. But I knew these students. They were bright, their secondary preparation was better than mine had been and they worked diligently at what I told them to do. . . . I suspect that students never were as good as they used to be. (p. 94)

For many, transmission is the paradigm of choice. For others, they don't know other options. For still others, it is a paradigm that needs to be deconstructed. People tend to believe in it or not with passion. Each of us reading this page has learned within the transmission paradigm. However, if we are honest, very few of us like to be talked at—and very few of us retain much information when all that is required is memorization. We believe that this is a great place to begin your own personal and professional reflections. Write about your own experiences with transmission model learning and teaching (see Figure 3.4).

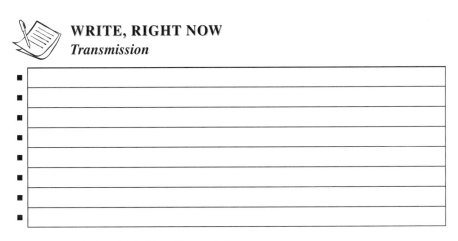

WRITE, RIGHT NOW
Transmission

-
-
-
-
-
-
-

FIGURE 3.4   Write, Right Now: Transmission

Generative

The generative approach to teaching and learning is based on the idea that we construct, or generate, knowledge in the learning process. Its historical roots reach back, not only to progressivist thought of the last century but also beyond that to the antiquities. Leaders of this educational paradigm are Socrates, Dewey, Vygotsky, Montessori, and Piaget. The Socratic method of dialogue was the impetus for generative teaching and learning of today. The generative approach is closely aligned with constructivist and interpretivist approaches. Transactive theory (Rosenblatt, 1978) is akin to generative pedagogy.

This school of thought is characterized by active communication. It is grounded in interaction, multiple perspectives, holistic learning, and social construction of knowledge. Students are responsible for negotiating meaning with the text and within their environment. Knowledge is socioculturally grounded. It frequently requires complex pedagogical skills of the teacher. Learners *construct* their own knowledge from the text or from the interactive processes of a experience-based, student-centered classroom. Students move from a passive role to be active learners.

As we write this paragraph, we as a nation are moving away from the constructivist approaches to learning, which were so popular during the 1980s and 1990s. Thus, it is safe to guess that readers of this text have had experience with generative teaching and learning.

Piaget and Vygotsky.   Below the surface of a discussion of generative learning are Piaget and Vygotsky who, although they each fall under a broad heading of construction of knowledge, bring their own unique perspectives. Both Piaget and Vygotsky were interested in learning and human development. However, for Piaget, human development leads learning and, thus, instruction needs to be adapted to the level of development of the child. Vygotsky, on the other hand, believed that learning leads human development and, thus, instruction enhances development.[2]

We begin with Piaget, as he is often the more commonly understood in the United States of the two educators. Piaget believed that knowledge was cognitively constructed; he focused on active construction and a restructuring of prior knowledge. Piaget was very intrigued with the construction of knowledge in the mind. For him, the teacher did not transmit knowledge but rather encouraged the learners to think in order to understand. He also taught that students progress through natural developmental levels. Yes, Piaget is associated with construction of knowledge, but it is often thought of as cognitive construction of knowledge. Transmission pedagogy posits that knowledge is what we memorize. Piaget had a different view; he said that knowledge was what we cognitively constructed with others. Piaget was a cognitive constructivist.

Vygotsky, on the other hand, is not as well known in schools in the United States. Vygotsky also believed that knowledge was socially constructed; however, he extended this view to highlight his understanding that knowledge and values are culturally grounded. Whereas Piaget was interested in the construction of knowledge within the mind, Vygotsky was more interested in the cultural and social factors that influence the construction of knowledge. Knowledge is mutually and collaboratively created and grounded on the experiences that the students bring to class. For Vygotsky, the teacher did not transmit knowledge but rather co-constructed knowledge, which was always based on social, cultural, political, and historical roots. Vygotsky did not envision predetermined developmental levels. He believed that learners continually move up to their next developmental level, in collaboration with a more capable peer. Vygotsky was a social constructionist (Wink & Putney, 2002).

Returning to Professor JS.   Returning to the saga of Professor JS, when we last left him, he had spent the first 20 years of his career as a professor vainly struggling to discover how to make the learning in his classroom meaningful, as he taught from his unexamined assumption about transmission or behaviorism being the only way to teach. At last glance, he had tried it *all* and had given up by blaming the students. Then an unexpected event in his life caused him to reexamine his long-held assumptions (Spencer, 2001–2002):

> About this time—beginning my third decade as a teacher—I chaired a national task force on the teaching of general chemistry. From this diverse collection of teachers of first-year chemistry, I began to learn about teaching. . . . I found that no erudite body had established the accepted method of delivery for the classroom. (p. 94)

Yes, Professor JS, there is no magic recipe. No one size fits all. The imposition of sameness on such diversity will not work. As Professor JS collaborated with two colleagues, they made some startling and upsetting discoveries. From the literature, they read that the way they had been teaching students had been deemed useless 40 years ago. You can understand their frustration. The most significant concept that they learned from the literature was: "The crucial point: What goes on in the learner's head is dramatically influenced by what is already there. Knowledge is personal" (p. 95). As Professor JS so clearly stated it, "Telling is not teaching" (p. 95).

> In the past, I had assumed that, if I could give examples that were clear to me, these examples would be equally clear to the students. I believed that I could make direct transfer from my mind to theirs. I had what educational psychologists term an egocentric point of view. The student would see exactly what I was seeing. But I was wrong. (p. 95)

Now, we will take a brief detour on the multiple meanings of construction of knowledge before we return to the inspiring conclusion to the saga of Professor JS.

ConstrucTIVist and ConstrucTIONist.   We said that we had chosen to look at education through three perspectives. However, we recognize that even within these three categories there are other perspectives. For example, as U.S. education moved from behaviorist to cognitivist to constructivist, decades passed and different interpretations of constructing knowledge together arose.

Although the construction of knowledge in classrooms has varying names with varying understandings, they are linked by the belief that people generate knowledge and are influenced by values and culture (Scheurman, 1998, p. 31). However, even the categories can be categorized. For example, constructivism (Scheurman, 1998) found at least 12 different categories or interpretations.

It appears that many have a common understanding that we construct knowledge jointly with another or with others. We come together; we read, inquire, explore; we learn together. Thus, the word *construcTIVist* has a broad base of mutual understanding. Or did we mean *construcTIONist*? Fasten your seat belts; let's see if we can *construct* knowledge about this *construct* of the *construction* of knowledge.

At a time when many share these understandings about the social construction or generation of knowledge, among some academics there is developing a more complex understanding of both of the words *construcTIVist* and *construcTIONist*. For educators, we need to understand the evolving concepts. In what follows, we will focus directly on construcTIVist and construcTIONist. The capital letters in the two words serve only as mnemonic learning aides. In addition we provide the following cognitive coat hooks that precede our explanation (see Figure 3.5).

Here is an example of construcTIVist learning. When Joan and Dawn talk about Piaget's developmental levels, they are socially learning. Or, as the graduate students walk through the classroom door, talking about their teaching contexts and the night's assignments, this is social learning. The focus is on INTER, or knowledge construction BETWEEN people.

By reflecting on the following example of construcTIONist learning, the focus is on a deeper sense of construcTIONist. If Dawn is sitting alone, reading a book about Vygotsky, it still has the potential to be social construction of knowledge. However, it is not simply interaction with Joan. It can also be interaction with the social, cultural, and historical context she brings with her and that which is within her environment. For example, as Dawn reads the Vygotsky book all alone, she is bringing other cultural artifacts to the learning as well: Her computer is in front of her; another Vygotsky book is within reach; an educational foundational text is lying open on the table by her computer. She uses the computer and the two other books to make meaning. In addition, she uses her language, as she mumbles to herself while searching for a specific file she knows is in her computer, to help her make more meaning. Dawn socially interacts with her social/cultural/historical context, including a cultural tool (language) and cultural artifacts (her computer and two books).

Here is another example of social construcTIONist learning. The next time you are in a teachers' lounge, watch people as they interact with the copy machine in an attempt to copy, collate, staple, and count. This is what you might see:

They begin to use a cultural tool (their language); you can hear the muttering. They might even get a little testy if you interrupt their social interaction with their own

---

ConstrucTIVist is to Piaget as construcTIONist is to Vygotsky.

ConstrucTIVist is to cognitive construction as construcTIONist is to social construction.

ConstrucTIVist is to interaction as construcTIONist is to collaboration.

FIGURE 3.5   Constructivist and Constructionist

language and the copier. The cultural artifacts can be almost anything that is handy, such as the various buttons to push, instructions taped on the top, or another colleague's example. It might, perhaps, even be another person who, unfortunately, happens to pass by—providing it is the right person, preferably an office person who runs the machine daily and brings a wealth of social, cultural, and certainly historical context to the machine. (See Figure 3.6.)

Now armed with real-life examples and a couple of summary statements, let's make one last mnemonic learning tool (see Figures 3.7 and 3.8).

Because of the different meanings of constructivist and constructionist, we will use the word *generative* to imply a broad semantic understanding of building knowledge as opposed to transmitting knowledge.

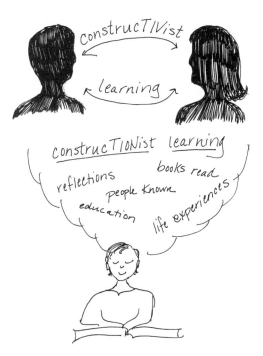

FIGURE 3.6   ConstrucTIVist and ConstrucTIONist

ConstrucTIVist: think Piaget; think cognitive; think interaction.

ConstrucTIONist: think Vygotsky; think critical reflection; think intramental.

FIGURE 3.7   Think Piaget; Think Vygotsky

WRITE, RIGHT NOW
ConstrucTIVist and ConstrucTIONist

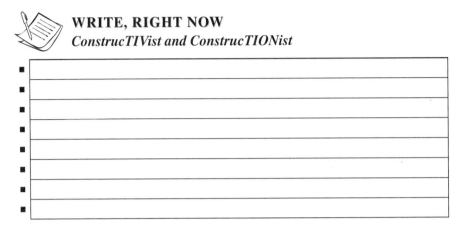

FIGURE 3.8   Write, Right Now: ConstrucTIVist and ConstrucTIONist

The entire previous discussion raises another question for us: What does *to know* mean? For example, in schools we want students to know the curriculum, to know the times tables, to know the theorems, and to know the proper grammatical rules. Some even suggest that there are specific things that all students *should know*. What does *to know* mean? Looking back on the discussion of construcTIVist and contrucTIONist, check yourself to see how much you know (see Figure 3.9). Imagine that the first test question is: What is construcTIVist and construcTIONist? Choose the right answer for you.

Returning to Professor JS.   Returning to the saga of Professor JS, we see that he had discovered the meaning of cognitive constructivist (Spencer, 2001–2002).

> The crucial point: What goes on in the learner's head is dramatically influenced by what is already there. Knowledge is personal. To effectively promote learning, the instructor needs to know what the students already know and what is going on in their minds and must be able to ascertain when a student is having difficulty. These cognitive students have shown that it is not possible for me as an instructor to transfer an idea intact from my head to the heads of students. This realization was profoundly unsettling but enlightening. The basic assumptions on which I organized my classes were turned upside down. (p. 95)

> Level one: not a clue
>
> Level two: a vague notion, but I cannot explain it.
>
> Level three: I can articulate it, but I will only confuse anyone who listened, but it would help me.
>
> Level four: I can articulate it, and you would "get" it.

FIGURE 3.9   Check Yourself

> **First,** the learners approach the new learning (data, information) with a hands-on, discovery approach.
>
> **Second,** only when the learners can ascertain patterns and trends to form their own concepts about the new learning are the new terms and definitions attached to the ideas of the new learning.
>
> **Third,** learners apply what has been learned, so that the new learning organizes itself and leads to a higher level of thinking.

FIGURE 3.10   A Basic Scientific Approach

Next, Professor JS, to his continuing credit, discussed his new learning with the students and devised an alternative approach to teach his college chemistry class. His basic premise was that students would be learners and teachers. He followed the basic approach that scientists follow when they do a study (see Figure 3.10).

If you should ever become confused with generative, or construcTIVist or construcTIONist, or social, cultural, or political mediation of knowledge, keep in mind what Patrick, a 13-year-old boy, said after he visited a three-hour university class that his father, Professor Young, was teaching. Patrick was a home-schooled student, who was doing well with his understandings of Western philosophies, but he really knew very little about Eastern philosophies, which was his father's area of expertise. The family created a plan for Patrick to begin his studies of Eastern thought, and part of the plan included Patrick attending a certain number of his father's evening classes. To appreciate this story, we must tell you that Professor Young has a great reputation as an instructor, and he is well loved and respected by students and faculty. The story is poignant and revealing, as we heard it from Professor Young.

At the end of the first class, Patrick and his dad were walking out to the car in the parking lot.

"Well, Pat, what did you think of class tonight?" Professor Young asked.

"Dad," Patrick replied, "maybe if you got the people involved with their learning, it would help."

Yes, Patrick, getting people involved with their learning is what the generative model of teaching and learning is all about (see Figure 3.11).

Transformative

The transformation model of teaching and learning is about getting people involved with their own learning and *taking action* on that new learning. It is often referred to in the literature as democratic, emancipatory, critical pedagogy, or critical theory, Freirian pedagogy, participatory, and/or feminist pedagogy. It is in the tradition of the Socratic method of teaching and learning with dialogue central to inquiry. The purpose of socially and culturally constructed knowledge within the classroom is to lead

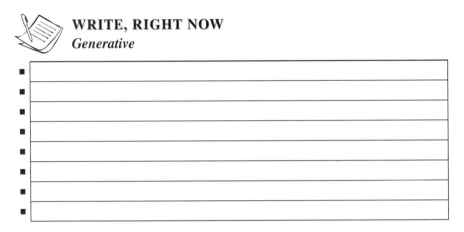

WRITE, RIGHT NOW
Generative

FIGURE 3.11   Write, Right Now: Generative

to self and social transformation out of the classroom. The transformation model of teaching and learning is grounded in multiple realities that are socially, culturally, historically, and politically shaped. This pedagogy calls us to name, to reflect critically, and to act (Freire, 1974).

We are often asked how transformative is different from generative because they are both grounded on socially constructed knowledge. The difference is that good generative teaching can be good generative teaching and still stay only in the classroom, whereas the challenge of transformative teaching leads to transformation in and outside of the classroom. The idea is to link the learning to the lives of the students, to inquire into their worlds, and to take the learning back into the community. Action always follows the learning. Action is the link back to the community, and action can come in many varieties.

At this point, we ask you to reflect on your own experiences. When did you experience transformative education, and what was the effect on you and your surrounding community? (See Figure 3.12.)

Multiple perspectives on teaching and learning abound because multiple ways of teaching and learning exist. As we conclude this discussion of these three perspectives, we encourage you to think deeply. Go vertically: What prior knowledge of theory do you bring? Go horizontally: What prior knowledge of practice do you bring? No one way is perfect for all learners. As teachers, it is our responsibility to understand as many perspectives as possible. We need to reflect on what is visible and what is below the surface.

Transmission and generative pedagogies are the dominant models of education that moved through the last century simultaneously and in contradiction to one another. These two adversarial schools of thought are what Bracey refers to as the "dueling visions" (Bracey, 2002). However, transformative pedagogy offers possibilities for schools and communities to create new and powerful human connections for self and social transformation.

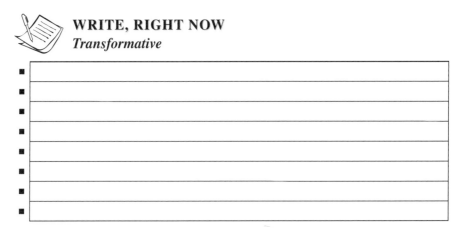

FIGURE 3.12   Write, Right Now: Transformative

The Voice of Life

This chapter is about the *ologies, ivists,* and *isms.* However, if these terms are baffling, our goal is to make them meaningful. In what follows, we share a metaphor of three gardens to capture the essence of the three pedagogical perspectives: transmission, generative, and transformative.

> *If you can't say it simply, you don't understand it.*
>
> ALBERT EINSTEIN

A Pedagogical Garden

The transmission garden appears as straight rows ending in precise right angles standing neatly at attention (see Figure 3.13). The only plants allowed to grow here have been planted deliberately and are sure to match the color scheme of the preplanned plant arrangement. Heaven help any stray seed that may have floated in on the wind or may have been deposited gently by the tiny foot of a passing hummingbird.

"You are throwing everything off!" the transmissive gardener bellows and promptly rips the emerging bud out by the roots.

A highly technical irrigation system has been constructed to encourage the growth of plants trucked in and intrusively planted in a new area not necessarily compatible to their natural requirements. These plants do not thrive, no matter how much external support the gardener gives them. Sunflowers stand staked efficiently in rows but the stakes prevent their large, seed-filled heads from following the natural course of the sun. In this garden, these flowers do not live up to their name in Spanish, *el girasol,* which means to rotate toward the sun.

FIGURE 3.13   A Pedagogical Garden

The behaviorist's garden is for show. Outside people are not invited in except on rare occasions when the gardener is showing off his control over his domain. The gardener does not pay any attention to natural climate and environment conducive to growing but rather forces the plants he wants into the ground.

"Some of them won't make it, but that's to be expected," he thinks to himself.

In the generative garden, a riot of color and a cacophony of various birds that have made this place their home greet us. Stone paths meander through the lush patches of free-flowing plants. An overall sense of order and symphony radiates throughout the garden. Maintained with a gentle and steady hand, the inherent wildness of the plants is allowed to flourish within the whole. Bright sprays of fuchsia zinnias ebb in and around the periwinkle bachelor buttons. Rose bushes laden with heavy, fragrant petals lean over against the wisteria vine, the purple flowers curling unbothered around the thorny stems. A huge cottonwood shades half of the yard, allowing shade-loving plants the protection to flourish. Benches and small tables dot the garden, providing an open invitation to sit and ponder, to read, or to reflect with a friend.

Unexpectedly, an errant raspberry bush springs up. Instead of being immediately weeded, it was allowed to grow and now provides support and shade for the clusters of Queen Anne's lace that would have otherwise withered in the sun's glare.

The gardener strolls through this garden admiring the natural growth of the flowers, guiding one stem away from the path here and coaxing a sunflower back upright there. Plants grow naturally, encouraged and guided with proper fertilizer, water, and oxygenation. Any unexpected plants are allowed to grow. The needs of individual plants are taken into account. The roses are given different care than the peonies.

The transformative garden contributes bounty and beauty for many. An abundance of color springs from a variety of flowers that complements the many vegetable and grain plants woven throughout. This garden is not for show, but rather its purpose is to enrich peoples' lives with its artistry and harvests. As with the generative garden, order and harmony shine through the multitude of plants. This garden differs from the generative garden in the fruit and vegetables it produces. This is a garden not only of reflection but also of action. This garden produces fruit and vegetables not only for the gardeners but also for a multitude of organizations. Portions of the harvest are sold at the local farmers' market, the proceeds going toward supporting organizations dedicated to social justice. Other portions are taken home to be eaten by the growers. One section of the garden is left unharvested for people in need to come and pick for their use. The gorgeous bouquets created from the flowers are given to neighbors and friends with the idea of sharing the grace of their beauty.

> *You will not learn from me philosophy, but how to philosophize—not thoughts to repeat, but how to think. Think for yourselves, enquire for yourselves, stand on your own feet.*
>
> IMMANUEL KANT

Praxis: Let the Magic Begin

> The lesson of Nietzsche may be summarized as follows: a philosophy is not something to be studied in a book—to be pondered in solitude and then, like any other book, shut up and put away—but something to be lived. Even if it exacts high or impossible stands, it must be tried and proved in action. (Tomlin, 1963, p. 276)

In the Praxis section of each chapter, our intention is to demonstrate how to take theoretical principles and turn them into practice. Pedagogical principles have no value if they do not turn into practice with students.

Principles to Practices

Throughout our careers, we have read many great pedagogical principles. We tuck these safely away in our brains and in our hearts, and we draw on them when teaching (and learning) in classes and inservices. In Figure 3.14, we share our four favorite pedagogical principles (Goodman, Bridges Bird, & Goodman, 1991).

When something seems to be going wrong with a class, we find that if we step back and quietly reflect on the four principles listed in Figure 3.14 we can usually get ourselves and the students back on track. We ask ourselves: Is this meaningful? Is this purposeful? Is this relevant? Is this respectful? It has become clear to us that when something is wrong in a class, and we can't quite put our finger on it, these four questions will guide us to a good answer.

How might these principles be turned into practice in a class? Lessons often follow a model or pattern with various phases. Whether you are philosophically grounded in transmission, generative, or transformative pedagogy, we have found

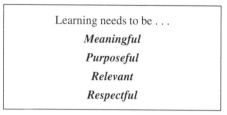

Learning needs to be . . .
Meaningful

Purposeful

Relevant

Respectful

FIGURE 3.14   Pedagogical Principles

that the four phases shown in Figure 3.15 provide structure for a lesson. The four phases are built on the needs and experiences of the students. We encourage teachers to link students' lives before beginning a lesson and to continue to seek linkages throughout the learning process.

More basics follow. Often teachers find it helpful to assign specific roles and responsibilities to students. Our preference is that the roles change, even on a regularly scheduled rotation basis, so that roles and responsibilities do not become fixed and slowly sink into *social sorting*. Figure 3.16 lists some archetypal roles that are often used in cooperative learning (Kagan, 1994).

First, Input
This is the initial state of a learning activity. Often teachers will model, pull in prior knowledge, focus students on the specific content or strategy to be learned, and develop the language that accompanies the learning. Teachers will often use this part of the lesson to spur the students' interest or to connect this to the world of the student.

Second, Guided Practice
After the initial phase of the learning activity, students are often provided a small group and relatively safe context to learn together. In literacy development, this phase is often accompanied by an adult, who provides guidance, when needed, on very specific aspects of the lesson. In content areas, often students will have read the same content and come together to practice something very specific.

Third, Independent Practice
This is the part of the learning cycle when students are required to read, to practice, and to learn alone without the support of another student.

Fourth, Assessment, Inquiry, Application
This is the part of learning that often depends on the knowledge or experience of the teacher. Based on the teacher's examined or unexamined assumptions, the teacher may test what was just learned; the teacher could ask students to demonstrate their knowledge in an inquiry-based application of the new knowledge; or the teacher could arrange for the new knowledge to be actually lived or applied in the real world.

FIGURE 3.15   Four Phases of a Lesson

Recorder—records the written information, ideas, and decisions for the group

Checker—checks for understanding and/or agreements

Facilitator—checks to see that all are included

Safety officer—responsible for safety issues

Materials manager—responsible for materials

Reporter—reports orally to the whole group

Praiser or encourager—praises effort and ideas

Taskmaster—brings team back to the task

Information organizer—helps to organize the information

Harmonizer or gatekeeper—makes sure all participate

Cleanup coordinator—makes sure that all help put everything away

Timekeeper—keeps the rhythm moving so all is accomplished

FIGURE 3.16   Archetypal Roles and Responsibilities

Often teachers create their own unique roles and responsibilities that tend to fit specific projects (see Figure 3.17). These roles also reflect the teacher's philosophical perspective; such is the case for Esmé Raji Codell, author of *Educating Esmé* (2001, p. 118), a book we thoroughly enjoyed.

Paradigm Paralysis

The point of this chapter is that there are multiple ways of knowing, many perspectives, and lots of different schools of thought. Many educational paradigms exist. The more we know about multiple perspectives, the deeper our reflections will be about ways of teaching and learning. We encourage you to revisit your own pedagogical paradigm. One danger to guard against is paradigm paralysis. Change is the only constant.

Time and experience often help us to see and to know in new ways. Reflection on our examined and unexamined assumptions is never easy. Often it feels as though the ground is moving when it is actually a paradigm shifting. It can be frightening, as

Discussion director—makes up questions

Literary luminary—reads aloud notable parts

Language lover—defines hardest words

Practical predictor—guesses or predicts what is coming

Process checker—sums it up; keeps track of each person's contributions

FIGURE 3.17   Individualized Roles and Responsibilities

we don't know where we will land. González (2001) describes her feelings as she emerged from her own paradigm paralysis. She had her particular notions about language and her prepackaged constructs about what she would see and learn in her research. However, when she went into the community, she was soon brought up short because her assumptions did not fit the people and the language. So, she tried harder, researched more, and tinkered with the data longer in her vain hope that her prefabricated package of expected patterns would emerge. It did not. Instead, she was jolted out of her complacency and into the previously unacknowledged and unseen world of the politics embedded in language. Only a painful abandonment of her previous assumptions opened her eyes to a new paradigm (pp. 18–19).

Can You Paradigm?

So, we ask you: Can you? As we have seen, Professor JS could. Now, we see that Professor Steph has another way of turning her theoretical principles into practice. She posts her pedagogical philosophy for all to see: the students and her peers. We know many teachers who do the same. A quick glance at the following professor's theoretical statement provides a look into the practice of her classes. (See Figure 3.18.)

The Literacy Link

In the first Literacy Link in the Introduction, we shared one way of making big books and said that we would add to this process in the following chapters. The next example is how Dawn made big books with students and families. At this time, she taught in a dual language program at the elementary level. She and the students made books almost daily.

Big Books: Dawn's Way

First, Dawn generated a dialogue with the students about content that they were preparing to learn. She did this to focus the students on the ideas and language. It also provided an opportunity for her to assess and to build on the prior knowledge of the group.

Second, as the students talked, Dawn wrote their ideas on the chalkboard.

Third, together the students and Dawn chose which sentences to put into the book-of-the-day.

Fourth, the students copied the new story onto their individual papers, as Dawn quickly copied the story onto large tagboard. She used markers to decorate and illustrate individual pages and quickly stapled ribbons to bind the book together. She discovered that she could make a book-of-the-day in about the same time that it took the students to write the same story on smaller sheets of paper at their desks.

Fifth, when finished, Dawn read the story with the students as she held up the big book for all to see. In the afternoon the students took their smaller copies home to

---

A Teaching Philosophy—Professor Steph

Dillard (1989) counsels that if you want to chop wood, aim for the chopping block, not the wood (p. 59). If you aim straight for the student, you will have nothing. If you aim for their answers on the test, their answers to questions asked, their demonstration of the knowledge that you have, you will have nothing. Aim past them, through them, to where they must go, to where you must go, if you and they are going to have a life. The students are pages they will write themselves. This is all I can really do.

1. *The Self Who Teaches:* As a teacher and writer who also quilts and paints I realize that teaching is every bit as creative an act as the artful methods used in painting, quilting, or writing. I bring my whole self into the writing classroom, the writing conference, and the in-class writing.

> *Excerpt from my teaching journal:* This week I noticed I felt the most creative in my writing conferences. After fifty-two writing conferences, I still have some strange energy when I should feel depleted. It comes from learning something about fifty-two lives and swapping ideas and listening carefully. Every fifteen minutes I make myself like a beach just after high tide, when the water starts to retreat, and what remains is just a smooth, clear surface without footprints, all promise. I make my mind like that after each conference so that the next writer gets a fresh ear.

Two adages sustain and direct me: (1) Less is more, and (2) suspend judgment. I show up eager to discuss the material. I prepare myself for uncomfortable surprises. I work at inviting students to talk more than I do while simultaneously helping them to connect with a wide range of texts.

> It is the quality of our own lives as we engage with the world that is one of the major sources of energy for our students. It is the questions you ask aloud about the world, your curiosity, the books you read, and your personal use of writing that teach far more than any methodological course you've ever taken.
> —Don Graves, *The Energy to Teach,* p. 35

2. *The classroom setting:* While flipping through a journal for professional pilots, I found a device that offers multifunction capabilities. Each screen assists the pilot in making informed rapid-fire decisions. I've always admired the situational awareness required to read both the instruments in the cockpit and the changing environment. Teaching allows me to channel a similar strength in a different venue. I, too, get flooded with information when I walk into a classroom. I have learned to cut, filter, highlight, streamline, listen very carefully, and act conscientiously. I have learned to keep us in flight for the semester.

FIGURE 3.18   One Way: Professor Steph

read with their families. The next day when the students entered the classroom, the larger book-of-the-day hung on a wooden clothes drying rack for students to read together on the floor during free reading time (Wink & Putney, 2000).

The Reading Café

In the following reading activity Laura, the teacher, combines her understandings of generative and transformative education. Laura shares that this process encourages students to follow their own curiosity within a dialectical process and then to take action on their learning.

The Reading Café involves discussions of facts, perceptions, and personal connections from text to personal life. Students come together to talk about text and life in their "café," just as adults do over a cup of coffee or tea in a real café. When the teacher says, "It's time to go to the café," students know what this means. This activity is designed to encourage students to bring in their ideas from their homes, books, and life experiences.

Laura teaches in a rural school district. Most of the students live in a low socioeconomic community, and many of the students are recent immigrants to the United States. Laura reports that they are always very interested in learning more about their new country. In this particular case, they were fascinated with chocolate milk.

Laura followed their curiosity with this specific activity. The students first generated language for and questions about this strange new beverage, chocolate milk. They then wrote letters to their principal requesting to try chocolate milk at lunch. Next, they wrote to a local vendor. Eventually, the vendor sent a distributor, who happened to be dressed like a clown, to visit the class and bring milk for the entire school.

In the process, they talked, they read, they wrote, they interviewed community and family members about the dairy industry, and they generated more questions from their own research. They linked their language learning with the science learning. Eventually, they learned about peer editing and process writing as they created their five-paragraph letters, and they learned about the power of language (Smith, 1998). However, the lesson in itself could be insignificant, except that Laura brought her teaching expertise to it. She had faith in the learners (Freemans, 1994); their *unofficial worlds* (Dyson, 1993) were embraced; Laura listened to the kids (Graves, 2001).

During the Reading Café, the teacher is as much a participant as the students. Student-generated questions are answered in five different ways: (1) by their classmates; (2) with other books that students find in class; (3) with books from home; (4) with interviews of their parents; and (5) from the Internet. When students report back to class the next day, they must state their intent by saying one of the following.

> "I have a fact to share."
> "I have an opinion to share."
> "I have a text-to-text connection."
> "I have a text-to-life connection."

Each student shares one fact, perception, or connection. If others have a question to ask this person, they may do so when the person is finished sharing the fact, perception, or connection. If that person cannot answer the question, it is opened up to the rest of the group for other opinions or connections. The timekeeper allows a maximum of three minutes.

In the Reading Café students learn the beauty of real-life discussion of ideas in a fun, safe manner. Talking and sharing their human responses to text and life create a provocative and intellectual climate that students carry with them out of the classroom and into their lives.

WHAT CAN BE LEARNED FROM THIS?

Theory matters. Practice matters. Theory and practice join together to create praxis. Praxis is the daily life of our pedagogy.

We have asked you to reflect on the past to rescue the future. Reflection helps us see more deeply, as in the saga of Professor JS. His courageous approach to personal reflection took him deeply into his own cherished assumptions about how to teach. The answers he found were the antithesis of his previous assumptions. He looked deeply within himself and revolutionized his teaching because of his respect for students and their learning. Previously, we wrote that methods are horizontal and theory is vertical. This has been the vertical chapter, which takes us below the surface, as in the iceberg. The purpose of this chapter has been to demonstrate that ideas run deep—often so deep that they are difficult to see.

CHAPTER NOTES

1. Our understandings of all that lies below the surface and the use of an iceberg to represent that have influenced through the years by the large volume of work of Jim Cummins.

2. The entire discussion of Vygotsky, Piaget, constructivist, and constructionist is informed by our ongoing collaborative dialogue with Le Putney of University of Nevada Las Vegas. For more on this, see Wink and Putney, 2002.

4 Teaching Passionately— Collaboratively

What the child can do in cooperation today he can do alone tomorrow.
VYGOTSKY, 1986, p. 188

This chapter will look at ways that collaboration can enhance teaching and learning. The centrality of caring across and within communities unifies the collaborative projects that we will describe in this chapter.

The Voice of Schools

Collaboration for us is not a selection of methods; rather, it is an approach to learning and living that is grounded in a critical and caring perspective. Critical, for us, does not mean to criticize; rather, it means to see below the visible surface, to reflect deeply, and to take action. Caring is not in opposition to being critical; rather, it is having a sense of respect, honor, or love. The pedagogical principles of collaboration and caring within the framework of a critical perspective can be turned into practice in various ways in multiple contexts. In this chapter, we will describe classroom practices that represent this understanding of collaboration.

Our understandings of collaboration do not exist in isolation. They are heavily influenced by the collaborative notions of the collected writings of Vygotsky and Cummins. Vygotsky (1986) theorized that collaboration was socially and culturally grounded interaction with others. Higher cognitive functions were a mediated action whereby language was more than a symbol carrying meaning. It was also a part of the co-construction of knowledge.

> Vygotsky believed that the child's reasoning was socially constructed through interaction with adults and peers. The development of higher cognitive functions was a mediated activity, which occurred first during social interaction. Understanding occurs through our historical, social, and cultural relations with others. Our language is more than a symbolic system through which we make meaning. Language also carries with it the meanings and intentionality of those who came before us, and who now use the same tool to make meaning for us. (Wink & Putney, 2002, p. 30)

Cummins (2001) expands on this construct by looking at what collaboration is and what it is not, within a framework of coercive and collaborative relations of power, linked together by the primacy of human connections in schools and communities.

Coercive and Collaborative Relations of Power

Coercive relations of power assume there is a limited amount of power; power is fixed and subtractive. It is fear based on the supposition that if one person gets more, someone else must get less. It is as if power is like pie—if someone eats a piece, there will be less for others. Thus, the person with the most holds on tightly in order to maintain what he or she has. This assumption sometimes lies just below the surface, unseen, and/or unacknowledged. However, this assumption often provides the unexamined pedagogical principle that drives practices.

We, like many others, have experienced coercive relations of power in schools, although we did not reflect on it at the time. Each of us has worked in schools run by coercive relations of power. In such situations, we now realize that we did less, we did it less effectively, and we were not happy while doing it. It made us subversive educators. The bottom line is that we were not very nice, which certainly must have had a negative effect on students and their learning.

Collaborative relations of power assume that power is infinite and dynamic. In addition, when we work together collaboratively, power grows.

We, like many others, have also experienced collaborative relations of power in schools. With further reflection, we now can see that when we were in that environment, we did more, we did it more effectively, and we were happier while doing it. It made us powerful educators. The bottom line is that we were nicer, which certainly must have had a positive effect on students and their learning.

If we have learned one thing in education it is that power and problems have one thing in common: There will always be enough for all. The challenge for educators is to learn how to negotiate their own identity when they are experiencing coercive relations of power. Cummins finds answers in the fact that the most important work we do includes the ways in which we create human connections with students. No one, no mandate, no regulations can take that away from an educator. Each person has the power to establish the most positive human connections possible so that students and colleagues can continue to negotiate their own identities and to control their own learning and future. We are living through a time when this is a greater challenge than 10 or 20 years ago. Recently, while Joan was teaching outside of the United States in an international education program, an international teacher quietly raised her hand from the back of the classroom and said, "Dr. Wink, I think that teaching in public education in the United States must be one of the hardest jobs in the world right now. Why would anyone do it?" Even more shocking was the fact that most in the classroom, who represented education in many countries, nodded their heads in agreement with her. In the following reflective writing activity in Figure 4.1 we ask you to reflect on your own experiences with coercive relations of power in schools and with collaborative relations of power in schools.

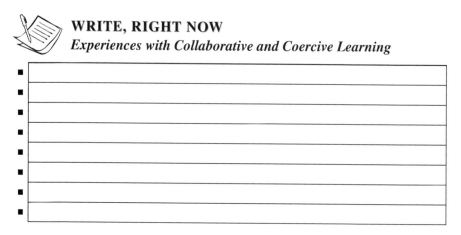

WRITE, RIGHT NOW
Experiences with Collaborative and Coercive Learning

FIGURE 4.1   Write, Right Now: Experiences with Collaborative and Coercive Learning

Inert and Catalytic Learning

The discussion of coercive and collaborative relations in schools leads us to another construct from Cummins (2001): inert and catalytic teaching and learning. Inert teaching and learning, as we have all experienced, is lifeless. Catalytic teaching and learning is filled with life (see Figure 4.2).

FIGURE 4.2   Inert and Catalytic Learning

Our experiences with inert learning, and we have had far too many of them, were always filled with lots of passive learning: We read; we listened; we memorized; we took tests and did well. One problem is that we forgot; or, in fairness to ourselves, we could say that we didn't *always* forget *all,* but it does seem that inert learning brings back mostly memories of memorizing followed by walking out of the class and not caring about the memorized knowledge. In fact, much of it immediately became meaningless after the good grade on a test. Our experiences with catalytic learning are vastly different. We remember much about the people, the context, and the content. We remember love and caring and fellowship. We remember chatter, gentle smiles, interaction, and moments of a-ha. We remember taking the ideas and building on them and using them today. At least in our experiences with collaborative relations of power, they involved catalytic learning. So, the more difficult reflective question then is: Did coercive relations of power lead to inert learning? Far too often, our answer is yes. (See Figure 4.3.)

Intentional and Incidental Learning

This leads us to Krashen's (1999) notions about intentional and incidental learning. Intentional knowledge is that which we studied hard for. Intentional learning involved a lot of memory work, followed by our ever-present forgetting process.

Joan remembers a specific French class; she intentionally learned the inert knowledge under somewhat coercive conditions. You guessed it; she doesn't speak French today. Dawn's experiences with intentional learning are highlighted by a German history class. Today her primary memory is the stacks of books and an orange highlighter pen. You guessed it; she knows nothing about what those books say today. In addition, she is still mad today that she got an A–. We emphasize the minus because that is what she remembers. We can look at our old texts and our class notes and see our own underlining, highlighting, and margin notes, but not even remember what we learned.

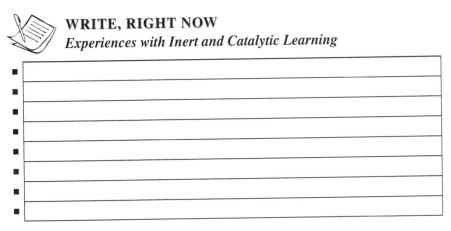

WRITE, RIGHT NOW
Experiences with Inert and Catalytic Learning

FIGURE 4.3   Write, Right Now: Experiences wth Inert and Catalytic Learning

Incidental learning is that unexpected, spontaneous learning that simply happens, but we never forget it. For example, in Joan's intentional studying of French, she remembers very little of French; however, in that class she incidentally learned a lot about birding and still loves to do it today. The professor and her husband were avid naturalists and loved to study birds. Joan was intrigued by their passionate interest in birds and eventually went out into the fields with them. At that time, their passion attracted Joan's interest, even though their interest in birds seemed odd at the time. Incidentally, today Joan is an amateur birder. (See Figures 4.4 and 4.5.)

It is safe to guess that the chemistry undergraduate students in Professor JS's classes studied intentionally. But, after a couple of decades, he started to worry that his students only had inert knowledge. Finally, he entered into collaboration with colleagues and suddenly the learning in his classes became catalytic. Based on his descriptions of the interactive processes he now facilitates, we will even guess that the students in his classes are leaving with some incidental learning.

Collaborating and Negotiating Identities

Reflecting on the preceding notions of coercive/collaborative relations of power, inert/catalytic learning, and intentional/incidental learning, it is safe to say that what

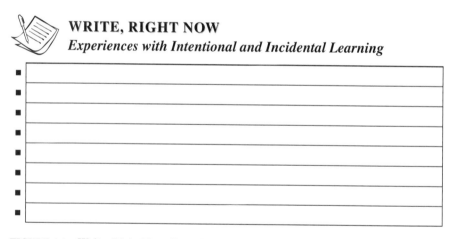

WRITE, RIGHT NOW
Experiences with Intentional and Incidental Learning

FIGURE 4.4   Write, Right Now: Experiences with Intentional and Incidental Learning

Coercive relations lead to intentional, inert teaching and learning. Collaborative relations lead to incidental, catalytic teaching and learning.

FIGURE 4.5   Coercive/Collaborative

we do matters. Following the framework of Cummins (2001), we believe that one thing we can do is to create collaborative processes in which students learn as they negotiate their own identities. If we do this with passion, all the better. The connections we create in classrooms are central to students' growth as they negotiate their own identities. These interactions trigger a process whereby students create their own sense of self. Furthermore, these human relationships can have a negative or positive effect. Students may be failing not because they are not motivated, or not because they need intervention, or not because they are nonnative speakers of English, but rather because of what is being communicated to them by their teachers. The social messages we send to students have the potential to send students' spirits soaring or crashing.

Human relationships are the ways we negotiate identities in our classrooms (Cummins, 2001). These relationships are evident when students transform their own self-image, discover who they are, redefine themselves, and, thus, create the future. And none of this takes place in a vacuum. These new and emerging identities are surrounded by the powerful relationships between teachers and students.

When teachers respect and like students, the students negotiate their identities to higher levels of human potentiality. When teachers don't like and don't respect students, the students have the potential to become less than they were before they entered the classroom. The interactions between students and educators are never neutral; these human connections either encourage or discourage collaboration and self-development (Cummins, 2001). Coercive relationships of power are used in the sociopolitical context to subvert the achievement of marginalized students. Affirmation and respect for students is a catalyst for academic development.[1]

An Example: Negotiating Identities with Passion.   The purpose of the following authentic classroom experience is to make visible what negotiating identities actually means within a collaborative classroom. This example of passionate pedagogy began quite unexpectedly in a graduate class filled with teachers. It evolved into an all-consuming project for the last six weeks of class. The story is a testimony to the power of collaboration in life and in a classroom.

We hear a lot of talk about *those people* these days. Who in the world are *those people?* Everyone talks about *them.* We are wondering who *they* are. It certainly couldn't be *us.* An unexpected reflection on *those people* started very simply after a colleague came to our graduate class to discuss culture. She discussed that there are many definitions of cultures, but essentially they all have two commonalties: Cultures are learned and they are shared.

When she left, I spontaneously shared with the class some of the things I could remember learning from my own culture. When I left home to attend college, I met my future husband. I remember our initial conversation because he told me several things about himself that bothered me. I remember the discomfort I felt when I learned he was from Iowa. I was from South Dakota, and you know how *those people* from Iowa are. He added to my anguish when he said that he was from a farm. I was from a ranch, and you know how *those farmers* are. He further told me that his family belonged to the Farmers' Union. Horrors! My family belonged to the Farm Bureau, and you know how *those* Farmers' Union people are. I didn't ask any more questions because I was afraid of what he might say about his home culture. However, I very clearly remember wondering what his politics and religion were. You know how *those* Democrats and Catholics are!

The class and I laughed about the things that I had learned from my own culture: ranchers were good, and farmers were bad; Republicans were good, and Democrats were bad; Protestants were good, and Catholics were bad. As we were laughing together, a young grad student slowly raised her hand and shared her culture with the class.

"I went to private Catholic school for 12 years," Heather shared with the class.

"And, you know how *those* private school kids are," one of her friends said, which relieved the tension we were feeling. The class and I laughed nervously.

"Do you know who I learned to hate when I was in private school all those years?" she asked us.

"No," we answered curiously.

"Public school kids and teachers," she quietly and seriously told us.

"That's us," someone blurted out.

"You know how *those* public school kids and teachers are," another student offered weakly.

A third student responded to my initial comments, "And it wasn't the Democrats who were bad either. It was the Republicans. I learned they were only interested in making the rich richer and the poor poorer."

This sudden outburst about Protestants versus Catholics and Democrats versus Republicans made the class and me realize that we were on a slippery slope. We were entering new territory. It was exciting and dangerous—ripe with potential and disaster. This was not a part of our prescribed curriculum; this was not on the syllabus. I was not transmitting knowledge. We were generating ideas together, and we sensed transformation could not be far behind. However, the truth is that we raced up that learning curve with reckless abandon.

Within the first 20 minutes of this spontaneous and powerful class dialogue, I noticed tears in the eyes of one particular grad student, Susan, who was sitting beside Constance, who was very, very quiet. As the class continued to share, I noticed that the five students at this table were listening to all the comments but were only sharing privately. Soon, I saw more tears in the eyes of the other students at this table. Susan is white; she learned to hate blacks. Constance is black; she learned to hate whites.

As the evening wore on, all the students in the class became aware of the intense pain of these five students. The rest of the class demonstrated their empathy and respect by leaving this small group alone. Finally, the tension was broken when someone referred to the small group as "the crying table."

Somehow, it made it okay for tears and laughter to be a part of meaningful teaching and learning about multicultural education. After this comment, Susan told the whole group that as each of them had shared who *those people* were, she suddenly realized that she had been taught to hate each group that had been named. In retrospect, we believe that this painfully honest moment was the impetus for further dialogue, which led to their collaborative process to generate passionate pedagogy. Later in the evening, I sat down to visit with this group of five tearful students.

"Constance, you are the only African American student in class, and you did not share with the whole group." Constance quietly nodded in agreement.

"Why?" I asked.

Silence.

"Constance," I continued quietly, "you were taught to hate *me,* weren't you?" Constance quietly nodded in agreement.

On our journey to discover who *those people* were, we started to examine hate, fear, and distrust. We began by talking about when we were young. In small groups, we reflected on our own experiences and reactions to *those people.* As we did this, we realized that our old yearbooks would be a great place to begin the painful process of critically reflecting on some of our previously held assumptions. When the semester began, none of us ever thought that our old high school yearbooks would become part of the curriculum. However, that is exactly what happened. When we took time to reflect critically, we were surprised to see what we learned.

Carolyn came to class with her high school yearbook, circa 1970, to share with her colleagues. Just as Susan's honest emotions had triggered the first phase of the dialogue, so now the faces in the yearbook served as a catalyst for an intense discussion about ethnic diversity within specific geographical locations and time frames. Some yearbooks were as white as snow, whereas others were filled with the colors of diversity.

As one small group reflected on their past by rediscovering their yearbooks, another small group of graduate students reflected on our use of language. We will be honest: We just don't know what verb to use. As we shared and dialogued in class, the students often said: I was taught to *hate* black people. I was taught to *hate* white people. I was taught to *hate* rich people. I was taught to *hate* poor people. However, when we wrote the word *hate,* it seemed so powerful on paper. This raised another painful question: Is hate more dangerous when it is visible on paper or hidden in the heart?

As we were struggling with our own use of the verb *hate,* suddenly another dangerous verb emerged among the students. Hate led us to fear. Several students suddenly added that they were never taught to hate; rather, they learned to fear certain groups.

"*Those people* in my family were the African Americans, Hispanic Americans, and Asian Americans. My family taught me not to hate but to fear them," a third student said.

"We feared having to go to school with the normal, underprivileged public," Heather, from the Catholic school experience, added in the dialogue.

Again the class and I sensed the steep learning curve of this dialogue about hate and fear. The word *fear* led us to immigrants.

"I am the perfect example of one of those people who were not taught to hate, but to fear. I am suddenly realizing that there is no difference. One of my clearest examples comes from my grandfather's open opposition to *any* type of immigrant. Plain and simple, he hates them. Incidentally, I love him," Carrie shared. "I recently told him that I was going to teach a group of 22 Japanese exchange students for eight weeks. In addition, my sister and I were each going to host one student in our homes."

" 'I can't believe you girls would have anything to do with *them*,' Grandpa said to me. He blames *them* for the death of his brother in World War II," Carrie told us.

"Now, I understand what the textbooks mean when they say that the social, cultural, and political context affects kids in schools," another grad student added.

"After listening to all of this," Lisa told her classmates, "I realize that I was taught to fear *those Mexicans*. This all makes me wonder who fears *me* now. This is frightening to think about because, as you know, I have many Mexican American students in my first-grade class."

The students were amazed at some of their personal and painful reflections about *those people*. We were horrified to see just how inclusive our list of people to hate had become. It seemed no one was spared.

It had all started so simply. We thought we would share and learn about cultures. It seemed safe when the visiting professor came to share with us. However, it didn't always feel safe and simple as we critically confronted our old assumptions about *those people*. Our reflections caused some of us to struggle with our old ideas, beliefs, assumptions, and stereotypes that were learned while growing up. It was painful when we came to understand that fear is very much like hate, and that much of our hate is covert and not overt.

Many adults in this class grew up believing they were the norm, the standard. All other groups were measured as being different from them. By realizing that we are not the norm—we are all different compared to someone—we can respect difference in others and in ourselves. This has been the story of what happened to us when we learned and shared about ourselves. We cried. We laughed. We ached. We cringed. We talked. We reflected. We wrote. We learned. A lot.

Everyone wanted to share; we all wanted to learn. This conversation of our lived experiences mattered to us. It was real. For the remaining six weeks of the semester, we wrote, read, and reflected on the "other," which was new and disturbing language for many in the class. Not every moment was wonderful.

But, in the end, we all learned far more than was on the original syllabus.

What is the *other*? It is all I haven't experienced. It is what I don't know and understand. It is the upside-down to my right-side-up. For each of us, the *other* is unique. My *other* need not be yours. However, many of us are often uncomfortable with the *other*. The antithesis does not affirm. The *other* asks us questions, and our answers don't fit.

During these weeks in class, we finally came to a point where we could agree that hope helps and hate hurts. We also learned that to hate and to love are powerful parts of teaching and learning, even when we ignore or deny them;

to *tolerate* difference is demeaning; to *respect* difference is empowering for all;

to reflect critically is one way to challenge our old assumptions;

to think carefully about what we are passing on to our own children;

to realize that *those people* are us;

to share passionately and honestly is central to pedagogy.

Rudyard Kipling's poem, "We and They," helped us to end our semester with some perspective. The following two lines made us laugh at ourselves again.[2]

All the people like Us are We,
And, everyone else is They.

The Voice of Life

Collaborative Learning in a Rural Context

Collaboration is not just for schools; it is also for communities. In the subsequent story, we will find collaboration in the most surprising places—when one can get there. The story opens with the daily adventures and struggles of a young 13-year-old girl as she tries to cross a river to attend her one-room schoolhouse on the prairies. Depending on the day, she wades the river, goes in a boat, drives a tractor, or sometimes her dad carries her across on his back. The story ends in her senior year, which takes place in a school 50 miles from her home. Funds of knowledge (Moll, 2000) are bodies of culturally grounded knowledge that exist in families. These are the human resources that come into school daily with the students who carry this knowledge inherently, because they grew up in their unique family constellation. These bodies of knowledge can be brought into schools when collaborative learning is encouraged.

The collective nature of the funds of knowledge can be seen in a one-room country schoolhouse. In the following conversation, Tracey, a 13-year-old girl on her way to school, shares her funds of knowledge with Joan. Her route to school includes crossing the river near her home daily during every season. Tracey and her family did not consider her abilities to cross the river as a unique family and culturally grounded body of knowledge. Joan did, as will be seen as she relates her experiences going to school for a day with Tracey.

"Tracey, how in the world are we going to get across the river?" I asked, looking down at the ice on that cold January day.

"Walk," she replied as she took off with determined 13-year-old strides across one hundred yards of the frozen (I hoped) river. "Come on," she called to me as I hesitated on the bank of snow.

I headed onto the ice; I stood as tall as I could; I swung my arms; I kept my head up; I did all of this to try to hide my terror from Tracey.

I had come to visit this little school of seven students because I wanted to articulate the differences and similarities between rural and urban education. I thought I would ask Tracey leading questions like: "So, tell me what you are reading at school. Do you have a school library? Do you and your classmates work together on projects?" Instead, I asked: "What in the world do you do in the spring when the ice starts to melt?"

"Sometimes, we use the four-wheeler. Other times, we take the Argo (a little open vehicle that resembles a tub with six wheels). Or, we use the 4 × 4 pickup, the tractor, the john-boat (a small oblong boat that resembles a floating block of wood), and sometimes we have to ride horses. But a lot of the year we can wade across except when we have to use planks to cover the ice and water," she matter-of-factly listed her means of transportation as she scrambled up the bank of snow on the south side of the frozen river.

"What? Planks?" I asked as I hurried to catch up with her.

"Yes, planks to connect the pieces of ice. Don't worry, we have life jackets we wear that we hang on that tree when we get to the other side. Sometimes we have to use a rope to tie my sister and me together. Dad usually goes ahead to check where the river is safest. But the worst time was when we were on horseback, and my horse fell into a hole in the river, and I had to swim. There was water coming over the saddle," she explained to me (Wink, 2000, p. 27).

Tracey drew on the collective funds of knowledge of her family to get across the river. She had experienced this problem-solving activity every winter of her life (Wink & Putney, 2002, pp. 97–99). This was how her father and older sister had attended school. It was "the way it is."

Ideally in schools, teachers and students draw on collective and individual funds of knowledge. Tracey was able to get to school because her dad and sister taught her how to do it and frequently helped her across. In the classroom, teachers may draw on students' funds of knowledge to make the curriculum meaningful and enrich the class with the often surprising and passionate funds of knowledge students bring to school.

In the following story, collaboration is found in a vastly different area of the world. In this case it is not a rural school on the prairies of North America but rather is found in the desert of the Middle East during war. In this example, it was only through collaboration with her in-laws that enabled the Iowa-born Jean to learn to live within a Muslim family. And it was the human connections that kept Ahmad, her husband, alive in the desert. Although the stories are vastly different in many respects, they are linked through the power of collaboration.

Collaborative Learning in an International Context

In her work with international education, Joan has discovered that when she speaks of collaboration, human connections, and passion, the international educators link these concepts to the four guiding principles of international teaching and learning: interconnectedness, context, multiple perspectives, and conflict management. The language may be different but the ideas are the same. Ahmad's funds of knowledge (his family knowledge) enabled him to stay alive. Jean's funds of knowledge from the Iowa farm enabled her to connect with her new family, culture, and religion.

Increasingly, life at the local level affects and is affected by numerous interconnected systems operating at the global level. Many of the most critical problems faced by the world today cannot be solved by individuals or nations working alone. Students need to understand interconnectedness, its benefits, its costs, and its requirement of cooperative efforts in working toward mutually beneficial solutions to contemporary issues in the classroom and in the world.

One of the most vivid examples of the interconnectedness of international education was recently made clear to us. A teacher in international education, Jean was 33 years old. She had grown up on a farm in Iowa in a large and loving stereotypical midwestern family. She went to the local state university and fell in love with a young man from Kuwait. Eventually, she moved to his country, married, and had four beautiful children. Jean and her new family lived in the same house with her new extended family of in-laws. She often commented that there were very few difference between his large and loving family and hers in Iowa. She and her husband, Ahmad, continued to be involved with international education in the United States, in Kuwait, in Spain, and in Israel.

One night in 1991, Jean awoke to horrible noise and thought it was a thunderstorm that she remembered from her childhood. As the entire family gathered in the kitchen, she slowly began to realize that what she was hearing was the noise of bombs, not thunder. Desert Storm had begun, and the Iraqis were retaliating against the U.S. bombs by using artillery against any family with connections to the United States. Her husband fled into the desert that very night.

For the next several months, Jean, who was pregnant with her fourth child at the time, and her extended in-law family never heard another word from him. Jean could not get out of the country; she could not call to her parents in Iowa. During the long months, she and her new family survived day to day; they were never safe. Life became a series of artillery fire, unwelcome and threatening banging on their door, and long and stealthy searches for food in the night.

When Desert Storm ended, Ahmad came walking out of the desert one night and back to his family. This experience emphasizes the interconnectedness of us all. Jean's multiple perspectives helped her connect with the new ways of knowing of her new family. Jean and Ahmad both used their conflict management skills innumerably during the separation. The context for each of them determined their daily lives. When all of the pain had ended, they discovered that human connections may be at the heart of school, but they are also very much at the heart of living.

These four principles of interconnectedness, context, multiple perspectives, and conflict management highlight the inherent undercurrent of interconnection encompassing every aspect of education and of life. Collaboration between teachers, teachers and students, teachers and political leaders, teachers and communities, and teachers and families acknowledges and embraces this intrinsic value of collaboration and positive human connections. The principles also reveal the very real local consequences of national and international occurrences. It is tempting to ignore this interconnectedness. When this happens, we create isolation and alienation, neither of which has any place in education.

Every event, situation, or problem has a context from which it emerged and that continues to shape it. The context and its interpretation define both the constraints and the opportunities for responding to human problems. Developing the ability to search for and understand the context of contemporary issues is crucial to the process of analysis, decision making, and problem solving in today's complex classroom and world.

Each of us brings a unique perspective to our assessment of the world. That perspective is conditioned by our membership in various groups (e.g., gender, class, race, and ethnicity). Students and teachers need to recognize the sources of their own viewpoints and to value their own perspectives while appreciating the existence of other points of view. Understanding the process by which individuals come to have different perspectives will prepare students to better handle the inevitable conflicts that arise in a diverse, interconnected classroom and world.

Conflict is a natural, recurring part of the human experience. Strategies of conflict management and resolution include peaceful approaches such as mediation and political or legal activities. The ability to communicate effectively with students and people of diverse backgrounds, worldviews, and languages is crucial to processes of nonviolent conflict management.

Collaborative Learning in a Virtual Context

Long-distance collaboration and connection is easier now than it has ever been in history. Cummins and Sayers (1995) envision a world in which students, teachers, and parents are globally connected through the Internet. This medium bridges cultural and geographic barriers once thought impenetrable. In one example, a young man in a Croatian refugee camp sends out an e-mail message describing prisoner abuse, which is received and translated by a Long Island high school student. Through the Internet, this student shares the translation with the world, resulting in forthcoming humanitarian aid. The Internet facilitates international cooperation and collaboration to previously impossible heights.

Although we heartily support the use of the Internet and the collaboration that it provides for all, of course, we also are very aware that we need to supervise and use caution with children's access to the Internet and time spent learning electronically. Used appropriately, the Internet and computers enrich and stimulate learning. Used inappropriately, they become time wasters at best and conveyers of unsuitable images at worse. The temptation for teachers can be to use technology to "plug students in" so that they, the teachers, can grab time to grade papers. The only appropriate use of technology in the classroom is as a tool for enhancing specific academic curriculum and collaborative learning opportunities.

Jalongo (2003) provides examples of these international possibilities. Students can connect immediately with other students around the world, seeing their work and discovering pen pals through sites such as Web Kids' Village (www.ks-connection. org/village/village.html) and Poetry Pals (www.geocities.com/EnchantedForest/ 5165/index1.html) (Jalongo, 2003, p. 247). Children can take a virtual field trip anywhere in the world via the Internet, for example, a virtual field trip of Brazil at www. vivabrazil.com (p. 249).

Elementary students can access National Geographic Kids, and the world of nature and discovery, at www.nationalgeographic.com and Ranger Rick magazine at www.nwf.org. Jalongo guides educators and parents to reflect on the ultimate desired outcome of technological use. She offers guidelines to help teachers and parents in their use of technology.

- Have I provided parents and families with recommendations about the media and young children (as we would add youth of any age)? Parents and families, whose children often know more about computers and the Internet than they do, may be dazzled by this superior knowledge. Parents and families may also be convinced (by the media) that computer access today will mean high-paying jobs tomorrow. As you work with parents and families, help them realize that technology is a tool, rather than a solution (p. 250).
- Have I taught children in the primary grades to use the Internet to research a question? Jukes, Dosaj, and Macdonald (2000) describe the five A's that can be used to address information needs: (1) asking key questions, (2) accessing relevant data, (3) what it suggests or appears to say, (4) applying the data to the task, and (5) assessing both the result and the process (p. 246).

The Internet throws open the doors to encourage literacy development. Something as simple as exchanging e-mail messages with pen pals, whether they be across the world or in the next classroom, is meaningful to the students.

Students can interact with other family members via e-mail; aunts, uncles, and grandparents provide excellent resources in literacy development. Students can use school time to exchange correspondence. This correspondence can be printed out and pasted into a blank journal, capturing the beauty of these memories. In our own family, Joan (Grammie to the grandchildren) writes e-mails to the kids. They adore receiving these personal messages. Even reluctant readers really want to know what their own message contains.

Computers can provide alternate routes of accessibility to the curriculum. Gurian, Henley, and Trueman (2001) found students respond positively to curriculum introduced through games and activities on the computer, when they find these skills difficult with pen and paper. They do include a cautionary note regarding how much time young children spend in front of the computer. Recent brain research reveals too much or inappropriate computer and media images are detrimental to development.

As districts and communities debate computer use, it is very important to remember this fact: A child who learns to use a computer at age 6 and a child who learns at age 16 show little or no difference in proficiency after a few months of use. Quite simply, to learn computer or other screen proficiencies can be learned later in life, thus, with no risk to natural brain development (Gurian et al., 2001, p. 35).

Although the previous examples have all been grounded in K–12 education, the graduate students in Joan's classes also are active users of the Internet to learn collaboratively. The vast majority of these students are also full-time teachers and parents; thus, their time is exceedingly valuable. The Net provides equal access to knowledge and communication later in the evening when children have gone to bed. As we write, the Web sites listed in Figure 4.6 provide a sampling of sites that students are using in class.

In the previous section, we shared authentic and diverse examples of the power of passionate pedagogy grounded in collaboration. Before moving into a classroom activity, which teachers can use and/or adapt, we ask that you reflect on your learning using Figure 4.7.

Praxis: Let the Magic Begin

Spiders, Rats, and Transformation

Spiders, rats, and transformation (Meyers, 1999) provide an example of the powers of collaboration. In this actual experience two elementary teachers and their colleagues at the local university modeled collaborative teaching and learning. As will be seen, the students in their classes soon were collaborating also. We doubt we have ever *intentionally* studied contagious collaboration, but it seems that it is one of those common understandings hiding under the surface that we all understand. The students, teachers, and teacher educators in this project learned *incidentally* the *catalytic* knowledge about spiders and rats, which certainly are not *inert*.

AltaVista's Babelfish world.altavista.com/tr	**Neil Brick, a teacher in Holyoke Public Schools maintains this site on bilingual education** http://members.aol.com/neilesl
Educational Research www.EdResearch.info	
ERIC—Educational Resources Information Center www.accesseric.org/index.html	**NMCI—National MultiCultural Institute** www.nmci.org
Steve Krashen www.sdkrashen.com	**Language Teaching and Technology** http://polyglot.cal.msu.edu/llt/default.html
CAL—Center for Applied Linguistics www.cal.org	**Dave's ESL Café** www.pacificnet.net/~sperling/eslcafe.html
CBER—Center for Bilingual Education & Research, Arizona State University www.asu.edu/educ/cber/	**James Crawford's Language Policy Website & Emporium** http://ourworld.compuserve.com/homepages/jwcrawford/
CMMR—Center for Multilingual Multicultural Research, University of Southern California www-bfc.usc.edu/~cmmr/	**Researchville** www.researchville.com
	Statistics www.statistics.com
CREDE—Center for Research on Education, Diversity, and Excellence University of California, Santa Cruz www.crede.uscsc.edu/HomePage/home.html	**TESL/TEFL/TESOL/ESL/EFL/ESOL Links** www.aitech.ac.jp/~iteslj/links
NCBE—National Clearinghouse for Bilingual Education The George Washington University www.ncbe.gwu.edu	**University of Michigan Internet Public Library** www.ipl.org
	YourDictionary.com www.yourdictionary.com

FIGURE 4.6   Web Site List

The curriculum for this project was not prescribed, not planned—and that was exactly its power. Through their expertise, the teachers recognized the possibility and potential of the imaginary spiders in the basement, which were scaring a group of elementary students. The teachers talked with each other and decided simply to follow the curiosity of their real-world fear. They asked the students more about the basement, the spiders, and their fears. This one pedagogical act eventually rippled through not only the lives of these students but also of a community of learners, composed of classroom teachers and professors from the local university. Soon the students decided to write a letter to the principal to request his presence on a field trip to the basement to confront their fears. Research groups were formed. The Basement

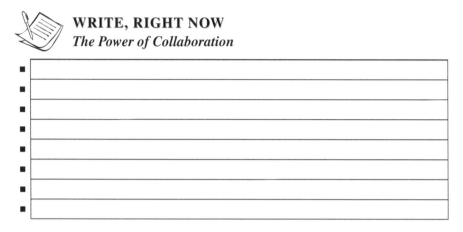

WRITE, RIGHT NOW
The Power of Collaboration

FIGURE 4.7   Write, Right Now: The Power of Collaboration

Group created a video presentation of going into the basement with the principal to uncover the truth that there were no spiders. The Spider Group created a 2-foot by 3-foot model of a spider web to share with the other students. Eventually, other research groups were formed to collaboratively study other scary living things: sharks, rats, snakes, owls, and dinosaurs.

The various research groups shared with their classmates. All students joined together to author and publish "The Basement Book," which they donated to the school library. The class shared all at a Learning Celebration, to the delight of 75 guests ". . . and they sent ripples through the first-grade classroom, through our teacher students group, and through the school" (Meyers, 1999, p. 4).

This model of collaborative learning is a stellar example of the role of collaboration in transformative pedagogy. It was thrilling, disturbing, and disruptive because it certainly did not conform to the mandated curriculum. However, because teachers and teacher educators collaborated as they inquired into the lives of students, their relationships to each other and to the community deepened, as did their understanding of teaching and learning. Their collaborative efforts led directly to more positive human connections (Cummins, 2001) within their classes, the school, and the community.

The Literacy Link

In previous chapters, we have demonstrated ways of making books with students. Many ways exist for authoring and publishing books with students (Wink & Putney, 2000). (See Chapter Note 1.) At this point, we are assuming that the teacher and students have multiple pages written and illustrated, and it is time to bind the book.

Big Books: How to Bind

It is preferable that each author be sitting at a table because the binding process for big books requires a little room. If you are making smaller books, an individual desk will suffice.

Tape is needed for the binding. For very small books, cellophane tape will function. For larger books (8 × 11), cellophane tape is less efficient; masking tape will work better for this size. For large books, which can be used with a small or whole group, you will need at least masking-tape strength, if not something stronger. Strapping tape is often used if the participants want to laminate each page prior to the binding process. Remember to laminate first.

Before beginning with tape, it is helpful to practice the following 10 steps with Post-it Notes. Begin with a five-page book only (Wink & Putney, 2000). (See Figure 4.8.)

At this point, we offer other ways of establishing literacy practices grounded in collaboration. A suggestion is to turn the classroom into a book club. Better yet, let the students create their own book clubs. If you were going to join a book club, what are the first questions you might ask: What do they read? Who is in the club? Do we have to do anything with the book other than read it and talk about it? In this case, it is truly the voice of life that is informing the voice of schools. From our own preferences in

---

1. Place the last page, face up, on the desk in front of you.

2. Tape the left (vertical) side of the page; half of the long strip of tape will be on the edge of the page and the other half of the long strip of tape will be taped to the desk. Remember: half on, half off.

3. Place the second-to-last page on top of last page, which is now taped to the desk. Place the tape exactly as directed in step 2.

4. Repeat step 2 with all pages, including title page and cover. All pages of your book are taped to each other and to the desk. You will be looking at the cover of your book.

5. Detach all pages of the book from the desk and turn over face down on the desk with the sticky side of tape facing up.

6. Place half of another long piece of tape on top of sticky part of the tape (which is facing you) and the other half of the tape on the desk. The front of the book is now facing down and is still taped to the desk.

7. Detach the book from the desk. Fold the only remaining sticky part over to the back of the spine of the book.

8. Take another long piece of tape and tape half vertically to the front of the book and the other half vertically to the back of the book.

9. Cut excess tape from top and bottom.

10. Share your book.

FIGURE 4.8   How to Bind Big Books

Form the group.

Choose a book.

Read the book.

Talk about the book with friends.

FIGURE 4.9   Book Club Basics

life and our own experiences in classes with students of all ages, we have created some basic guidelines for your classroom book club rules and regulations (See Figure 4.9).

Book Club Basics

Becky, a 10-year-old, seemed to grasp the importance of collaboration and real reading. For two years Becky attended the evening graduate classes twice a week with her mother, a single mom who was working on her master's degree. Imagine this: Becky with a room full of tired teachers who adored her. We have often thought that you can't have too many adults loving a child. In her own quiet way, Becky was a part of the group. She listened intently to discussions, she joined in the group discussions and projects, and she always had a book to read. The professor had a hunch that Becky, certainly the youngest "grad" student, learned a lot in those two years.

One night, with a twinkle in her, Becky walked into the class holding a rather crumpled assignment, which her fifth-grade teacher had returned to her that day in her own class. The question typed along the top of the paper said simply: What are 10 rules for learning to read? See Figure 4.10 for Becky's rules.

Obviously, Becky had been listening, and on that night she taught the adult graduate students a lot.

Read

Read

Read

Read

Read

Read

Read

Read

Read

Read

FIGURE 4.10   Becky's Rules

A disclaimer: We know teachers who will immediately sigh and say that, given the mandated curriculum, they simply do not have the time to do what their professional expertise tells them. As we write this book, we, too, know many teachers who simply have every minute of the day so tightly controlled that they are right—they cannot read with or for students in their classes. More on this in Chapter Eight, Teaching Passionately—Politically.

However, sometimes we can do things when we change our assumptions and/or perceptions. Okay. Not always, but sometimes. Pataray-Ching and Roberson (2002) confront this I-don't-have-time assumption and call it a misconception that hinders teaching and learning. Following their lead, if we think of real reading as an add-on to the curriculum, then perhaps there is no extra time for it for classrooms. However, if we approach reading as a philosophical overview that frames and guides instruction, then maybe we can find ways. "Researchers argue that in order for children to become readers and writers, they need to inquire as readers and writers. Similarly, in order to become mathematicians, historians, scientists, artists, and musicians, students need to inquire from and through those perspectives" (p. 503). We encourage readers to think of literacy as the framework for all curricula. Having said that, we still know public school teachers using tightly scripted programs who truly do not have the minutes in the day to read for or with students.

That Grating Problem

As we share the various Literacy Links throughout each chapter, it is inevitable that we will bump into that grating problem: *Kids who read real books do better than kids who read textbooks* (Nash, 2002). For us, it seems that Becky, at her young age, knew and understood this already, as does Bill in the story that follows.

Bill, a high school teacher, inspires us with his passion for reading in the same way that Becky did during her mom's M.A. studies. Bill teaches in a rural town in the southern tip of the Central Valley of California. Bill was hired to teach remedial reading and writing to reluctant teenage readers. To even be placed in Bill's "remedial classes," the students had to have met one of the following criteria: (a) scored below the 25th percentile on the SAT9 (or other standardized test), (b) failed an English class, and/or (c) failed the writing proficiency test, which was essentially a five-paragraph expository essay. Let's be honest: Bill had a challenging teaching assignment.

Bill was highly motivated to motivate the students. He collaborated with colleagues on the Internet to enhance learning in his classroom.

First, he read the literacy research on the Internet and connected with colleagues and experts. He entered into collaboration to learn more.

Second, he chose to create a classroom library that rivaled the school library for fiction and teen-relevant nonfiction.

Third, he filled his classroom with books: his personal collection; books from garage sales; books from friends; books from used-book stores; books that were purchased from fund-raising activities. Bill admits to spending a few thousand dollars on books and unabridged books-on-tape and 30 personal Walkman cassette players and headphones.

This is an important point. If you are a beginning teacher, do not be discouraged that you, too, need to spend this money for books. Go to garage sales and used book-stores. Use every library available to you. However, we know too many teachers through the years who have subsidized public education on their limited salaries. Celebrate these teachers. Honor these teachers. They are transforming the students and communities.

Now, in his fourth year at this high school, Bill has a classroom library, which fills two large bookcases, an old library display case, and a spinner rack. Bill writes:

> You cannot walk into my room without seeing and feeling the presence of BOOKS, everywhere. I sing the praises of books and the reading experience nearly every day. I also tell them about the different types of books I have, sorted by category, labeled on the front of each shelf. (in personal communication, October 1, 2002)

This is a book about passionate teaching and learning—Bill does that daily, and so can you. Just as interesting, Bill gives credit to the students' improved literacy and newly acquired interest in school to others. First, he acknowledged the collaborative support he received from his administration; second, he praised the district for spending the money needed to support his interest in books; and third, he honored the knowledge that he had acquired from Krashen (1993) and McQuillan (1998) and other literacy specialists he found on the Internet. Without these human connections, he never would have become the teacher he is today, nor would he have been as aware of the importance of real reading and books.

However, we particularly want to highlight Bill's very first step when he was hired initially to teach "remedial" reading; he read the literacy research and very creatively turned it into practice in his own classroom. You can, too. Go to www. EdResearch.info, as did Bill, who teaches at Taft Union High School. We believe that the *Teacher from Taft* has a lot to teach us about teaching and learning. Here is something else he taught us.

Book Pass: Bill's Way

Here is an activity from the *Teacher from Taft:* Bill gives everyone a book and a few minutes to scan the book before reading a few pages. It's like a sampler plate. Then they pass their book onto the next student, and so forth, for an entire class period. Each student samples about a dozen books of varying genres and reading levels. They keep a log of every book they sample and note the ones that they might like to read.

Bill then takes their individual lists and creates a class list with each student's name and the books he or she was interested in as a future reference in the event they can't remember the titles or can't find a book to read. At the end of class on the day of Book Pass, several students always snap up books they liked before anyone else gets them. During the rest of the week, Bill encourages students to check out one of the books they liked or ask him to help them find something. It works. Within a week, nearly every student has a book and is reading. Bill continues in what follows.

> So, what's my point? Last week, during our second week of school, I asked my classes if they wanted some quiet time to read. I received a unanimous, "Yes!" Within a few minutes, every student was immersed in a novel, reading silently. No one was talking, goofing around, or trying to sleep. They had all selected books within days of beginning the school year, and they were reading them! Seeing students reading warms my heart. I have always felt that if a young person is a reader, everything else will fall into place, sooner or later. (in personal communication, October 1, 2002)

Back to the Basics

What does this mean for your classroom? Real books lead to real reading; however, access is the issue lurking below the surface. Some kids have lots of books at home, and some kids do not. Some families read a lot, and some families do not. The playing field simply is not level. The kids who come from homes with books are advantaged. However, teachers have the power to create classrooms with books and to bring library books into the classroom. We can do a lot to level the playing field.

Take time to read for pleasure. Let the students see you reading. Talk with the students about what you are reading. Be sure that books are lying around in your classroom. Frankly, we are sometimes bothered about teachers complaining because students don't read, and we ask: Do you read? (See Figure 4.11.)

WHAT CAN BE LEARNED FROM THIS?

Collaboration matters. Caring counts. Collaboration has primacy in real life. Learning to work with a group is important for the students' future success in life. Learning to solve problems together is a required skill for the future. The truth is that none of us can do this alone—it takes us all.

> **Back to the Basics**
>
> Access to books matters.
>
> Time to read matters.
>
> A teacher who reads with great passion matters.

FIGURE 4.11   Back to the Basics

CHAPTER NOTES

1. For a more comprehensive approach to creating books with students, we encourage readers to see Ada and Campoy (2003, pp. 121–129).

2. This story has been adapted from Wink (1977 and 2001). We wish to thank the contributing students of the first article: Allene Beck, Carolyn Caporgno, Samantha Ericksen, Lisa Fasel, Susan Glectcher, Hope Hansen, Patrick Helms, Katherine Hill, Margaret Lima, Carrie Martin, Barbara Mesa, Heather Morganson, Kelly Pinheiro, Liza Runkel, Rosalva Salcedo, Constance Sharpe, Dennis Simpson, Susan Thompson, Mai Vang, Marcia Vineyard, Diana Wildenberg, and James Witter.

5 Teaching Passionately— Parentally

Parenthood is just the world's most intensive course in love.
POLLY BERENDS, 1983, p. 20

Parents are the first and most important teachers of their own children. In this chapter, we explore what families and caregivers can do to facilitate learning in school and in life. Our assumption is that readers of this book are students and/or teachers and much more. The personal and the professional cannot be separated; the personal *is* the professional. In addition to being teachers and learners, we are members of families as daughters, sons, fathers, mothers, cousins, brothers, sisters, and grandparents. This chapter addresses human connections that are at the heart of schooling and life.

The home is a child's first learning environment. Children spend far fewer hours in school than at home. By age 6, a child has spent 700 hours in school and 52,000 hours outside of school (Trelease, 2001, p. xviii). What takes place in the home becomes the child's foundation when he or she enters school. These experiences enrich or hinder a child's learning in schools. Each child is unique. Each child has inherent interests and strengths. We encourage families to find, celebrate, and enhance the approach to learning and life unique within each child. "Instruction, after all, does not begin in school" (Vygotsky, 1986, p. 208).

Flashback 25 years: Dawn reflects on a childhood memory.

Every Sunday evening, when I was a child growing up, I remember Mom sitting at her little desk, writing letters to family friends, most of whom were a generation older than she. Mom still writes letters to the same people, and now I write to them, also.

They are all over 80 years old now, and they have enriched our lives immensely. These friends have shared their wisdom and passions with me: One opened the door to Australia for me; another brought the flora and fauna of the Arizona desert alive; and another helped me to appreciate art in all aspects of life. They have taught me the richness of extended family. Each brings a unique view of the beauties of life. The greatest gift we have received is the love that is a daily part of our lives now.

By witnessing this correspondence and the love and beauty that stem from it, I experienced the grace of correspondence, which we unexpectedly receive when we write. Letter writing led to love, learning, and literacy.

Flashforward 25 years: Dawn is a mother now.

"Mom, I want a notebook to write," Luke, age 4, told me.

"Okay, Lukie, if you want to write, I'll buy the notebook," I told him. We jumped into the car and drove to the local grocery store and bought a pocket-sized spiral notebook. When we got home, he put his pen into the spiral on top and began to solemnly survey his surroundings.

"Now, I need someplace to write," he instructed me.

I looked around. The kids' blue table had a medieval castle set up, so that was not available. We eyed the Lego table, and I slid the Legos aside, and said, "Here ya go, big guy. A writing space."

"I have some deep and serious thoughts. I'm going to write them down right here," he said more to himself than to me, and he began making squiggly lines, left to right, top to bottom, across the page.

"Are you ready to read me your story, Luke?" I asked a little later as I was drying the dishes.

"No, I don't want you to read this one."

"You know, a lot of my writing I do for myself, Luke. I don't read it or share it with anybody. You don't have to share any of your writing if you don't want to."

"Okay, well, this is just for me," and he bent his strawberry-blond head down and intently began drawing lines again.

Today: Joan reflects on Dawn and Luke.

This was a literacy practice grounded in the context of one family's culture. Dawn grew up watching me write at my little desk surrounded by the Mexican cobalt blue tile in the kitchen. Dawn is now a writer. As Luke grows up, he is watching his mom, Dawn, write. We will leave it up to the imagination as to what Luke might do with his memory of watching his mother write daily at her little desk surrounded by the brilliant colors of the Mexican art in her office.

In this chapter, we want to share our "deep and serious" thoughts about what teachers and parents can do to create homes that are places of learning and refuge for children. So much of our society parents cannot control, but we can control the atmosphere we create in our own homes. "We need to take back our streets and our living rooms" (Pipher, 1996, p. 32).

Bearing witness and tending to children's unique needs *outside* school helps foster happiness and performance *inside* school. "Parents have a special responsibility and joy as they get to know well and to cultivate their children's individual minds. Tragic results are seen when we misconstrue and possibly even misuse a child's kind of mind! And that happens all the time" (Levine, 2002, p. 13). In this chapter we explore academic and familial ways of honoring individual styles of learning.

The Voice of Schools

Models of Family Involvement

Schools and families working together promote stronger academic and social development of students. Thus, the question is: What kind of family involvement? In order to answer this question, we again must look below the surface for the theory undergirding a family involvement program. Years ago, Joan and Dawn asked themselves this very question on a cold Saturday morning. Dawn, in her first year of teaching, asked Joan how to do it. This simple question was followed by meaningful dialogue and the resulting chart, which we rapidly scribbled on a yellow legal pad (Wink, 2000). Joan tells the story in what follows.

> I reminded her of the various family and school activities she had experienced while she was growing up. While she was describing various experiences, it suddenly occurred to us that we were recounting two very different approaches to school-sponsored family involvement. One approach is much more democratic. It seems that even when we do not see our beliefs, they tend to be visible to others. Each of us has hidden assumptions that we do not recognize. Our beliefs lead us as they turn into behaviors for all the world to see. I reminded her of two school districts we both knew very well, each of which had a family involvement program. I asked her which district had a more democratic approach to working with families. She knew immediately, and so did I. However, I am equally confident that both these districts would say they had democratic family models of involvement. This caused us to quickly draw the two approaches to family involvement seen in Figure 5.1, which represents our experiences with many programs and districts.

In this section, we will highlight successful models of family involvement that are filled with passion because they are collaborative and democratic.[1] Nieto (2000) refers to family involvement that extends well beyond the traditional processes of PTA meetings or assistance with homework. She and her colleagues speak of family involvement that brings in the family attributes (p. 297) to make schools more caring places that teach lessons with heart. These family attributes are the very funds of knowledge (Moll, 2000) that enhance school communities.

First, an example of family involvement illustrates how teachers taking the time to visit students' homes can inform curriculum, making it more contextualized and meaningful for the students (McIntyre, Kyle, Moore, Sweazy, & Greer, 2001). A group of educators set out to gain insight into each family's funds of knowledge in order to build on students' previous knowledge and create curriculum. The teachers in this school community visit the homes of all of the students. Later follow-up visits are scheduled based on multiple factors, for example, the needs of the students, the receptivity of the family, and the complex time schedules for all. These visits dispel

Models for Family Involvement

The We-Are-Going-To-Do-This-To-You Model of Parental Involvement

Or

The We-Are-Going-To-Do-This-With-You Model of Parental Involvement

DOIN' IT TO 'EM   **DOIN' IT WITH 'EM**

Goal

change the parents   *change the schools*

Objectives

to melt into the pot   to melt the pot
to discuss building community   to build community

Characteristics of the Meetings

teachers talk   teachers listen
families listen   families talk
families sit still   families interact
everyone leaves immediately after   people hang around
people leave space between them   people hug
kids go to a room with a sitter   kids work with families
teachers tell objectives   families tell stories

Result

Dysfunctional School   Functional School

FIGURE 5.1   Models of Family Involvement
(Wink, 2000, p. 133)

incorrect assumptions about the students, build a sense of trust and respect between teacher and family, and bring together the two worlds children inhabit daily.

In our own public school experiences, probably nothing else enhanced our passion for teaching and learning more than the family visits we made. "More than anything else, the family visits for me turned a student into someone's dear child. It made me understand that child in a concrete way. It helped me see the child through the parent's eyes," Dawn said as we wrote this paragraph.

A second example demonstrates how even tension-filled interactions with students' families can provide otherwise hidden insights to the teacher and parent. Wilson-Keenan, Solsken, and Willett (2001) invite parents into the classroom to share a skill or passion with the class. In one particular parent presentation, the teacher felt uneasiness and tension at what she perceived as an inappropriate topic for the parent to present. Further reflection on her own interpretation and her possible misunderstanding led this teacher to learn more about this parent's ethnic history and culture. In doing so, she learned that not only did what the parent do make perfect sense, but she also acknowledged the difficult position she had placed on the students by imposing her perceptions on the discussion. By reflecting on this one tension-filled visit, the community came to understand each other better. The simple democratic act of inviting parents to share in the classroom and to bring in their funds of knowledge taught a lesson with heart.

A third example reveals how a teacher's understanding of the families' literacy beliefs can positively affect teaching and learning. Klassen-Endrizzi (2000) explores the influence of the parents' literacy experience on her students' literacy acquisition and fluency. Through using parent–teacher journals in which parents described their own experiences with literacy, the teacher discovered that many of the parents' own struggles with reading were being instilled in their children. Many did not like to read and thought of reading only as the decoding of sounds rather than as a process of meaning-making. In addressing the parents' struggles and providing parent education, the teacher had access to the students' background knowledge and was better able to serve their needs.

We close this section of the Voice of Schools with library mapping (Wink & Putney, 2002), which is a process bringing families and school personnel together in libraries. In this concluding section, we will first provide one generic mapping activity, designed as an initial mapping activity for teachers and families. Its purpose is to create a safe place where family involvement can begin around positive human connection and eventually to lead the group to discover libraries together. Next, we will expand on this mapping activity with the story of library mapping specifically. Finally, we will provide a more detailed overview of the activity for readers to adapt and use in their own contexts.

First, we will share a generic approach to mapping. When bringing the families and teachers together for the initial activity, it is safe to guess that the two groups could feel a bit separated from one another. In this process, we need two lead people, one a teacher and one a family member, who ensure that the participants are not separated. Teachers and families need to be sitting together. The two leaders ask the participants to visualize a favorite geographical location from their childhood. After visualizing the location, the two leaders ask the participants each to draw a map of it. Next, the leaders instruct each person to place numbers or symbols on the map where the stories or events happened.

The teachers and family members now have to choose one spot on the map and write their individual memories, using all five senses: the sights, the sounds, the smells, the tastes, and the touch of it. At this point, the teachers and families are invited to share in small groups their memories and their maps. For an initial activity, this would be enough for the first meeting of the two groups.

Second, we want to share a story from a university context, when a colleague tried this activity. Our purpose in sharing this context is to encourage readers to adapt this activity to their own needs, as did the professor in the following true story.

Professor Le taught a foundations course for preservice teachers, which focused heavily on the social, cultural, historical, and political contexts. One specific assignment for the future teachers was designed to lead the students into the community—not necessarily "their" community, but the community of the students who were in the process of acquiring English as another language. Professor Le started concretely with maps, representing various neighborhoods. On the maps, the library or libraries were high-lighted. Slowly the students began to realize that the "neighborhood map" was that of the schools in which they were being placed for student teaching.

The maps were clearly marked with the bus routes, the homes of the students, and the localities of the libraries. The first thing that the preservice teachers noticed when looking at the maps was the proximity to the school and library for many of the students. The first assignment was deceptively simple: They were to visit the library and map where the bilingual books were located. If the students wanted to simply read a book in a language that they could understand, where were those books located? Professor Le told the preservice students to ask for help from the librarians for bilingual books and then to map the area made available for families to sit and read.

The range of findings by these preservice teachers is worth noting. Of the 18 in that university cohort, two came back with glowing reports of how esthetically pleasing and inviting the reading areas were. The bilingual books were easy to find, the librarians were wonderfully helpful, the library even had outreach programs in place that invited the parents to come in and read with their children. Not surprisingly, these libraries had good attendance, as noticed by the students when they did their observations.

Now, for the rest of the story. Most of the university students were outraged at the conditions of the libraries they observed. The bilingual books were located on high shelves and not easily accessible to anyone. One of the future teachers even went in and asked for help in Spanish. She was completely ignored until she "code-switched" to English. She was furious. Others talked about how easy it was to get to the library *if* you had access to a car. Some of the preservice students decided to make this a "real" experience so they took the bus to the library. After multiple transfers, they decided that they would not do *that* again. It was just too hard to get there and back in a reasonable amount of time. These university students could find no other public outreach programs at these local centers. The preservice teachers experienced firsthand a glimpse into the frustration that parents and children whose first language is not English feel when they are trying to do something as *simple* as checking books out of the library.

The availability of the books was an issue; the ease of transport to the libraries was an issue; the way in which the patrons were treated was an issue; lack of outreach was an issue. Bookmobiles would be one way to make the books more accessible, but the real issue is money being spent on part of the population who has the least access to any kind of reading materials. The books have to be in place, hopefully in schools first and then in public libraries. Then we have to move forward on making access to the books more inviting and available.

It is not that parents do not value reading and books; rather, it is that the contexts make it hard for them to access the books. This activity in the "real" sociocultural context of the future students caused the preservice teachers to reflect critically on some of their long-held assumptions about literacy of students who are in the process of acquiring an additional language (Wink & Putney, 2002).

Third, now we want to share the library-mapping activity in a more detailed lesson approach, so that readers can see it from a different perspective. (See Figures 5.2 and 5.3.)

Purpose: to introduce families and teachers to the libraries that are available for the students in their own neighborhoods. This activity is designed specifically for the collaborative group to experience a community library from the perspective of a student who is still in the process of acquiring English. This activity could easily be adapted for other target groups of students; for example, a teacher who lives in an upper-middle-class community and who teaches students from lower socioeconomic communities is encouraged to visit libraries in the neighborhood of the students where he or she teaches.

Introduction to the Activity

The leader begins by preparing a map of the community. This can be done on an overhead transparency, the chalkboard, large paper, a handout, and so on.

However, the point is to begin with the something very concrete, a map, so the participants can visualize it as the activity is introduced. During the introduction, the lead person marks the libraries, the various communities, and the public transportation routes. During the week, the families and teachers are asked to visit the libraries with the following instructions.

- Find the library in the neighborhood of the students in your school.
- Use public transportation to go to this library.
- Before entering the library, sit outside alone for 10 to 15 minutes. Take notes to capture your experiences with public transportation. In your field notes, write anything that captures your five senses as you sit in front of the library.
- Before entering the library, visualize yourself as a 10-year-old who has recently moved to this country from Mexico. You are an avid reader and want to find a good book for the weekend. Spanish is your dominant language; you are still very uncomfortable using any of your emerging oral English.
- Enter the library alone.
- Do not use English while in the library.
- Map the inside of the library; locate the books in your language.
- Sit at a table near these books.
- Describe the library in one paragraph from this vantage point.
- Describe the quality and quantity of books in your language.
- Check out two books.

Reflection in the Following Family/Teacher Program Evening

The leaders graph the range of findings into the following categories:

- The availability of the books (quality and quantity)
- The availability of transportation to the libraries
- Personal interactions within the library

Follow-Up Action

The best part of this activity: What do you as a group and as an individual decide to do with what you have learned? You tell us.

FIGURE 5.2   Library Mapping

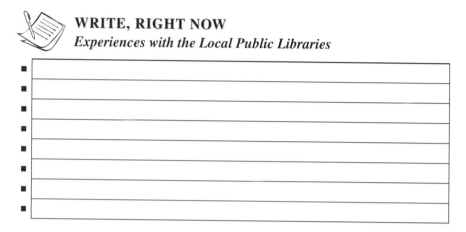

✎ **WRITE, RIGHT NOW**
Experiences with the Local Public Libraries

FIGURE 5.3   Write, Right Now: Experiences with the Local Public Libraries

The Voice of Life

Parents' primary role is to love and protect children. Providing protection is a complex process. Parents and teachers today feel battered on all sides. Our awareness is heightened to possible dangers. It is precisely because of this level of awareness that children seek a strong sense of connection and safety at home and in school. They crave "walls of love."

Walls of Love

The protective walls of a family are made not of stone, but of love.

MARY PIPHER, *1996, p. 246*

Walls of love separate the family from the rest of the world (see Figure 5.4). These walls are designed to nurture and protect from within, working as a sieve, filtering outside influences. Walls of love protect, breathe, and include family rituals, traditions, and stories.

In modern society, these walls include filtering messages the mass media expounds as crucial. Today's media-soaked environment can bring the outside world into our homes and into the lives of children with alarming constancy. Although there are many benefits to this access, it brings challenges as well. The avalanche of information can bury a family. The current trend to process this information is for family members to look outward to TV, radio, the Internet, video games, and other electronics more often than inward to the bonds of family. Televisions in the home are disruptive to families on three levels: The inherent separateness, consumerism, and passivity it fosters tear at the fabric of a family. (See Figure 5.5.)

FIGURE 5.4   Walls of Love

Television can invite separation. Often now, instead of gathering together as a family, members sit isolated in front of some piece of electronic machinery, disrupting the natural flow of conversation, creativity, and time spent together that creates a strong family. Before electricity, when people depended on lanterns and candles for light, the limited sources of light, frequently only one in the house, naturally drew

FIGURE 5.5   Children Not at Play

people together in the evenings to talk, sew, read, and take part in a variety of other creative endeavors (see Figure 5.6).

> Now, most families sit in front of the television or go off to their own interests. Families gather round the glow of the TV as the Lakota once gathered around the glow of a fire on the Great Plains or as the Vikings huddled around fires in the Caves of Scandinavia. They gather as New England families gathered in the 1800s around a fireplace that kept them warm and safe. But our TVs do not keep us warm, safe, and together. Rapidly our technology is creating a new kind of human being, one who is plugged into our machines instead of relationships, one who lives in a virtual reality rather than a family. (Pipher, 1996, p. 92)

This is by no means meant to glorify the past. The extreme poverty, abuse, precarious medical care, hard work, and lack of opportunity for education ensured that only the fortunate actually survived to sit around the hearth in the evenings. Many people could not read. We do not wish those days back. What we do admire, though, is a sense of unity and interdependence that comes with gathering as a family in the evening.

Television invites consumerism. As families gather around the TV, they are subjected to the 400 ads a day, which adds up to over 4 million ads in a lifetime. Research also confirms that the more television we watch, the more we spend. One study demonstrated that each additional hour of television watched per week reduces annual savings by $208. So watching just 10 hours of TV per week costs, on average, over $2,000 in increased spending (Dunham, 2001, p. 5).

Mass media is bent on instilling in our children the concept that everything worth having in life is external. Children have the potential to be assaulted regularly

The Family Hearth of Old   The Family Hearth of Present

FIGURE 5.6   The Changing Family Hearth

by violent video games, back-talking children on TV, graphic movies, and highly effective advertising. Walls of love create a safety zone in the house from the outside culture. Parents cannot always control which video game will be at the pizza place, what kind of music kids will hear with their friends, or what will be seen flashing on 30 televisions in a department store, but parents can control the atmosphere and environment in the home.

Consider what children miss during the 15,000 hours (from birth to age 17) that they spend in front of the TV screen. They are not working in the garage with their fathers or in the garden with their mothers. They are not doing homework, reading, or collecting stamps. They are not cleaning their rooms, washing the supper dishes, or cutting the lawn. They are not listening to a discussion about community politics among their parents and their friends. They are not playing baseball, going fishing, or painting pictures. Exactly what does television offer that is so valuable that it can replace these activities that transform an impulsive, self-absorbed child into a critically thinking adult (Trelease, 2001, p. 201)?

I De-TV'd My Home

Television viewing invites passivity. Following are Dawn's experiences when she got rid of the television in her home.

"Enough," I said to myself, "that TV is out of our house." I did show considerable restraint, I thought, by not just throwing it out the two-story window. Instead, I lugged the TV to the garage, packed up all the videos in a box, and put the entire kit-and-kaboodle downstairs in the garage under a blanket.

This happened a few weeks ago when I was reading yet another article about the detrimental effects of TV on children's creative and intellectual development and family closeness. Ironically, I read this while my three children were, of course, watching TV.

I will admit to a history of needing and hating the TV, since I became a parent. My children were only allowed to watch PBS and the Animal Planet channels. Nothing else. The truth is that during the several years that my husband was away from home for weeks at a time, this selective TV watching helped me maintain the shreds of sanity of those long days with three preschoolers. Before our third child was born, I have wonderful memories of Wyatt, Luke, and me curled up in front of *The Crocodile Hunter* on weekday afternoons: All of us being at peace, laughing and enjoying. In addition, it was one of the few times during the day that I didn't have to do anything!

But, I, like many parents, have used TV as an electronic babysitter. The TV always seemed to loom and seduce us. It was an addictive voice, even when turned off. It beckoned the kids and me. It was the basis for too many of our decisions about what to do. This was particularly true for my youngest, Wynn. When she was 3 years old, I noticed that it seemed like she constantly asked to watch TV and cried when I said, "No." Everything, for her, was measured against this.

So, how has our life changed since I tossed the TV? We are amazed at how much more peaceful our home is now without the constant lure of the TV. I was prepared to grit my teeth and endure the rebellion for a couple of weeks, but it just has not happened. For example, today when Wyatt, 6 years old, came home from school, a time he usually got to watch a half-hour show on PBS, he came running in the house, grabbed his makeshift bow and arrow, and headed out the door seeking rabbit in the juniper and piñon trees that surround our house. Let me qualify, there is no way he could actually hit one.

Watching him outdoors, intent on his physical surroundings, independent and at peace with himself, was a sharp contrast to his glazed-over expression in front of the TV. Wynn asked only three times, and after an initial crying spat, seems to have accepted the disappearance of the TV much more easily than I'd anticipated. In addition, I am not tempted to plop the kids down in front of it while I get something done. The lesson for me: My kids know how to entertain themselves better than I knew.

This week during times the kids would have been watching TV they have jumped on the trampoline, played with Play Dough, played with blow pens, played on the swing set, read books in the book nook, asked me to read to them, played with the dog, played dress-up, and listened to kids' audiotapes.

Sure, they did all these things before, but now they do them more often. I have read that in a home without television, children come to entertain themselves creatively much more readily. It was only when the TV and VCR were out of our house completely that we were freed from the eternal lure and tug of the great black box in the house. Without its looming presence, my children and our family dynamics blossomed. We all breathe easier and are more at peace.

The homogenization of children's culture saddens us. Children spend too many hours absorbing the messages of the TV instead of being immersed in the richness of literature, spending time reading cuddled up with parents, or gathered with the family.

Family stories and metaphors create unity among family members. Stories link us as a family together, as a unit in the world. In our family, Dean's infamous horse stories are a part of the glue holding us together in our own special place of mutual understanding, surrounded by a large and complex world. Remember, Dean is Joan's husband and Dawn's dad. It does not matter that we have heard these stories countless times. Still, Dawn and Bo ask "Dad, tell us about the time the horse you were riding jumped down and over the cliff; or, tell us about the time the horse you were riding in the riverbed went down in the quicksand; or, tell us about that huge horse you were riding when it ran straight through the barn door." In fact, it is the nature of the familiarity of the stories that is so comforting. Stories are the glue that binds families together. We create what we believe. "A friend of mine told me about her trip to Singapore. She talked to a local woman about the different living arrangements in the two countries. In Singapore several generations of family live together. My friend explained that here each nuclear family lives separately. The woman from Singapore asked in amazement, 'Where do the children get their stories?'" (Pipher, 1996, p. 150).

Stories build walls of love. Walls of love are diverse and unique. One mother writes of her journey to find a cure for her son's autism (Seroussi, 2000). She found through research and trial and error that her son's autism was related to his allergies to wheat, dairy, and soy, among other things. She builds a strong case that its onset began when he received his MMR (measles, mumps, and rubella) vaccination at 19 months. Creating her own path, she discovered and created a special diet for Miles, her son, and because of her passionate belief that there is no symptom without a cause, the effects of autism were reversed and he is now a happy, healthy little boy attending public school. Miles's kindergarten teacher was surprised when Seroussi shared with him Miles's history of autism. He described Miles as an exceptionally bright, social boy. Seroussi's walls of love helped Miles's walls of isolation crumble.

Writer Isabel Allende describes in her book, *Paula,* the passionate love of a parent. The book begins with Allende being told that her only daughter, Paula, has fallen into a coma in a hospital in Spain. Allende initially begins the book as a history for Paula to read when she wakes up, in case she has lost some of her memory, and ends with Paula dying in her mother's arms after a year of being in a coma in which her mother tended to her. By sharing this experience, Allende created a wall of love, enveloping Paula and the readers. It is this love and gratitude readers take into their relationships with their own children that embody passionate parental pedagogy. (See Figure 5.7.)

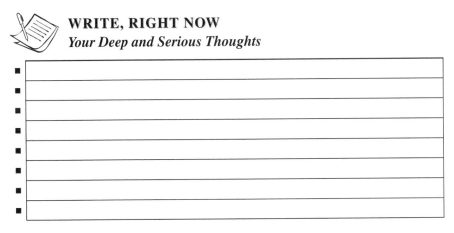

WRITE, RIGHT NOW
Your Deep and Serious Thoughts

FIGURE 5.7　Write, Right Now: Your Deep and Serious Thoughts

Reading Aloud

"There is one skill that matters above all others, because it is the prime predictor of school success or failure: the child's vocabulary upon entering school," (Trelease, 2001). The best method to build that vocabulary is to read aloud to our children as much as possible from a variety of genres. The most complex vocabulary and sentence structure are found in printed text. Daily conversation provides a limited vocabulary range, but through books children gain experience with formal language and rare vocabulary necessary for academic success.

"Because words are essential in building the thought connections in the brain," writes Fox (2001), "the more language a child experiences—through books and through conversation with others, *not passively from television*—the more advantages socially, educationally, and in every way that child will have for the rest of his or her life" (p. 18).

Enriching children's vocabulary and lives with literature expands their worlds and their critical thinking processes. Reading a wide variety of literature with our children is a political act in itself; it helps to prepare them to think for themselves and create independent lives as adults. In a study commissioned by the government (Neuman, 2001a), the data demonstrated the importance of surrounding kids with books, reading with them, and creating time for them to read alone. The bottom line of this study indicated that children who are exposed to print read more, and they "read up," whereas children who have little access to book and print material read less, and they "read down" (Moustafa, 2002).

> The more limited our language is, the more limited we are; the more limited the literature we give our children, the more limited their capacity to respond, and therefore, in their turn, to create. The more our vocabulary is controlled, the less we will be able to think for ourselves. We do think in words, and the fewer words we know, the more restricted our thoughts. As our vocabulary expands, so does our power to think. (L'Engle, 1972, p. 149)

When reading aloud, the more rich and varied the language read, the better. Don't stick only to what you think your children already know. Make them reach. That is precisely how children learn new vocabulary, by hearing it and either asking the meaning or figuring it out through context.

The one exception we recommend when reading to very young children whose language is still developing is using correct grammar when reading aloud. Dawn and Joan learned this lesson one summer on the ranch while reading the *Little Britches* series by Ralph Moody.

"I'm wearing my Australia shirt today, ain't I, Mom?" 4-year-old Luke greeted us one morning.

"What did you say, Lukie?" Dawn managed to stammer after just about dropping her coffee cup in surprise.

"I'm wearing my Australia shirt today, ain't I?" he said again.

"Ain't? AIN'T?" she turned over in her head, "Where on earth did he hear that?" Then she remembered the *Little Britches* series is written in language appropriate to the time and place the author writes about, and *ain't* is a primary word in the text, along with several other idiomatic language uses that enrich the books immensely. The language of the text paints the portrait of the story; however, due to the *Ain't Incident,* we recommend improvising correct grammar until children's language is developed enough to recognize it and enjoy various forms of speech without necessarily acquiring them.

Academic success does not depend on the plethora of educational toys, computer games, television shows, flashcards, and expensive reading programs so actively marketed. A far more significant factor is for the child to be exposed to as much rich vocabulary as possible, from the earliest age possible, and for as much time as possible, in a *pleasurable and interactive* setting. Reading aloud also requires the most inexpensive preparation available: a free library card.

Parents who cannot read can still talk about the pictures and the story with their children together. Sitting with a parent, the feel of a book in the hands, talking about what the story must be and the details in the pictures, all of this promotes literacy.

Parents who are dominant in languages other than English still need to read to children in their primary language. The higher the literacy development in the first language, the higher the literacy in the second language because literacy transfers.

Reading aloud to older children is just as important as reading to young children. We stop far too soon. As children get older, the complexity of read-aloud material increases. Many parents assume that as soon as children are old enough to read to themselves, the reading aloud together comes to an end.

Equally as important as the literacy development is the time together. Reading is often the bridge between parent and child. Dawn describes the role reading plays in her relationship with her young son, Wyatt.

> Wyatt is very interested in many things that do not naturally interest me: for example, dinosaurs, insects, reptiles, and fishing. I encourage those passions for him, I foster them, and I join along, because I know that is important. However, we are both passionate about reading. No matter what has happened during the day, how crazy it has been, how badly things have deteriorated, when we crawl into bed to read, the rest of the world evaporates. We are in our own little world of books and love. It is a central way that we connect. I've found that with Wyatt, it is when we are reading that we communicate best about everything else. When we read, the other tensions and conflicts of the day disintegrate as we're swept along in the story and in each other.

Reading enjoyable books aloud together is a fundamental building block in the relationship between parent and child. It opens the world and the heart. This is no coincidence. The first sound a baby hears, his or her mother's heart in the womb, has rhythm, as do reading rhymes and stories aloud. Hearing a book read aloud continues to be a soothing human experience throughout life.

Passionate Play

Dawn grew up on a cattle ranch in southeastern Arizona. Her days were filled with riding horses, reading books, and following her dad around the ranch, usually bouncing along in a dirty pickup truck or trotting along behind in well-worn cowboy boots. She never wore pink and had no time for dolls. Now Dawn is the parent of a little girl who covets pink and dolls of any kind. The following is a conversation that took place, leaning over a barbed-wire fence, between Joan and Dawn on the ranch in South Dakota:

"Well, Mom, do I break down and actually enroll her in ballet classes?" Dawn said, as they stood watching Wynn bouncing on the trampoline in her favorite piece of clothing, a pink tutu, complete with a stiff little tulle ruffle encircling her pink leotard.

"Who just told me that parents should introduce children to a wide variety of experiences, encourage their interests, and foster their inherent passions?" Joan replied with an ironic smile.

"Oh, yes, I did just say that. However, somehow I had never envisioned pink tutus and tulle would be involved," Dawn sighed.

Inherent interest and passion provide our life's directions; interests are like a tiny acorn that has the potential to grow into a giant tree of dreams. In Chapter Seven, Teaching Passionately—Spiritually, we continue to explore the acorn theory in schools. Here we explore what that idea means for parents and teachers. From Vygotsky we have learned that play has purpose in that it creates an imaginary situation and is a means of developing abstract thought (Wink & Putney, 2002).

Play can also be an indicator of the acorn, with children naturally drawn toward what brings them meaning and purpose, as exemplified in the following story of Marie Curie.

> In a dark corner of her childhood house, her father sometimes set up a makeshift laboratory. She used to sneak in and play there, watching the bubbling liquids, measuring the weight of her little hands on the scale. . . . When her sisters were outside playing, she escaped to the laboratory, a sanctuary of quiet, concentration, and potential. Marie Curie's mystical attitude toward the laboratory never changed. . . . The conception of the laboratory as a place of serious play, a continuous present moment that could hold her captive with eternity's questions, was born in her childhood through a simple ritual. (Lloyd, 1997, p. 3)

As with Marie Curie, children discover their acorn, their personal truth, through play. The parents' role is to introduce their children to a wide variety of experiences, including music, dance, outdoor activities, sports, and even pink tutus, if necessary. Children will not be attracted to them all. "So it is that we all live with minds wired to excel in one area and crash in another" (Levine, 2002, p. 23). Parents then follow their children's inherent and unique passions, trusting that within each child lies an instinctive attraction to what will bring him or her meaning, purpose, and joy. (See Figure 5.8.)

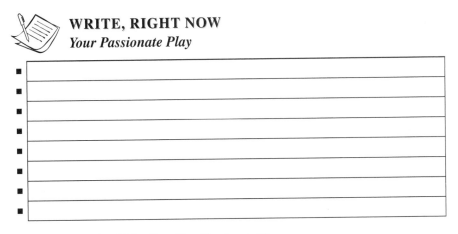

WRITE, RIGHT NOW
Your Passionate Play

FIGURE 5.8   Write, Right Now: Your Passionate Play

Rethinking Play

It is incorrect to conceive of play as activity without purpose . . .
creating an imaginary situation can be regarded as a means
of developing abstract thought.
VYGOTSKY, *1978, p. 103*

Kids need to play not only to work off an overabundance of energy but also for their social, intellectual, and academic development. Through imaginative play, their intellectual development matures by leaps and bounds. A person's potential play is limitless. Children become adults, trying on being serious or funny or smart for size. Although play is especially for children, it is by no means only for children. Adults require imaginative dreaming and play. How do we discover our dreams and set those plans in motion? Through daydreaming, through going for a long walk, through having fun and *playing*. Human beings must have time to have fun, experiment, and just enjoy being alive in their own skin to discover who they really are. Without this time, this be-ing time, this playing time, human beings' potential remains stunted. Playing time cracks open our shells of resistance, self-doubt, and self-consciousness, freeing the potential within.

Play needs to be a part of schooling. Recent studies suggest that the United States, by shortening or doing away with recess completely in a fervor to instill ever more facts, is in fact shooting itself in the foot.

The latest installment of one of the few longitudinal research projects currently looking at preschool education has just come out, and the results are particularly important in light of current federal policy. Rebecca Marcon has been following a cohort of mostly poor African American kids in Washington, D.C., who attended either "child-initiated," "academically directed," or "middle-of-the-road" preschools. By the end of the kids' sixth year in school, those who had been in academically oriented programs "earned significantly lower grades compared to children who had attended child-initiated preschool classes. . . . Their progress may have been slowed by overly academic preschool experiences that introduced formalized learning experiences too early" (Alfie Kohn, personal communication, December 10, 2002).

Let's rethink play. Instead of thinking of it as wasted time, let's think of it as time to expand a child's social, intellectual, and academic horizons. Let's think of it as time to be, as time to connect with personal passions that are our indicators in life. Let's rethink play and recognize it as a crucial enhancer of brain development. This recognition of the importance of play is reflected in a letter to the editor (retrieved October 18, 2002 from the *Philadelphia Inquirer Online*).

> I find it terribly shocking and frightening that the idea of all-day kindergarten is being embraced by so many across the country (Editorial, "It's Not Play Time," October 6). What type of "brave new world" are we moving into when our children are being judged on the basis of "significantly outperforming" each other at the ripe old age of 5? Consider this idea: Children need less school and more playtime. Play is how children learn, grow, interact with their communities.

Children learn to read on their own timetable; it is not controlled by mandates that vary from state to state or with benchmarks that differ from place to place. Many children read without arbitrary benchmarks—actually, it seems most people we know learned without benchmarks. Books are better than benchmarks. Some read earlier than others. Learning does not occur solely in the classroom. Learning occurs in the real world and, sadly, our children are becoming less and less a part of it.

Rethinking Homework

The assignment of more and more homework is a growing trend in the United States. Daily homework now starts in kindergarten and progressively increases as students move through the grades. We question the mounting commitment of time dedicated to homework this requires of students and parents.

Joan reflects: As parents, we dreaded homework that Dawn and Bo brought home. It was usually meaningless and invasive for our family. Homework seemed to mean that we had to stop living and "do" something because it was required the next day. Of course, at that time, I would never have mentioned this outside of our family, as homework was perceived to be honorable. If we didn't like it, the problem must have been with us and not with the work.

Of course, we did all the homework; remember, I was a teacher, and in our little family unit, we had several college degrees, in addition to which my husband and I both grew up on the Northern Prairies—we were weaned on character-building experiences. . . .

As a teacher, I assigned homework, and I continued to dread it. I spent hours and days collecting homework, reading homework, recording homework, and looking for lost homework. When I think of homework, I remember Alisa, who was a marvelous student. She was very involved in all school activities. She went on to be class valedictorian. Her classmates and I spent considerable time that year simply looking for her homework, which was often misplaced in the depths of her book bag or somewhere in her messy desk. We knew that if we could find it, it would be fantastic, but finding it was the challenge. Her classmates adored her and must have felt that she needed their help. I have fond memories of the daily and loving search for Alisa's homework, so I could record it in the grade book. Did she learn much from my homework? I doubt it. It is the love and camaraderie of the search that I remember.

I also remember Danny, who never brought his homework because he had not done it. The best part of Danny's life was the safe time he spent in school with us. When the school day ended, chaos and pain consumed his life. Homework was completely irrelevant.

Slowly, I began to realize that homework privileged a particular type of student: those who are safe, well fed, and surrounded by supportive families. I also came to realize that the six hours a day (or, for those of us with secondary experiences, the hour a day) is the only human and learning time we are guaranteed with students. In addition, I came to trust the fact that sometimes it is enough. For example, I am sure most of us have been profoundly enriched by at least one teacher in our past, who only was with us for an hour a day.

Now, as a grandparent, I watch with discomfort as I see Dawn having similar experiences. Each day it is a long process of checking the book bags for instructions, filling in the blanks, circling the words, recording which book was read when followed by the obligatory parental signature, and looking for the right paper on the right day and getting it into the right folder and book bag again. Of course, the irony is that Dawn typically reads with her children two to three hours a day, and when she is not reading with them, they are snuggled in the book nook reading alone.

We realize that questioning homework is heresy, so we are always so pleased to read others' reflections. While writing this short piece on homework, the following reflection popped up on e-mail this morning.

> As the year winds down the postings suggest that education remains one of the most crucial issues. I think about these things more personally lately as I see what I do for my kids and marvel at the obvious difference such efforts make. Examples: We ask about homework and keep track of it; what of the kid who does not get asked (for whatever reasons)? I spent hours in IKEA with the kids this weekend trying to find a good desk setup and new bookcase for the boys; what of the child who has no dedicated space to study, or someone who makes that kind of investment in their education? We bought the kids many books for Christmas; what of the kids who never get books and have none in the house? I read every night to my sons (*Where the Red Fern Grows* is the current selection); what of the child who never has this experience? And so on. We all know the difference these things make; the implications of my own investments (or the lack of such investments) just became more clear to me lately and it makes me feel like I better understand those factors

(in the classroom) over that I do have control and that can make a powerful difference in my students' lives. (J. Burke, personal communication, December 30, 2002)

Reflection to Action.   Funwork, as opposed to homework, has been suggested by Enright and McCloskey (1998) and captures the concept that our learning together within family units can be fun, interesting, and pedagogically sound. Ada (2003) extends this idea to say that homework should not be additional schoolwork, but rather that it is homework because it requires the interaction of students with their families.

We are reflecting on ways of putting the *home* back in homework, and we offer our suggestions in what follows. However, if we could offer an opposite idea, simultaneously, it seems that taking the *home* out of homework might also offer some options. If we take the *home* out of homework, the school creates safe times and places where students can informally go for support while they do their homework. Some students come from families who have computers, books, papers, calculators, papers, and pencils, and families who will encourage their work. However, some students come from homes where there is much less available that is supportive of homework. Often family members are away from home working long hours. In order to level the playing field, we suggest districts and schools consider safe and friendly locations with music, snacks, and supportive adults working with students on their homework. In these days of limited funds, it seems heresy to suggest more cost for schools; however, we ask it anyway with the hope that some reader somewhere will take this idea and bring it to fruition for the sake of kids. It seems that tutors, mentors, senior citizens, and/or civic groups might provide some support.

Putting the HOME Back in Homework.   Here we offer five suggestions for ways of putting *home* back into homework (see also Figure 5.9).

1. Interview a family member and write a short biography. Questions can be generated in class to begin the interview process. Time in class needs to be arranged so that the students read their written biographies of family members. Following is a listing of a few examples of interview questions that Dawn has used.

    "Tell me about the funniest thing I did as a baby."
    "Tell me about the funniest thing that ever happened to you."
    "Tell me about my grandparents."
    "Tell me about where you grew up."
    "Tell me about what you did as a child."
    "Tell me about your favorite memory."
    "Tell me about how you and Dad/Mom met."
    "Tell me about your favorite book and why it is your favorite."

2. Students choose books from the classroom or the school library to take home to read with parents, or students can choose reading materials from their public li-

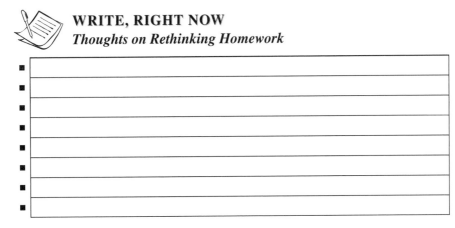

WRITE, RIGHT NOW
Thoughts on Rethinking Homework

FIGURE 5.9   **Write, Right Now: Thoughts on Rethinking Homework**

brary or reading materials that are in the home. Arrange for time in class for students to share orally their reading experiences at home. Celebrate the students who are reading with families at home.

3. Students write about projects or experiences they have with their families in the evenings. Students create a book that captures their families. In school, time is arranged to share their individual books.

4. Students write about the various literacy activities at home. Students list all of the contexts of literacy in their life, for example, comic books, magazines, how-to books used at home, grocery lists, computer activities, reading mail at home, and so on. Arrange time in class to chart the home reading activities of all students.

5. Students, with family members at home, write letters to extended family members outside of the home.

Praxis: Let the Magic Begin

In this section, we address what parents and teachers can do with love to enhance the learning of their children. Families of all cultures can do much to enhance their child's development, but often various cultures do different things to enhance the learning and developing of children. "The ways families support children in their learning are complex and sometimes not what one might expect" (Nieto, 2000, p. 194). For example, families who are nonnative speakers of English can enhance the academic development of their children by maintaining the native language and encouraging communication within the family (Nieto, 2000). In what follows, we are highlighting family practices that we hope cut across cultures. As we do so, we acknowledge the "cultural capital" assigned in schools and in society to Dawn's three children and Joan's four grandchildren.

First, talk with children and read from a variety of genres. Talk is the precursor to literacy development and success in schools. The more we converse with our children, talking about grocery lists, events in school, and family happenings, the more experience with language children have. Reading from a variety of genres exposes children to the various melodies of language. "Children need to hear 'the song' of a wide range of texts" (Calkins & Bellino, 1997, p. 39).

Second, create a book nook in the living room or kitchen. Choose a well-lit corner or space for the nook. This can be done very economically, and the rewards are infinite. Place the book nook where it will be the focus of attention for the kids when they enter the room. The nook is composed of a floor rug, an assortment of pillows, a reading light, and a basket full of books. We have found that wicker laundry baskets work well for this. Rotate books frequently.

Third, do family chores together. "One way to have more time is to work together. Rather than divide chores, everyone can help with the dishes, yard work, laundry, and home repair. Children like communal work that's genuinely useful. They learn things with this work. And while they work, they can visit with adults" (Pipher, 1996, p. 232).

Fourth, have dinner together. "A couple of years ago, there was a study to determine what caused children to get high scores on the SATs (Scholastic Aptitude Tests). I.Q., social circumstances, and economic states all seemed less important than another subtler factor. Youngsters who got the highest SAT scores all regularly had dinner with their parents" (Calkins & Bellino, 1997, p. 14). Take time to relish the stories and events of the day. Too often we haphazardly rush through a meal, barely taking time to make eye contact or talk. "We even light a candle, which has an amazingly calming effect. Everyone makes eye contact, and we slow down internally. It is a time of connection, of touching base" (Fuchs, 1996, p. 93).

A child who has been read to and conversed with daily and who has explored a variety of experiences begins school well prepared to learn. Children who have not had these experiences begin school at a great disadvantage. It is like a potato sack race: One child stands primed and ready at the starting line, clutching the sack tightly around her chest, and the other child remains tied inside the sack and must first struggle to find a way to begin.

The Literacy Link

First, read books that interest you aloud with your child. We now know that the single most important thing we can do to prepare our children for academic success is to read aloud to them. Aside from the requisite thousand-plus readings of *The Big Red Barn,* read books that interest you as well as your child. If the parent is bored, children intuitively pick up that books are boring. However, if the parent is interested and engaged, children will sense that as well.

We can share our old favorites, but following children's interests can introduce adults to new worlds of literature. We have been surprised and delighted how reading to Wyatt, Luke, and Wynn has introduced us to new books. We are reading books that did not interest either of us in our youth, and we are suddenly intrigued and interested in *Call of the Wild, The Hobbit,* and *The Legends of King Arthur.* After reading *The Legends of King Arthur,* we wanted to go back and reread *The Mists of Avalon.* We love that we are reading *Harry Potter* together for the first time. Each is as excited as the other to open the book.

Second, create a stationary box for your child. A box full of gorgeous stationary, writing and coloring pens, stickers, and sealing wax invites children to experience the fun and love of writing. Designating a specific letter-writing time is helpful for both children and parents. By watching Joan write letters, Dawn learned the meaning of literacy and love. Giving kids gorgeous stationary to write letters, notebooks for journals, and time to write encourages writing to become a part of their lives.

Teachers can create writing boxes in the classroom full of fun writing implements. Opportunities for correspondence are endless: Students of every age can write to parents, to administrators, to authors, to friends within the classroom, and to historical figures. If a student writes to a historical figure, another student can respond as if he or she were that person. An integral part of what makes writing letters fulfilling is the anxious waiting for a response and the joy of seeing your name addressed on an envelope.

Third, consider the suggestions in the following editorial printed in the *New York Times* (Letters, September 4, 2002). (See Figure 5.10.)

Parents' and teachers' love of literacy has a profound impact on children. Instead of focusing only on their literacy development, we need to reflect on our own literacy practices also.

If we're serious about "Helping Struggling Readers," we should:

1. Encourage parents to subscribe to a newspaper, read interesting stories out loud, never make kids produce by putting them on the spot to repeat the ABCs, respond to flashcards, or read out loud alone.

2. Have every teacher in every class from kindergarten through twelfth grade read to the group, at least briefly, every day.

3. Make extensive use of reading in unison, either one-on-one or in a group of four led by an adult or older student.

4. Avoid, like the plague, quizzing and testing while occasionally asking the pupil to "Show me what you CAN do, and then I'll HELP you do better."

5. Encourage free reading for pleasure in both the library and at home.

FIGURE 5.10 **Helping Struggling Readers**

WHAT CAN BE LEARNED FROM THIS?

Kids matter. Parents matter. Teachers matter. Reading at home matters. In this chapter we explored what families and teachers can do to create an atmosphere of love and learning in the home and in the classroom.

CHAPTER NOTES

1. For more examples of passionate family involvement processes, we encourage you to read Ada and Campoy (2003).

6 Teaching Passionately— Bilingually

There is no equality of treatment merely by providing students with the same facilities, textbooks, teachers, and curriculum; for students who do not understand English are effectively foreclosed from any meaningful education. Basic English skills are at the very core of what these public schools teach. Imposition of a requirement that, before a child can effectively participate in the education program, he must already have acquired those basic skills is to make a mockery of public education. We know that those who do not understand English are certain to find their classroom experiences wholly incomprehensible and in no way meaningful.

Supreme Court Justice WILLIAM O. DOUGLAS
Writing for the majority, in Lau v. Nichols, *1974*

It's a tough time to be a bilingual teacher educator; it's a great time to be bilingual. Dickens was right: These are the best of times; these are the worst of times.

If we ask people if they want their kids to speak *English,* the answer is yes. Bilingual people want it; English-only people want it. However, we notice that when we ask people if they want their kids to be *bilingual,* the answer is often the same, yes: Bilingual people want it; English-only people want it.

So, what in the world is going on here in the public debate about bilingual education? Lots. When we ask people if they are for bilingual education, most will say no. When we ask people if they want their kids to be bilingual, most will say yes. As any parent knows (or as any researcher knows), how you ask the question determines the answer you get (Wink, 2001).

In this chapter our purpose is to establish the principles and practices of bilingual education by telling stories of our shared experiences with multiple language programs. It may appear at first glance that some of the narratives have little to do with bilingual education. However, taken as a whole, we anticipate at the end of the chapter, readers will have generated their own answers to: What is bilingual? How do you do it? Why does it matter? Some of the stories within this chapter speak directly to nonbilingual education majors and teachers; some of the stories are for the battered and bruised bilingual educators, who are trying to survive in the trenches as we write; and other stories here are for your families and neighbors and ours. As this chapter is written in layperson language only, all supporting research will be shared in the Chapter Notes.

Language acquisition is a complex topic, but it pales in comparison to that of the politics swirling around it. Much is visible and even more is below the surface in the public debate. For example, in the following experience, two superintendents are talking to Joan at an education forum. It is not what they say; rather, it is what they mean. The subtext of the following dialogue is often where assumptions suddenly surface in any dialogue. Joan tells the following story.

In an evil state, far, far away, public school superintendents were invited to share their expertise with other state educational leaders. I was curious and went to listen. I arrived early in the morning and two tall, distinguished gentlemen superintendents, whom I did not know, came to introduce themselves. After the initial introductions, this is the conversation that followed.

"Well, *Miss* Wink, what do you do?" Superintendent 1 asked me. As I had not been addressed as *Miss* for several decades, I was intrigued. I was curious and wanted to be sure I heard not only what he said, but also what he meant.

"I am a professor in teacher education," I answered.

"Oh, but, what in particular do you *do?*" he continued.

"I spend most of my energies in the multilingual master's program, and I work with the bilingual credential candidates," I answered.

"Well, I have finally learned what multilingual education means," he immediately responded.

"Then you can tell me," I added.

"One who talks with a forked tongue," he said to me.

Superintendents 1 and 2 laughed.

"And, I know what bilingual education means," offered Superintendent 2.

"Oh, then you can tell me," I added.

"It means one who talks out of both sides of his mouth," Superintendent 2 said.

Superintendents 1 and 2 continued to chuckle to themselves as they strolled away. This entire conversation took about two minutes. It was not yet 8:00 A.M. I wondered what these two men would say to the new state educational leaders. The truth is I was wondering about a lot of things.

I know both of these school districts very well. They essentially have English-dominant teachers, working with English-only curriculum. English is the language of the classroom. The students and the community are Spanish dominant. The schools are constructed around the needs of the teachers—not the needs of the students.

Later in the morning, Superintendent 1 spoke to the assembled group and told us of all the problems in "his" district and how he was going to *fix* them. The room was filled with educational leaders, university administrators, professors, and other superintendents. At the end of his monologue, he told us that just six months prior to this, he was happily employed elsewhere—as a lawyer.

We leave you to ponder all that was below the surface. This chapter will address three central questions: What is bilingual education? How do you do it? Why does it matter? Our definitions and understandings will differ from those of the two superintendents in the previous story. Our understandings have evolved from decades of experiences within multiple language programs, not law school.

The Voice of Schools

In this section, we will share our understandings of language acquisition programs. As with other pedagogical programs, we do not believe in a one-size-fits-all approach for bilingual education. However, there are some pedagogical principles that can become practice in various contexts for bilingual and multilingual programs.

Recently, Joan flew to a literacy conference in a large urban area of the United States. As she arrived at the airport, she unexpectedly met two former colleagues, whom she had not seen in more than a decade since they had all been teachers in the same district. Now they were principals at schools in a very high-status district. After the initial greetings, Joan was a bit surprised by what they said to her.

"Joan, what are you doing here?" the first principal asked.

"We thought you were in bilingual education," the second principal added. "This is a literacy conference."

This brief encounter made us realize how badly we need to generate and articulate what bilingual education is and what it is not. For us, bilingual education is centered on the development of literacy. Of course Joan would be at a literacy conference. (See Figure 6.1.)

Defining Bilingual Education in Various Contexts

Through the years, we have had the opportunity to define bilingual education on many occasions. Our definitions are not meant to be memorized. They are contextually grounded because we have noticed that we adapt them to fit the context. For example, what we say in an in-service might differ a little from what we say during Thanksgiving dinner with family and friends. Our definitions are also grounded in narratives. As educators, we feel we are each called on to find the power of the narrative to make our complex pedagogical understandings more meaningful to the public. As a bilingual teacher educator (Joan) and a bilingual educator (Dawn), we notice that we get to explain bilingual education on airplane trips, trips to the grocery store, and social gatherings. We have also noticed that this is not true for all academics. For example, a dear colleague is a statistician; very few understand what she does, and very few ever ask her to explain it. Not true in bilingual education.

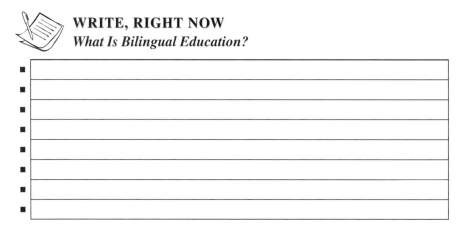

WRITE, RIGHT NOW
What Is Bilingual Education?

FIGURE 6.1   Write, Right Now: What Is Bilingual Education?

As we begin the following narratives, we first want to provide some of our understandings of English as a second language (ESL) and sheltered content instruction. ESL, which is known as English language development (ELD) in some areas, focuses on the development of conversational language for students who are not yet speaking English. The goal is the acquisition of English. Some programs, such as ESL in the Content Area, use content as a vehicle for the development of English. The students are often early language learners in the various models of ESL.

Sheltered content instruction is sometimes referred to as specially designed academic English instruction. The goal is to make grade-level content (math, social studies, science) understandable and meaningful for nonnative speakers of English. Academic language is used to link prior knowledge and experiences with the generation of new concepts and cognition. The students are often intermediate language learners.

First, *if we are in an in-service filled with principals, curriculum directors, and teachers who are interested and eager to understand, we say the following.*

The goal of bilingual education is English: understanding, speaking, reading, and writing. A program consists of good oral language development, often referred to as ESL (English as a Second Language); good sheltered content instruction; access to the core curriculum in the students' dominant language; and good mainstream activities and integration with all students. The way each school or district divides up the day or week to provide the various components depends on the needs of the students, the human resources within the district, and the political will to provide the best services possible to the students who need them the most.

Early language learners of any age need more oral language (English, in this case) development and more time learning content in their primary language. *Intermediate language learners* need a little less time with oral English and a little more time with sheltered content instruction. Intermediate language learners still need good primary language instruction. *Later language learners* need even less oral English development and more sheltered content instruction. Later language learners still need good primary language learning experiences. For example, we can classify Joan and Dawn as *later language learners* in Spanish, but they still need good primary language (English) experiences.

When we do an in-service in California, we make small changes to fit the context. For example, in California when we are talking about *early language learners* and their need for good oral English, instead of saying ESL (English as a Second Language), we say ELD (English Language Development). From our perspective it does not matter if we say ESL or ELD or simply oral language development. What matters is that teachers understand how important oral language acquisition is particularly for the *early language learners.* Even *intermediate language learners* need lots of good oral English, as it will increase comprehension and make literacy more accessible. In addition, remember Joan and Dawn, *later language learners* in Spanish, still need their primary language. People all around the world like to use their primary language. It increases comprehension and makes literacy more accessible.

One other change we make in California is that we say specially designed academic instruction in English (SDAIE) instead of sheltered English or sheltered content instruction. *Intermediate language learners,* in particular, need lots of good SDAIE or sheltered content instruction. It increases comprehension and makes literacy more accessible. Once again, for us it doesn't matter what terminology is used—what matters is that teachers understand the importance of making content and language meaningful for students who are in the process of acquiring English as another language.

Second, *if we are with a group of highly resistant, English-only mainstream classroom teachers, who for one reason or another have been mandated to come listen to us, we usually say something like:*

The goal of bilingual education is English. If you have students who are dominant in languages other than English, you, too, are a part of bilingual education. We know you didn't plan it this way. We know this was not your career goal. We know that in some cases you might not even want it this way, but this is the way it is.

Bilingual education is far more than bilingual teachers. It is pedagogically grounded principals, secretaries, bus drivers, board members, and interested community members. If your community has students who speak other languages, you are a part of a bilingual/multilingual context. Each of you has talents and gifts to contribute. Each has something to offer to a total program for students. A total program includes ESL, sheltered content instruction, primary language support, and mainstream experiences.

ESL is nothing more than oral English. It is speaking and listening; it is good chatting skills in English. ESL is important for early language learners of any age. If the students know very little English, they desperately need a great oral English teacher. Early language learner needs are unique. Often the learners are frightened because they don't have friends. They can't express themselves. The total school experience is overwhelming. Good oral English with a great teacher who loves kids is what is needed. Often primary teachers understand this need better than others on the staff. They have studied the importance of language development. They understand the integration of ideas and words. They know that students need to feel safe as their language develops. They often know it takes time to acquire a language.

At other times, we have found the best ESL teachers to be those who have taught for about 10 years and are looking for new challenges. They now understand the system, the kids, and their own pedagogy. They often are eager to apply their knowledge of teaching and learning in new contexts.

ESL teachers or oral language teachers do not necessarily have to speak other languages in addition to English. It is great if they do, but it is not necessary. It is important that the teacher be caring and pedagogically grounded.

Sheltered content instruction, often referred to as sheltered English, is another important part of bilingual education. It is important, in particular, for the *intermediate language learner.* Good sheltered content is for the student who has been here awhile and is well along in oral English development. Sheltered content is for the student who can speak and understand conversational English but still needs support in the more demanding content areas. It is often very helpful if the sheltered content teacher understands and even speaks the language of the learner, but it is not absolutely necessary. A good sheltered content teacher needs to understand the process of language acquisition. This could very well be a mainstream teacher who understands that there is a difference between conversational and academic language, who understands that it takes a long time to acquire a language, who understands that all students need access to the core curriculum, and who understands that this is still a very difficult and challenging experience for the intermediate language learner.

In any school setting, there are always teachers with much to offer students. However, sometimes there is a limited number of teachers who speak the multiple languages of the students. Difficult decisions have to be made. The pedagogical principle guiding these decisions is: How best can we meet the needs of all students and effectively use the multiple human resources at the site? In a school district with a limited number of bilingual teachers, the first principle is to get the bilingual teachers to the site closest to the bilingual students. Link the students' needs with the human resources in the district.

The students need to continue learning; education is the bedrock of bilingual education. The students need access to core curriculum. If they cannot yet learn the new content in English, they need to learn it in a language they understand. Primary or heritage language instruction is the one part of an entire bilingual program where we must have teachers who speak the language of the students. This is another unique pedagogical skill designed to serve the complex needs of language learners.

Students who are in the process of acquiring English also need to be integrated with students in the mainstream classes. All students need to be with all students. Of course, we cannot do this for six hours of each day, but certainly for part of the bilingual program, all students need to come together to learn and to also learn about each other. We often fear what we don't understand. Again, the teacher does not have to be bilingual or multilingual. But, hopefully, this is a caring and pedagogically grounded teacher whose expertise is bringing students together and creating safe and challenging dynamics where all students inquire into knowledge and seek answers together. These teachers tend to have very noisy classrooms. They also tend to adore teaching and learning. Above all, they are grounded in justice and equity. Just as bilingual teachers bring unique talents to facilitate learning in a whole program, so, too, do English-dominant teachers bring unique talents, serving the greater community of learners. No student knows it all; no student can do it all; no teacher knows it all; no teacher can do it all. None of us can do it alone. Each of must contribute our unique gift. Each of us has hidden human resources.

Third, *if we are with a group of embattled bilingual teachers, we listen; we affirm; we validate. We seek to create a healing context.*

With bilingual educators, we facilitate a discussion of morally, politically, and ethically grounded pedagogy. We are each challenged to act responsibly and morally based on our knowledge and our experience. Bilingual teachers often have very comprehensive understandings of the social, cultural, and political context of language and learning. We cannot expect everyone to understand. It took us a long time to come to our understandings about languages, and we only learned it from students.

To this point, we have shared with you answers to the question: What is bilingual education? Our definitions are contextually grounded in narratives of our experiences. We will conclude this section with two other definitions.

Remember Professor Beto from the beginning of the book? He always said that bilingual education is all about education that happens to be in two languages. This definition serves as a great cognitive coat hook on which to hang further understandings. Later in the semester Professor Beto would add to his definition: Bilingual education is all about literacy and knowledge. That's it: literacy and knowledge; literacy and knowledge; literacy and knowledge.

Krashen (1996) states that bilingual education consists of good, comprehensible input in English, good subject matter teaching in the primary language, and continued literacy development in the primary language. Given these three components, kids will get literacy and knowledge (pp. 3–4). (See Figure 6.2.)

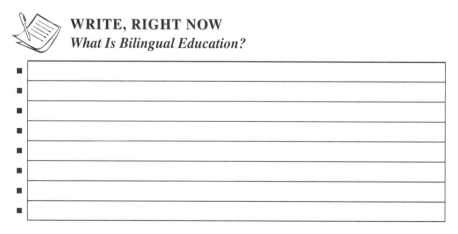

WRITE, RIGHT NOW
What Is Bilingual Education?

FIGURE 6.2   Write, Right Now: What Is Bilingual Education?

The Voice of Life

In the previous section, we asked the question that we often hear when we are in schools working with teachers and administrators: What is bilingual education? However, we have noticed that often in the grocery store or on a plane, we hear a different type of question. Sometimes people ask questions about bilingual education, and they don't really want to hear our answer. They want to tell us that this is America, and kids need to learn English. Incidentally, the answer to that is: Yes, you're right, yup, sí, or you betcha.

In this section, The Voice of Life, our intention is to tell stories because sometimes the answers we use in schools don't work as well in life—at least, not in our lives. For example, when Krashen (1993) speaks of comprehensible input and low affective filter in the language acquisition process, teachers "get it." However, not everyone understands comprehensible input and low affective filter, much less first and second language acquisition. The following story is one we have used with our relatives and friends, as they struggle to understand language acquisition, which is the foundation of bilingual education. These are people who truly wanted to understand how one "gets" (acquires) a language.

First, a disclaimer: This story is very gender centric. Remember, these stories are based on our lived experiences. We know about being a mom, and we don't know about being a dad. In addition, we needed an *m* word. Thus, in the following story, when we say "Mama," please know that we mean *everyone*—women and men.

As we write this, we cannot help but reflect on the early days of gender-free language, when women gently mentioned that *he* or *him* didn't seem to include us, but we were told not to worry because, "Of course, *he* or *him* meant women, too." Men, when we say "mamas," in what follows, we want you to think, "papas." To bring us back to focus, this story is not about *he, him, she,* or *her.* It is about something we all have in common: first language acquisition.

Mamas, Meaning, and Motivation

Families around the world know about first language acquisition. Apparently, you don't need a Ph.D., an ESL certificate, or teacher credentials to understand language acquisition. Most kids everywhere grow up talking. Someone, somewhere must be doing something right. They are. Families do what is necessary for language acquisition.

Envision a small baby you know very well. Think about what happens when that baby comes home to begin life with her new family. I know exactly what happened when I brought Dawn and Bo home from the hospital: I started to talk meaningfully and lovingly with them: "Do you want your baba? Did you take a good nap? You are such a love-bug. Are you hungry? Oh, poor baby, you have a dirty diaper. Do you want to cuddle? Oh, look at that face." Dawn and Bo didn't have to do anything; I didn't expect anything, I just kept sending loving, meaningful messages. I knew (and so do families everywhere) that if I just kept speaking in this manner, sooner or later, Dawn and Bo would begin to understand and then respond.

Now, imagine that the baby you are thinking about is between one and two years of age. Probably, the baby is beginning to respond physically and even verbally. I know what we did when this happened with Dawn and Bo: We continued to talk and model and show, and we began to celebrate every response—no matter how small.

When I said, "See the light?" if Dawn or Bo looked toward the light, I was delighted with their understanding. If I said, "Here comes Daddy," and they ran to the door, I was thrilled that they understood. The happier I was about each incremental bit of understanding, the more motivated Dawn and Bo were. Mamas around the world do exactly as I did: They provide meaning in a loving way that motivates their children. Papas, grandparents, and caregivers do the very same thing, and most children eventually start to speak—each child at his or her own rate. Some speak earlier. Some speak later. But most start to speak and understand. Language acquisition is very natural.

Now imagine that this child is between two and three years old. She is probably beginning to respond more rapidly. Words come one by one, and we are thrilled. I used to run to the baby book and record and date each new word as it developed. I celebrated. I called my friends and told them about the new words. I kept talking in meaningful ways and I hope in a loving way, too.

When words started to come two by two, I was sure I had birthed gifted children. When Dawn and Bo began to string nouns together, I didn't worry about noun pileups. I just focused on the meaning and their understanding. Soon they knew too many words, and I couldn't record them in the baby books fast enough. When language starts to emerge, it comes first as a dribble, and then it is a raging river.

Comprehensible input and low affective filter are fundamental to language acquisition. We have known a lot of families in our lives, and they all seem to know this and they are all mostly doing it right because the kids are growing up with language. It is only when the kids go to school that we stop doing what we know works.

First, think about what families do right. In the first year, they know that it is inappropriate to expect their children to speak. They give their babies lots of time to acquire language naturally. If you are an adult second language learner, you appreciate how long it takes to acquire a language. In the first year, families don't give vocabulary and comprehension tests; families don't worry about errors in language. Families give meaningful messages; families give time; and families give love.

In the second year, families are thrilled with physical responses that indicate that the child understands; "yes" and even "no" become benchmarks in a family life. Individual sounds that mean something specific send all the family members into action to do whatever the 2-year-old is indicating. Families respond to the 2-year-old's initial sounds. The 2-year-old can see that language has purpose; language has power.

In the third year, families love to hear the natural progression of more and more words and more and more complex groups of words. Families respond appropriately to the child's language, and families are thrilled when the child responds appropriately to more complex sentences.

Families don't give language and comprehension tests; families don't expect perfect pronunciation at first—in fact, many are thrilled with the creative use of sounds. Families don't send their babies off to special classes the minute a new word is used incorrectly. Families know that language is an individual developmental process. I remember feeling so nostalgic when Bo's /r/ sound finally developed. For of his early years, I had loved the sound of his childlike speech without that bothersome /r/ sound.

Meaning, meaning, meaning is what bilingual education is all about. First language acquisition takes place when mamas provide meaning, and kids are motivated to speak. Krashen (1993) tells a similar story when he works with teachers: He says that students need comprehensible input (a.k.a., meaning) with a low affective filter (a.k.a., mamas and motivation). A low affective filter refers to the state of ease and comfort of the language learner. Babies learning their first language generally have low affective filters during their language acquisition. They are comfortable, and the emphasis is on providing meaning and love. A high affective filter refers to the anxiety produced in stressful situations. A high affective filter in the classroom inhibits language acquisition because people do not acquire languages as well in high-stress situations. If you understand this story, you know a lot about bilingual education, which is second language acquisition—not first language acquisition. However, there are some easy comparisons, which will hopefully help you ponder bilingual education.

My People Made It without Bilingual Education

A second story follows in answer to the many times we have been asked a question, which tends to follow this line of inquiry: My people made it without bilingual education. What's the matter with yours (Betances, 1986)?

Joan thought a lot about this as she tried to find an answer based on her own life's experiences.

Yes, my Grandma Grace made it without bilingual education, too. In fact, she made it without any education. Now that I think about it, all my husband's grandparents and my grandparents made it without bilingual education, and they all made it without education. It didn't matter in their world.

The men raised cattle, sheep, pigs, and chickens; they planted corn; they dug wells; they panned for gold; they built sod huts. The women took care of children, fed the chickens, planted gardens, cleaned houses, pumped water, canned beef, and fed people. It didn't matter if they didn't speak English—the corn still grew; the baby calves were still born; men still needed to eat when they came in from the fields. It only mattered that they worked just as hard as they could for years and years. Schools must have been nearly irrelevant in their worlds.

Those economic avenues are not open to my grandchildren whose educational needs are vastly different from those of my grandparents. Society's needs are different, too. Today, even if you have a willingness to work and even if you have a strong back, it just isn't enough.

It seems that the basics aren't so basic anymore. My Grampy lived from the horse and buggy days to see a man walk on the moon. In my wildest dreams, I cannot imagine what my grandchildren will live to see.

> Their world will be totally different from anything we know or used to know. I don't know what my grandchildren will need to know, but I will guess that they will need high levels of literacy, know how to solve problems, and be able to get along with lots of people who are different from them. They will need to be able to access and to generate new information via technology that isn't even in science fiction yet. I suspect that those citizens who will thrive economically and socially in the next century are those who can speak English and other languages. Being bilingual will be basic.

As Joan reflected on her grandparents and her husband's grandparents, it became clear that the educational needs of the past are not the future.

Previous generations gradually learned to talk and understand oral English, and that was enough. Future generations will need complex levels of literacies. Whereas Joan's grandma only needed oral English to thrive in her world, this will not be enough for Joan's grandchildren.

Conversational English might have served previous generations well, but the future demands academic English (Cummins, 2000b). Drawing on the legacy of many linguists, language educators, and scholars, Cummins's constructs of conversational and academic language demonstrate the complexity of language proficiency. As a student moves up through the grades, the cognitive demands grow, and the contextual supports diminish, whether it be in written or in oral language. The challenge for schools is to enhance the academic language of students who are in the process of acquiring English. Academic language leads to success.

Yes, English is the goal of bilingual education. More kids are learning English faster than ever before. You can't stop it. No matter what you do, kids are going to speak English. We, in schools, are taking the credit and/or blame for kids acquiring English, but really they are learning English on the playground, on television, at the mall. Speaking English is good, but it is not good enough. Schools need to focus on literacy and knowledge.

Lucy: A Chinese-English Bilingual

When Lucy reflected on her previous educational experiences, she discovered something different.

> "If we learned English and succeeded in school without bilingual education, then why can't others?" True enough. Some immigrants do well in public schools with little or no assistance in their native language.
>
> I was one of those students. Arriving in the United States at the age of 8, I was placed in a third-grade class. The school had few limited-English-proficient students and even fewer Asian language speakers. I believe I've succeeded in school, having graduated from high school and college. And until several years

ago, I was one of those people who didn't see the need for bilingual education. That is, until I realized that I did get bilingual education, just not in school. I had what some call de facto bilingual education.

I got help in my schoolwork from my parents and my older and more English-fluent sisters—in Chinese. Other immigrant students get help in their native language from hired tutors or bilingual classmates. In some subjects like math, I had already learned the concepts being taught in class in my native country and understood the lessons in English, at least initially, without much assistance.

I was exposed to good English instruction from my siblings and from the English-speaking children on our block. Some immigrant students have English tutors or get help in community after-school programs.

I already knew how to read and write in Chinese. Other children learn to read and write in their native language in the home, in community language schools, or like me, in their native country. Knowing how to read and write in the native language helps tremendously when facing the same task in another tongue.

However, not all students get, outside of school, the three things that good bilingual programs provide: help with school subjects in the native language, quality English instruction, and literacy development in the native tongue so that reading and writing are easier in the new language. Unless these students get bilingual education through school, they are unlikely to learn well and succeed in school.

Isn't the goal of education to help all students succeed academically? If so, then we need to give them the best possible schooling. These students need well-implemented bilingual education programs, ones that researchers, parents, and teachers overwhelmingly support (Tse, 1997, p. B7).

Lucy discovered that she had experienced de facto bilingual education (Krashen, 1996) in her family. Lucy's knowledge of subject matter that she gained in the first language made English more comprehensible. In addition, Lucy's first language facilitated her literacy development in English. Good bilingual programs attempt to provide these same two components: subject matter knowledge and literacy. In addition, Lucy's primary language continued to develop, another component of effective bilingual programs.

Lucy received all of this at home, de facto bilingual education, but she recognizes that not all students have that opportunity at home. In spite of that, knowledge and literacy are still worthy goals for schools.

Praxis: Let the Magic Begin

Let's be honest: the magic is gone, in spite of the overwhelming data supporting good bilingual programs. The zeitgeist is xenophobic, in spite of an overwhelming need for

U.S. schools to produce bilingual and multilingual citizens with broad international perspectives. As we write, the future is racing to us, in spite of the fact that we are racing backward.

In California the word *bilingual* has been banished and replaced by *English-language learning.* The change has taken hold, as we consistently hear teachers talk about the "English learners." Even the word *culture* has been expunged by the state board of education as the state mandates rigid standards, high-stakes testing, an inflexible Euro-centric curriculum and English-only teaching and learning (Katz & Kohl, 2002).

> These state mandates ignore the most significant language-acquisition research findings of the past twenty years: Students learn a second language best when they can build academically upon their first language. The policies also ignore a 1998 report of student achievement (as measured in standardized test scores) that showed that English-language learners enrolled in bilingual programs in San Francisco and San Jose schools outperformed native-born English speakers in all content areas. These programs are now at risk of being dismantled in favor of a uniform system that suppresses many children's first language. (p. 6)

Let's be even more honest: The magic is inherently still in being bilingual and multilingual. We know how to create programs that lead to high academic achievement, biliteracy, and positive group relationships, but the political will has been drummed out by a narrow perspective and a Eurocentric approach. How will Joan ever explain this to her grandkids when they are older and career paths are enhanced and accelerated by being bilingual?

Programmatic Models

Keeping with our assertion that one-size-does-not-fit-all, we offer some options for your consideration. Obviously, the program chosen is determined by the needs of the students. Javier was in a program that is fairly typical of transitional bilingual education in that it provides support in the primary language early in the program with more and more English added over three years. This program served him well; unfortunately, it has now been taken away by a public vote. Students who follow Javier will not have this opportunity. This story serves as a picture of what actually happens with immigrant kids in schools both yesterday and today.

Javier left an orphanage in Mexico and came to the United States when he was 6 years old. He had no formal education and he spoke no English. The family who adopted him used mainly Spanish at home, and he entered first grade in a public school not far from our house. His classroom was composed entirely of native Spanish speakers, and the children were taught to read in Spanish.

Today, some two years later, Javier is in a mainstream, English-language, third-grade classroom; he speaks English fluently, and he's now reading within the range of expectations established for native English speakers entering the third grade.

How did this happen? It seems upside down: More time in Spanish results in more English? How can that be? No wonder the public gets confused. Here is one hint: We learn to read once in our life, and it happens faster if we already know that language. Javier knew Spanish.

In first grade, their teacher initially taught students to read in Spanish, while ensuring that they progressed in math, science, and in other skills by using their native language. Even students with little to no early childhood education, like Javier, thereby lost no ground progressing in multiple academic disciplines while simultaneously being introduced to English. Here is another hint: Javier's developing Spanish made English more accessible.

By the middle of second grade, however, English instruction had all but taken over the classroom. Whereas words like *casa, una,* and *la* were on Javier's spelling lists at the beginning of the first grade, English words as complex as *blue, sleep,* and *paint* appeared by the end of the second.

Today, Javier and his peers are divided into mainstream English classrooms while taking part in a third and final year of English assistance, amounting to English tutoring for up to one-and-a-half hours a day.

Here is another hint: What we know in one language, we know in all languages.

At the end of the three-year transition program, which his district allowed, Javier entered the all-English program; this is a reasonable time period for transition. However, the students who follow Javier will only be allowed one year to transition into learning all curriculum in English. Laws recently passed in Colorado now penalize individual schools that do not adhere to this standard by threatening their accreditation and federal funding under President Bush's No Child Left Behind initiative.

> The George W. Bush Administration killed The Bilingual Education Act. This law, officially Title VII of the 1968 Elementary and Secondary Education Act, was replaced by a provision called No Child Left Behind, which requires that funds be used only for the explicit acquisition of English. The former Office of Bilingual Education and Minority Languages Affairs is now the Office of English Language Acquisition. Essentially, the words "bilingual education" have been excised from the federal government's lexicon. (Katz & Kohl, 2002, p. 275)

It is clear to Javier's new family that, even with all of the support within their family, that Javier simply would not have been ready to enter a mainstream classroom after only one year of English assistance.

The magic is gone.

There Is Immersion, and There Is Immersion

Immersion has many different and even contradictory meanings (Mora, Wink, & Wink, 2001; Wink, 1991; Wink, 2000). It seems that English-only people want it, and bilingual people want it. Dawn and Joan certainly want a good immersion program for Dawn's children. In addition, the most ardent bilingual education foe wants immersion. The confusion surrounding the use and abuse of the word *immersion* has the potential to hurt kids. No one (reading this book) wants that.

We are not fans of definitions for fear that a student somewhere might be made to memorize them, but in this particular instance we feel the need to define.

French Canadian immersion is terminology used in the United States to refer to a program in Canada. The program serves language majority students. The goals are English and another language (bilingualism/biliteracy) and high academic achievement in seven (K–6) years. The teachers are credentialed or certified bilingual or multilingual teachers. It has a long and successful history in Canada.

English immersion is very different from the Canadian model. It is designed to serve language minority students. The goal is English dominance within one year. Teachers are not required to speak the language of the students, and the language instruction is overwhelmingly in English.

English immersion is very much the exact opposite of the Canadian model, although the public often thinks they are the same. The goals are the exact opposite; the students represent two distinct groups; the teachers' preparation is vastly different; and the time in the program is completely different.

Bilingual (dual or two-way) immersion is designed to serve majority and minority language groups. The goals are English and another language (bilingualism/ biliteracy), high academic achievement, and positive intergroup relations in seven (K–6) years. The teachers are credential or certified bilingual or multilingual professionals.

Bilingual immersion is what Dawn and I want for her kids: biliteracy, high academic achievement, and positive human relations with kids regardless of ethnic, linguistic, or cultural groups. We are for this. This is very similar to what many call *enriched, maintenance bilingual education* that focuses on biliteracy and academic achievement for all. Bilingual immersion or enriched, maintenance bilingual education differs from what many have experienced with *transitional bilingual education,* which serves only the minority language groups by providing a little support early and then exiting the students rapidly (Mora, Wink, & Wink, 2001; Wink 2000), as in the case of Javier.

What we have provided here are generic definitions, as we quickly acknowledge that programs vary. Language education programs fall along a continuum with the two extremes being compensatory models versus enrichment models of dual language instruction (Mora, Wink, & Wink, 2001). How strange and sad to have a language program that seeks to "compensate" anyone for their language. At one end of the extreme we have monolingual/monocultural programs that view second language teaching and learning as compensatory. At the other end of the continuum, we have models of dual language teaching and learning that view languages as enrichment or as human resources (Ruiz, 1984), in which the goals are consistently grounded in academic achievement, biliteracy, and the ability to live and thrive in a diverse cultural setting, which leads to great career opportunities (Mora, Wink, & Wink 2001).

Hierarchy of Languages

To look only at programs *in isolation* is to deny the social, cultural, historical, and political context of each. People influence programs, which in turn influence students. As teachers, it's true, we are in those classrooms, and we have incredible power and potential to assist and/or hinder students' achievement and self-worth with not only what we do but also with what we think. Even if we do not recognize our power and our inner assumptions, they are apparent for all the world to see. Ask a student. Ask a colleague. It is as though our assumptions run around behind us like a shadow; when we turn to try to see them, they move. These hidden social, economic, political, ethnic, cultural, and linguistic assumptions play a role in the lives of students in good programs and in not-so-good programs.

The relationships we establish with students, be they coercive or collaborative (Cummins, 2001), very probably will have a more lasting effect on the lives and academic success of students than the majority of programs, curriculum, and methods we love and/or hate. Students may forget what we taught them but they will not forget how we made them feel. As we assist students in negotiating their identities, we affirm their past and their future. As we celebrate and honor students' past and present, we raise their academic achievement and their sense of self-efficacy. This is nothing more or less than we do for our own children; this is nothing more or less than what Joan and Dean wanted for Dawn and Bo.

The language programs, previously described, are often grounded in an unseen or unacknowledged (at least, by some) hierarchy of languages. For example, if our goal is to *compensate* students for their heritage language, we are not honoring the past of those students. If our goal is to *maintain* or *enrich,* we are honoring and respecting their language, their family, and their history, thereby fostering social and academic empowerment of students.

When one language group is more highly valued than another, the effects are good for the valued language group and bad for the devalued language group. This context hurts the achievement and the soul of the child whose language is not valued. For example, think of the different receptions Mexican Spanish-speaking children and European French-speaking children encounter when they enter school. The Mexican children's native Spanish is usually viewed as a detriment to learning English and to academic success. Their Spanish is an obstacle to be surmounted. French-speaking children who enter school in the United States are lauded for speaking French. Their language is not seen as a detriment but rather as a wonderful, cosmopolitan advantage. This tells us a lot, not about French or Spanish, per se, but rather about the people in the schools.

This hierarchy of languages is found throughout the world: Japanese and Korean; Turkish and Kurdish; English and Spanish; Spanish and Catalan; and Swedish and Finnish. It is often easier to acknowledge these contexts when they are farther away from us. For example, why is that Korean students often do well in schools in the United States but not as well in Japanese schools? Or why is it that Finnish students historically have a pattern of underachievement in Swedish schools? The answer lies in history and the continuing consequences of patterns of colonization. Sometimes it seems to us that *colonization is forever,* as the costs continue generations later. The memory of colonization matters.

In the Finnish-Swedish example, one needs to know that Finland was colonized by Sweden from 1155 to 1809 (Skutnabb-Kangas, 1988, 1998, 2000). The Finns have a history of migrant labor work in Sweden. The Finnish language, culture, and people continue to receive low-status recognition in Sweden. Predictably, the Finnish students had a history of underachievement in Sweden. Skutnabb-Kangas found that the expectations of the teachers combined with whether students felt pride or shame about their primary language and culture have a determining effect on students' academic success. Inherent in this is the common occurrence of then blaming the students for their failure.

Now the question is: Which brings it closer to home? Why is that Euro-American students have higher levels of academic achievement than African American (or Native American students) in the United States? When one group of people and their language and their culture are not valued in society, the children of that group have many hidden academic and unacknowledged barriers. We bring it even closer to home. We well remember a person we loved a lot; she taught for years, and the Native American students never achieved in her classes. She was sure it had to be their fault, or their families', or their culture. She could not understand it because she taught them with the exact same materials and the same curriculum and in the same classroom as the white students. There is no gentle way to say the truth: She hated Native Americans, although she would deny it to this day.

In our experiences in the United States, we see a pattern of *less* and *more* with the attitudes of teachers toward Spanish-dominant students of Mexican or Central American students. The students are treated as if their language and culture are a detriment to learning. The message they receive in subtle (and not so subtle) ways is that they are *less* in the United States.

Language rights are human rights, as stated in the guiding principles of the United Nations Universal Declaration of Human Rights, which was approved in 1948 (Skutnabb-Kangas, 2000). Inherent in the success or failure of any bilingual program is the school's overall atmosphere regarding linguistic human rights, which refer to a person's basic human right to speak his or her mother tongue. The United States has a dismal record in this area, summed up best with the prevailing attitude of "This is America and they'll speak American!" Students who come to school speaking other languages have historically have been prohibited from speaking their primary language and even corporally punished if they do. The teachers' and administrations' attitudes toward students' primary languages define the effectiveness of any program.

If the hierarchy of languages seems like an abstract concept, let us introduce you to a young girl for whom it was a concrete concept. This story also demonstrates the devastating effects of one teacher's belief structure, even if she could not see it. Mónica, a 10-year-old from a Mexican migrant family, was in a highly enriched dual language program for majority and minority students, with goals of biliteracy for all. We knew Mónica well, as Joan remembers when she was born while the family lived in a privately owned wretched camp for migrant laborers. Through the years, we came to know all of the children of the family and watched with awe as the family broke the migrant cycle to keep their children in one school community.

Suddenly, Mónica was not succeeding in the fourth grade despite a dual language program grounded in pluralistic goals, which we respected. Dawn periodically heard Mónica's teacher speak of Mónica in disparaging language. The teacher said that Mónica was lazy and not motivated. Mónica saw the situation differently. Mónica described the teacher's attitude toward the students of Mexican origin with these words: *"Las maestras piensan que los mexicanos somos sucios. (The teachers think we Mexicans are dirty.)"* Monica's reaction to the teacher is an example of a teacher's implicit message that clearly contradicted the dual language program's goal of providing equity and parity of participation for both majority and minority language students (Mora, Wink, & Wink, 2001; Wink, 1998).

Heritage Language Instruction

A heritage language is one not spoken by the dominant culture but is spoken in the family or associated with the heritage culture.

KRASHEN, TSE, & MCQUILLAN, 1998, p. 3

A heritage language is the language of the heart. It is the language spoken between parent and child to express love. It is the language of childhood and family stories. Each person carries within all of the norms, stories, politics, spirituality, expectations, and history of our heritage language. Experiences feel more real. For example, often Holocaust survivors cannot describe their experiences in the heritage language. The pain is too intense. They can describe these horrors only in their second or third languages. These languages, learned later, provide the necessary distance to make the words utterable. Our heritage language with all that it encompasses is a primary lens through which we experience the world.

The power and influence of this lens were captured recently by Yasmina, a Muslim Arab from Pakistan. Yasmina was a student of Joan's one summer in Mallorca, Spain, in a class for teachers in international education. English was the language of the classroom in addition to the multiple heritage languages: Serbian, German, Croatian, Czeck, Arabic, Japanese, Dutch, Berber, Pakistani, French, and Spanish. Yasmina was, quite simply, one of those magical people who not only attracts people to her with her own passion for life and learning but also makes it safe to expand one's understanding.

The class discussed heritage languages in class one morning. Yasmina remarked on the complete aversion to pigs that is part of being Muslim. This aversion was so strong that Yasmina could not even utter the word in her own heritage language, Berber, but could voice the word in her second and third languages.

Yasmina's inability to speak the word *pig* in Berber effectively demonstrates the ties of the heartstrings connected with our heritage language. Somehow, through the blanket of love and safety that slowly enwrapped the class, pigs became a source of discussion and jokes. A room of people overtly discussing pigs was completely irreverent and sacrilegious in Yasmina's heritage language and culture. However, the love and trusting human connections in the class made it okay. Even Yasmina, seated in her complete head and body covering in the Mallorquin heat, couldn't keep a straight face and laughed along with the rest.

Eventually, Joan asked one small group to review the concept of heritage language (Krashen, Tse, & McQuillan, 1998) for the entire class. They were not simply to transmit the ideas, but rather they were to engage the learners in an active process to experience the value of heritage languages. This was the context as the small group of students began their review of heritage languages. They walked to the chalkboard and wrote in large letters:

Never try to teach a pig to sing. It wastes your time and annoys the pig.

The class roared with laughter. The student leaders told the class that they were to translate it into as many heritage languages as possible. Each small group wrote their various translations on chart paper posted around the room; the more languages in each group, the more translations, an obvious advantage.

However, the class immediately jumped into all of the hidden advantages of languages and cultures. One group wanted to forgo the exact translation, as they preferred to use authentic expressions, which expressed the same meaning, in various languages. A second group quickly shared their translations and, with tongue firmly placed in cheek, launched in a soliloquy on the Dewey concept of beginning with the pig. Another group taught their translations from the point of view of a pig.

The example of the pig in the Muslim Arab culture captures the wide-reaching web encompassed in a heritage language. It is not merely the words. It is also all of the history, culture, norms, and *love* that go along with that language. The word *pig,* in the context of the Muslim Arab world, demonstrates the power of heritage language. Remember that Yasmina couldn't even speak the word *pig* in her native Berber. It was too close. Love amongst the students and teacher made discussion of pigs safe.

When we deny people the right to speak and develop their heritage language, we are also denying them access to dynamic relationships between thought, speech, and experience. When development of the heritage language is prohibited, family ties, cultural and historical norms, and expressions of love are essentially prohibited, as well.

The learning in that international context was fascinating to experience, and it was abundantly obvious that heritage languages are not only harmless but also actually quite beneficial. As Joan and Dawn have discovered numerous times in their lives, being bilingual is not bad; rather it is good, a distinct advantage. The development and maintenance of the heritage language have cognitive advantages and job-related advantages, and it encourages deeper communication among family members (Krashen, Tse, & McQuillan, 1998). Families and older children support the maintenance of heritage languages (Shin & Krashen, 1999), although many adolescents go through a stage in which they feel indifferent to the heritage language and may even avoid it.

This happens apparently due to the strong pressure for English and social integration in English-speaking society (Krashen, Tse, & McQuillan, 1998).

So, given the obvious: How do we maintain and develop heritage languages? We do it through comprehensible input, good books, TV, parents' use of the language, and recreational reading in the heritage language (Cho & Krashen, 2000; McQuillan, 1999; Tse, 2001); we do it the very same way we develop any language: meaning. It is the same thing we do daily in families. However, for heritage languages to thrive, the dominant culture must value them—the vital ingredient presently missing in the United States.

When we tell the people we love "I love you," it is most meaningful and powerful when we say it in our heritage language. Does anybody have the right to take that language and those feelings away? Heritage language has recently captured the attention of many and seems to be readily understandable by academics and laypersons. The development of the heritage language assumes the continual development of the dominant language (English, in this case) also.

The Literacy Link

Books are the best literacy link. Libraries are the links to literacy. Go to the library. Buy books at garage sales and annual library sales; trade books; write books; read with children; let children see you reading; talk about your reading. If you do all of these things in English, English will develop. In addition, if you do these things in a language other than English, you will get two languages, plus all of the cognitive, social, and job-related advantages that come with being bilingual.

WHAT CAN BE LEARNED FROM THIS?

When it comes to learning English, many believe the more, the better. The sooner, the better. The faster, the better. The harder, the better. Turns out it is not true. Many of the long-held assumptions about bilingual education do not stand up to the bright light of data; nor do these assumptions serve the United States well for the future. Properly organized bilingual programs hold the promise of high academic achievement in two languages and positive intergroup relations. The future calls us to create such vibrant programs. How dare we not? Being bilingual is not bad. "Bilingual is best" (Krashen, 2003).

Sometimes we can learn things in the most surprising places and in amazing ways. Probably some of our most memorable learning takes places when we least expect it. Such was the case with Lonnie, who actively resisted learning anything about being bilingual, until one day . . .

Joan was in Mallorca, Spain, teaching adult international educators ESL and bilingual theory and methods. One of the students, Lonnie, was particularly resistant to learning anything about bilingual education; she could tolerate a little ESL but no bilingual education. She came from a business background with very little experience in education and no experience in bilingual education. She had not experienced acquiring another language, although she was quite worldly and sophisticated in many ways.

As Lonnie resisted, Joan kept remembering how long it took her to understand bilingual education. Joan needed a meaningful story, and Lonnie needed time to make her own meaning.

One night as Joan sat looking at the Mediterranean Sea, she wrote her the following letter.

Dear Lonnie,

My trip from our ranch in the northern plains of the United States to our apartment, *Edificio Pelicano*, in Mallorca took 40 hours with many unexpected events. My husband is coming to visit next week, and in order to prevent him from experiencing some of my problems, I faxed him the following letter. (See Figure 6.3.)

The next day in class, Joan read the letter aloud to Lonnie and the class. They laughed.

"Lonnie, why did I write this letter in English to my husband?" Joan asked her.

"Because you wanted him to understand," she replied.

"Yes, Lonnie, if you understand why I wrote this letter in English, then you understand bilingual education," I replied. If I had written the letter in Mallorquín, the language of Mallorca, he would probably still be at Newark airport.

Bilingual education is grounded in meaning—in schools and in life. Kids have to make meaning in order to understand. Dean had to make meaning in order to get from Rapid City to Mallorca. Behind all the political rhetoric are children who are trying to understand. Their lives are currently on the line. When we think of bilingual education, we do not think in abstract terms. Instead we envision the faces of Manuel, Natalie, Victoria, and Margarita. Their lives will be forever touched by the political and educational policies of the day. Our future will forever be touched by what we do today.

Our mother tongue, our primary language, our heritage language: Each of us has one. Each of us feels passionately about it, as it is how we first came to know love. It is how we make sense of the world. It is central to our being. It links our heart with our heritage, as it is how we filter our past, present, and future. Our mother tongue is the language of the heart and soul.

Dean,

When you get to Rapid City, be sure to check your baggage all the way through to Mallorca. The woman who works in the airport in Rapid City will tell you that you can't do this, but you can and must. You do not want to go through customs in Madrid. In fact, you won't have time to go through customs there and catch your connecting flight to Mallorca.

When you get to Newark, do not go down the Continental National wing at the airport. You need to go farther to the right and find the International wing for Continental. We left from Gate 75 and a very competent Continental employee, named Judith, helped us as much as possible although the plane was delayed in Florida all night because of bad weather. We slept in the chairs at Gate 75, so we were all on first-name basis before the transatlantic flight even departed.

When you get to the Madrid airport, the minute you go through the passport area, turn immediately to your right and go to the end of the room to a very small desk with a sign above that says *Conecciones*. There will be two or three people at the desk to help several hundred other people. The woman at the computer yells at everyone and has total control over your life for the next several hours. If you are nice to her while she yells at you, the young woman behind her will reward you with a first-class seat to Mallorca. Smile, thank her, and get the heck out of there.

Turn around and go back to the main exit of the customs room. As you will not have luggage, this will be a breeze. Just keep walking like you know where you are going.

As soon as you leave the customs room, turn right again. Keep going and going and going until you find *Iberia Nacional*. Everyone will tell you *al fondo; al fondo; al fondo*. This is exactly what the Mexicans mean when they say *derecho; derecho; derecho*. No matter what, just keep going straight ahead; straight ahead; straight ahead.

Finally, you will come to the end of the building; we left from Gate D45. There is a very nice man there who seems to take care of all the gates in the 40's and 50's. He will insist you have time to go to the First-Class Lounge and have a drink . . . that is, if you were nice to the woman who yells at everyone back at the *Conecciones* desk near customs.

When you arrive in Mallorca, go to the luggage area and look for your luggage. The luggage handlers may be sitting on the luggage ramps because they are having a slowdown. It is not a complete strike—more like a brownout of baggage.

When you leave the Mallorca airport (with or without your bags), the taxi drivers will be waiting. Just go up to any one of them and tell them, *Edificio Pelicano* in *Cala Mayor.* They will charge you about $3000 pts. or about $20 to $25.

When you get to the *Pelicano Mayor,* walk up the hill. There is a building on the right—this is not the *Pelicano.* There is a building on the left—that is not the *Pelicano.* *Al fondo. Al fondo. Al fondo. Derecho. Derecho. Derecho.* This building will look like a little one-story cantina. Go into the front entrance and wait for one of the residents to open the locked door. *Al fondo. Derecho.* Straight to the Mediterranean. Look down. You will note that this is not a little one-story cantina; it is really an eight-story apartment complex built into the wall surrounding the sea.

Juan, in the bar, has all of the keys for the faculty apartments. I'll be waiting for you.

Love,

Joan

FIGURE 6.3   How to Get from South Dakota to Mallorca

Putting politics aside, we ask you to think of a child you love and imagine what you want for him or her. Would you voluntarily cut that child off from the language of family, culture, and roots *in addition* to giving him or her a handicap in academia and life? Of course not! None of us would. Bilingual education connects children's language of the heart with their new language of schools and life, and it does it all with no cost to learning English. In fact, bilingual education will enhance the acquisition of English.

CHAPTER NOTES

Because this chapter is filled with stories that demonstrate the data, we have chosen to list the research that support the narrative by the means of Chapter Notes. These specific citations were used in the development of the personal stories. Please note that we include a short annotated bibliography followed by three documents—the fallacies, Figure 6.4, and Figure 6.5.

August, D., & Hakuta, K. (1997). *Improving schooling for language minority children: A research agenda.* Washington, DC: National Academy Press.
> A comprehensive review of the basic and policy-centered research of schooling for language-minority students. It offers suggestions for how evaluation can be used to improve programmatic models.

Baker, C., & Hornberger, N. (Eds.). (2001). *An introductory reader to the writings of Jim Cummins.* Clevedon, England: Multilingual Matters.
> This text answers four specific questions that are embedded within the narratives of this chapters: (a) Does bilingual education work? The research clearly shows that successful programs exist throughout the world for linguistic minority and majority groups. In these programs students do not suffer academically or linguistically in the target language, even though much of their learning is in the minority language. (b) Does bilingual education work better than English-only programs? Until the term *bilingual education* has a clear definition that is accepted for research, it is difficult to be sure. However, to date the enriched models whose goals are bilingualism and biliteracy for both groups of learners show better outcomes. (c) Will students suffer academically if they are introduced to reading in their second language? No, the language of initial introduction of reading is not, in itself, a determinant in academic outcomes. (d) Will greater amounts of English instruction (time-on-task) result in greater English achievement? The data overwhelmingly fail to show any positive relationship between the amount of English instruction in a program and student outcomes.

Crawford, J. (1999). *Bilingual education: History, politics, theory, and practice* (4th ed.). Los Angeles: Bilingual Education Services.
> An excellent critical perspective on the history of bilingual education and present-day bilingual education, in addition to an extensive look at the federal policies governing bilingual education. This text serves undergraduates and graduates

well, whether they are new to bilingual education or veterans in the field who need a good resource book.

Crawford, J. (2000). *At war with diversity: U.S. language policy in an age of anxiety.* Clevedon, England: Multilingual Matters.

Crawford tackles the paradox of bilingual education. Pedagogically speaking, the preponderance of evidence demonstrates that a well-designed bilingual program can produce high levels of academic achievement at no cost to English. Politically speaking, the counterintuitive research has not persuaded the public.

http://ourworld.compuserve.com/homepages/JWCRAWFORD

This Web site has a wealth of current information relating to this chapter. Crawford reports how the English Only movement has advanced in all 50 states of the United States. E-mail discussions with Ron Unz, a major supporter of the English Only movement, are posted in this Web site. Mr. Unz clearly reveals his intentions of eliminating bilingual education in this country. The academic research on bilingual education enables readers to gain a well-balanced view of the language debate.

Cummins, J. (2000). Biliteracy, empowerment, and transformative pedagogy. In J. V. Tinajero and R. A. DeVillar (Eds.), *The power of two languages 2000: Effective dual-language use across the curriculum* (pp. 9–19). New York: McGraw-Hill School Diversion.

Applied linguists agree that research and evaluation results on bilingual education demonstrate its efficacy. The principles advanced by advocates have been found true in the data. In addition, instructional time spent on a student's first language does not adversely affect the acquisition of English as a second language.

Cummins, J. (2000). *Language, power and pedagogy: Bilingual children in the crossfire.* Clevedon, England: Multilingual Matters.

Framed in a critical perspective that grounds teaching and learning in a broader sociocultural context, this overview of research and theory relates to the instruction and assessment of bilingual learners. In this text Cummins focuses on the patterns of human interactions within school and within the wider societal structures. He concludes the text with a critique of the most recent and significant studies on bilingualism.

www.iteachilearn.com/cummins/researchbildebate.html

Cummins, using the construct of doublethink, critiques three people who have publicly condemned bilingual education. Cummins demonstrates how Rosalie Pedalino Porter, Keith Baker, and Christine Rossell contradict themselves in their arguments against bilingual education. As Porter, Baker, and Rossell oppose bilingual education, they have also spoken in support of the effectiveness of bilingual programs. Cummins admonishes that they need to be more ethically responsible for the information that they are presenting, especially since the public perceives them to be credible. Their arguments have helped with the passage of Proposition 227 in California and the denial of equal access to education for bilingual children.

Dolson, D. (1985). The effects of Spanish home language use on the scholastic performance of Hispanic pupils. *Journal of Multilingual and Multicultural Development, 6*(2),135–155.

Dolson examined school performance among fifth and sixth graders in one Los Angeles school who came from families that spoke only Spanish at home when the children entered elementary school. Children from families that kept using Spanish at home significantly outperformed children from families that switched to English at home on tests of mathematics and had higher grade point averages. There was also a tendency for those who kept using Spanish at home to excel in English reading. A plausible explanation for this effect is that use of the first language at home encourages more and higher-quality parent–child interaction, which has positive consequences for cognitive and affective development.

Fishman, J. (1990). Empirical explorations of two popular assumptions: Inter-polity perspective on the relationships between linguistic heterogeneity, civil strife, and per capita gross national product. In G. Imhoff (Ed.), *Learning in two languages* (pp. 209–225). New Brunswick, NJ: Transaction Publishers.

Fishman analyzed the impact of 230 possible predictors of civil strife and economic well-being in 170 countries. His results suggest that multilingualism is not to blame for political or economic problems.

Greene, J. (1997). A meta-analysis of the Rossell and Baker review of bilingual education research. *Bilingual Research Journal, 21*(2,3), 103–122.

In a recent review of research on the effectiveness of bilingual education Greene concluded that the use of the native language in instructing English learners has beneficial effects and that "efforts to eliminate the use of the native language in instruction . . . harm children by denying them access to beneficial approaches" (p. 115).

Krashen, S. (1992). *Fundamentals of language acquisition.* Torrence, CA: Laredo Publishing Co.

Krashen provides an overview of his second language acquisition hypotheses and their application to bilingual education. The "affective filter" prevents comprehensible input from the reaching the "language acquisition devise, as posited by Chomsky (1965).

Krashen, S. (1996). *Under attack: The case against bilingual education.* Culver City, CA: Language Education Associates.

The published research on bilingual education is consistent: Children in properly organized bilingual education programs acquire English at least as well as, and usually better than, children in all-English programs.

Krashen, S. (1998). Heritage language development: Some practical arguments. In S. Krashen, L. Tse, & J. McQuillan (Eds.), *Heritage language development* (pp. 3–13). Culver City, CA: Language Education Associates.

The development of heritage language results in modest advantages in cognitive development (it makes you smarter; Krashen, 1999); it has practical, job-related advantages (we need bilingual spies, sales personnel, interpreters) and it leads to smoother relationships between generations (Wong Fillmore, 1991).

Krashen, S. (2000). The two goals of bilingual education: Development of academic English and heritage language development. In J. V. Tinajero and R. A. DeVillar (Eds.), *The power of two languages 2000: Effective dual-language use across the curriculum* (pp. 20–27). New York: McGraw-Hill School Division.

The first goal of bilingual education is the development of academic English and academic success; the second goal is the development of the primary or heritage language. A bilingual citizenry is good for national security and diplomacy and carries additional economic and social advantages. Krashen posits that the way to increase good bilingual education is with a flood of books in the languages of children. It would cost less than the many tests, curriculum packages, and computers, and the rewards would be greater.

Krashen, S. (2002). Is all-English best? A response to Bengston. *TESOL Matters,* December 2, 2003, p. 5.

How can the first language help the second in school? Properly organized bilingual education programs use the first language in ways that accelerate and facilitate second language development. First, when teachers provide students with solid subject matter in the first language, it gives the students knowledge. This knowledge helps make the English children hear and read much more comprehensible. A child who speaks little English who is knowledgeable about history, thanks to education in the first language, will understand more in a history class taught in English than a limited-English-proficient child without this knowledge. The child with a background in history will learn more history and will acquire more English because the English heard in class will be more comprehensible. Second, developing literacy in the first language is a shortcut to literacy in the second language. It is easier to learn to read in a language you understand; once you can read in one language, this knowledge transfers rapidly to any other language you learn to read. Once you can read, you can read. This phenomenon has been confirmed in many studies and is well known to many teachers.

Kerper Mora, J. (2003). http://coe.sdsu.edu/people/jmora.

Mora provides the arguments supporting monolingual education and those arguments supporting bilingual education. The road map to the bilingual education debate presents the cultural, linguistic, and academic program issues from both points of view. The conclusion is clear. If bilingual students are not supported in their primary/heritage language, there will be great consequences for the rest of society. Since the public education system has failed to meet their needs, bilingual children will not contribute to the society.

Oller, D. K., & Eilers, R. E. (2002). *Language and literacy in bilingual children.* Clevedon, England: Multilingual Matters.
The most recent study of the effectiveness of bilingual education was done by a research team headed by Oller and Eilers. At grade 5, students in a bilingual program (60 percent English, 40 percent Spanish) did as well as comparisons in an all-English program (with an optional 10 percent of the day in Spanish) on tests of English literacy and did far better on tests of Spanish.

Ramírez, J. D., Yuen, S. D., & Ramey, D. R. (1991). *Executive summary: Final report: Longitudinal study of structured English immersion strategy, early-exit and late-exit transitional bilingual education programs for language-minority children.* Contract No. 300-87-0156. Submitted to the U.S. Department of Education. San Mateo: Aguirre International.
This longitudinal evaluation compared three distinct programs: English-only immersion; early-exit or transitional bilingual education; and late-exit or enrichment/maintenance bilingual education. This study followed over 2,000 elementary children for four years. The comprehensive data collection documented an array of child, family, classroom, teacher, school, district, and community information. The study concluded that providing language minority students with substantial instruction in their primary language does not interfere with or delay their acquisition of English language skills but actually helps them to "catch up" to their English-speaking peers in English language arts, English reading, and math. In contrast, providing language minority students with almost exclusive instruction in English does not accelerate their acquisition of English language arts, reading or math. That is, they do not appear to be "catching up." The data suggest that by grade 6, students provided with English-only instruction may actually fall further behind their English-speaking peers. Data also document that learning a second language will take six or more years. Retrieved from www.ncbe.gwu.edu/miscpubs/nabe/brj/v16/16_12_ramirez.htm.

Rand Reading Study Group (2002). *Reading for understanding: Toward an R&D program in reading comprehension.* Report prepared for the Office of Educational Research and Improvement. Stanley, N. (August 2002). Teaching non-native speakers to read. *Language Magazine,* p. 36.
According to a Rand Corporation report over 90 percent of Mexican Americans born in the United States say they are proficient in English, and among those born in Mexico who are permanent residents of the United States, over 75 percent said they spoke some English and nearly half said they spoke English well. The Rand researchers concluded that "the transition to English begins almost immediately and proceeds very rapidly." (See Tse, 2001, for additional evidence showing that immigrants and their families are acquiring English.) www.rand.org/publications/MR/MR1465/MR1465.pdf,

www.census.gov/population/socdemo/language/table5.txt, and www.census.gov/population/socdemo/language/table2.txt.

Skutnabb-Kangas, T. (1988). Resource power and autonomy through discourse in conflict—a Finnish migrant school strike in Sweden. In T. Skutnabb-Kangas & J. Cummins. (Eds.), *Minority education: From shame to struggle* (pp. 251–277). Clevedon, England: Multilingual Matters.
This book contains a collection of articles that reveals the impact of the societal power structure on minority language students throughout the world. Collectively, the articles demonstrate that the use of minority language for instruction lessens the ambivalence and hostility of the language minority students toward the dominant culture and languages, and the use of the minority language increases academic performance and feelings of self-worth. The history of struggle of the Finnish students in the context of Sweden is highlighted in several of the articles. One example describes a school strike by Finnish parents who withdrew their children from a Swedish school when they learned that instruction time in Finnish was to be cut. It is hypothesized that the resulting renewed sense of efficacy among the Finnish children led to higher levels of academic achievement.

Skutnabb-Kangas, T. (2000). *Linguistic genocide in education—Of worldwide diversity and human rights?* Mahwah, NJ: Lawrence Erlbaum Associates.
Thirty years of passion and dedication to linguistic human rights and scholarly contributions are shared in this 785-page synthesis of the author's life's work. Language rights are the glue that holds together her vast global perspectives regarding marginalized communities.

> Declaration of Children's Linguistic Human Rights
> Every child should have the right to identify with her original mother tongue and have her identification accepted and respected by others. Every child should have the right to learn the mother tongue fully. Every child should have the right to choose when she wants to use the mother tongue in all official situations.

Thomas, W. P., & Collier, V. P. (2002). A national study of school effectiveness for language minority students' long-term academic achievement. George Mason University, Fairfax, VA: Center for Research on Education, Diversity and Excellence.
English-language learners do better academically over the long term if they participate in special programs to learn English at the start of their school careers rather than attend only mainstream classes. Students who take bilingual education classes do much better on standardized tests after entering mainstream classes than students who take English-only classes. The study reports on student records from 1982 to 2000 provided by five school districts, including the 208,000-student Houston district, and is part of an ongoing, federally fi-

nanced study of programs for English-language learners in 16 school districts. www.crede.ucsc.edu/research/llaa/1.1_final.html.

Thomas, W. P., & Collier, V. P. (Winter/Spring, 2003). Reforming education policies for English learners: Research evidence from U.S. schools. *The Mutilingual Educator, 4* (1), 16–19.
A summary of their longitudinal research findings. It is particularly accessible information, as the data are all summarized and listed in bulleted items; for example:

- English Learners submersed in the English mainstream because their parents refused all bilingual and ESL services show large decreases in reading and math achievement by Grade 5, when compared to students who received bilingual/ESL services.

- The strongest predictor of L2 student achievement is amount of formal L1 schooling. The more L1 grade-level schooling, the higher L2 achievement.

Tse, L. (1997, December 17). A bilingual helping hand education: Many children get no help learning English outside school. *Los Angeles Times,* 7.
One can also argue that encouraging the use and development of heritage languages is in the national interest: Tse (2001) points out that "learning English while maintaining the heritage language is perhaps the easiest and most efficient way to achieve bilingualism, and being bilingual carries advantages in many domains" (p. 48). For the individual, bilingualism improves school performance, provides access to wider sources of information, and has career advantages. Bilingual citizens contribute to society economically, through improved trade and improved national security (Krashen, Tse, & McQuillan 1998; Tse, 2001).

WestEd Study (in progress). (2003). Effects of the Implementation of Proposition 227 on the Education of English Learners, K–12: Year 2 Report.
This is a legislatively mandated study to monitor and record the effects of California's 1998 move away from traditional bilingual education to immersion. Robert Linquanti is the lead investigator. The study compares the achievement of children in schools that maintained bilingual education through special waivers with the achievement of children in schools that dropped bilingual education; the increases in the reading scores of the two groups of students in grades 2 to 5 were identical. Some areas of concern for researchers remain; for example, in 2001 more children were tested than in 1998. In addition, this study demonstrates that even some "English-only" programs use considerable amounts of the child's first language. The data so far demonstrate that there is no substantial increase in English competence in California since 1998. The gap between English speakers and English learners has widened since the passage of Prop 227 in 1998. Currently, 4 percent of English learners in high school

made it to the 50th percentile on the statewide test—a score that is down from other years. Scores from other grades are either stagnant or down and continue to get worse as the students get older. www.wested.org/cs/wew/view/rs/661.

Crawford, J. (November, 1998). *Ten common fallacies about bilingual education.* Retrieved February 26, 2003, from www.cal.org/ericcll/digest/crawford01.html.

Cummins, J. (2001). *Negotiating identities: Education for empowerment in a diverse society.* Sacramento, CA: California Association of Bilingual Education.

Mora, J., Wink, J., & Wink, D. (Fall, 2001). Dueling models of dual language instruction: A critical review of the literature and program implementation guide. *Bilingual Research Journal, 25*(4), 435–460.

Crawford, J. (1997). *Ten common fallacies about bilingual education.* Retrieved February 26, 2003, from www.cal.org/ericc11/digest/crawford01.html. Researchers have made considerable advances in the fields of psycholinguistics, second language acquisition, bilingual pedagogy, and multicultural education. Today, we know a great deal more about the challenges faced by English language learners and about promising strategies for overcoming them. One such strategy, bilingual education, has been the subject of increasing controversy. Although a growing body of research points to the potential benefits, there are a number of commonly held beliefs about bilingual education that run counter to research findings. Based on current research, this digest clarifies some of the myths and misconceptions surrounding language use and bilingual education in the United States.

Fallacy 1: English is losing ground to other languages in the United States. More world languages are spoken in the United States today than ever before. However, this is a quantitative, not a qualitative change, from earlier periods. Concentrations of non-English-language speakers were common in the nineteenth century, as reflected by laws authorizing native language instruction in a dozen states and territories. In big cities as well as rural areas, children attended bilingual and non-English schools, learning in languages as diverse as French, Norwegian, Czech, and Cherokee. In 1900, there were at least 600,000 elementary school children receiving part or all of their instruction in German (Kloss, 1998). Yet English survived without any help from government, such as official-language legislation.

Fallacy 2: Newcomers to the United States are learning English more slowly now than in previous generations. To the contrary, today's immigrants appear to be acquiring English more rapidly than ever before. Whereas the number of minority-language speakers is projected to grow well into the next century, the number of bilinguals fluent in both English and another language is growing even faster. Between 1980 and 1990, the number of immigrants who spoke non-English languages at home increased by 59 percent, whereas the portion of this population that spoke English very well rose by 93 percent (Waggoner, 1995). In 1990, only 3 percent of U.S. residents reported speaking English less than *well* or *very well.* Only eight-tenths of 1 percent spoke no English at all. About three in four Hispanic immigrants, after 15 years in this country, speak English on a daily basis, whereas 70 percent of their children become dominant or monolingual in English (Veltman, 1988).

Fallacy 3: The best way to learn a language is through "total immersion." There is no credible evidence to support the "time-on-task" theory of language learning, the claim that the more children are exposed to English, the more English they will learn. Research shows that what counts is not just the quantity but also the quality of exposure. Second-language input must be *comprehensible* to promote second-language acquisition (Krashen, 1996). If students are left to sink or swim in mainstream classrooms, with little or no help in understanding their lessons, they won't learn much English. If native-language instruction is used to make lessons meaningful, they will learn more English and more subject matter, too.

Fallacy 4: Children learning English are retained too long in bilingual classrooms, at the expense of English acquisition.   Time spent learning in well-designed bilingual programs is learning time well spent. Knowledge and skills acquired in the native language—literacy in particular—are "transferable" to the second language. They do not need to be relearned in English (Cummins, 1992; Krashen, 1996). Thus, there is no reason to rush English-language-learner (ELL) students into the mainstream before they are ready.

Research over the past two decades has determined that, despite appearances, it takes children a long time to attain full proficiency in a second language. Often they are quick to learn the conversational English used on the playground, but normally they need several years to acquire the cognitively demanding, decontextualized language used for academic pursuits (Collier & Thomas, 1989).

Bilingual education programs that emphasize a gradual transition to English and offer native language instruction in declining amounts over time provide continuity in children's cognitive growth and lay a foundation for academic success in the second language. By contrast, English-only approaches and quick-exit bilingual programs can interrupt that growth at a crucial stage, with negative effects on achievement (Cummins, 1992).

Fallacy 5: School districts provide bilingual instruction in scores of native languages.   Where children speak a number of different languages, rarely are there sufficient numbers of each language group to make bilingual instruction practical for everyone. In any case, the shortage of qualified teachers usually makes it impossible. For example, in 1994 California enrolled recently arrived immigrants from 136 different countries, but bilingual teachers were certified in only 17 languages, 96 percent of them in Spanish (CDE, 1995).

Fallacy 6: Bilingual education means instruction mainly in students' native languages with little instruction in English.   Before 1994, the vast majority of U.S. bilingual education programs was designed to encourage an early exit to mainstream English language classrooms, whereas only a tiny fraction of programs was designed to maintain the native tongues of students.

Today, a majority of bilingual programs continue to deliver a substantial portion of the curriculum in English. According to one study, school districts reported that 28 percent of ELL elementary school students receive no native language instruction. Among those who do, about a third receive more than 75 percent of their instruction in English; a third receive from 40 to 75 percent in English; and one-third of these receive less than 40 percent in English. Secondary school students are less likely to be instructed in their native language than elementary school students (Hopstock et al., 1993).

Fallacy 7: Bilingual education is far more costly than English language instruction.   All programs serving ELL students—regardless of the language of instruction—require additional staff training, instructional materials, and administration. So they all cost a little more than regular programs for native English speakers. But in most cases the differential is modest. A study commissioned by the California legislature examined a variety of well-implemented program models and found no budgetary advantage for English-only approaches. The incremental cost was about the same each year ($175–$214) for bilingual and English immersion programs, as compared with $1,198 for English as a second language (ESL) "pullout" programs. The reason was simple: The pullout approach requires supplemental teachers, whereas in-class approaches do not (Chambers & Parrish, 1992). Nevertheless, ESL pullout remains the method of choice for many school districts, especially where ELL students are diverse, bilingual teachers are in short supply, or expertise is lacking in bilingual methodologies.

Fallacy 8: Disproportionate dropout rates for Hispanic students demonstrate the failure of bilingual education.   Hispanic dropout rates remain unacceptably high. Research has identified multiple factors associated with this problem, including recent arrival in the United States, family poverty, limited English proficiency, low academic achievement, and being retained in grade

(Lockwood, 1996). No credible studies, however, have identified bilingual education among the risk factors, because bilingual programs touch only a small minority of Hispanic children.

Fallacy 9: Research is inconclusive on the benefits of bilingual education.
Some critics argue that the great majority of bilingual program evaluations are so egregiously flawed that their findings are useless. After reviewing 300 such studies, Rossell and Baker (1996) judged only 72 to be methodologically acceptable. Of these, they determined that a mere 22 percent supported the superiority of transitional programs over English-only instruction in reading, 9 percent in math, and 7 percent in language. Moreover, they concluded that transitional bilingual education (TBE) is never better than structured immersion in English. In other words, they could find little evidence that bilingual education works.

Close analysis of Rossell and Baker's claims reveals some serious flaws of their own. Krashen (1996) questions the rigor of several studies the reviewers included as methodologically acceptable—all unfavorable to bilingual education and many unpublished in the professional literature. Moreover, Rossell and Baker relied heavily on program evaluations from the 1970s, when bilingual pedagogies were considerably less well developed. Compounding these weaknesses is their narrative review technique, which simply counts the votes for or against a program alternative—a method that leaves considerable room for subjectivity and reviewer bias (Dunkel, 1990). Meta-analysis, a more objective method that weighs numerous variables in each study under review, has yielded more positive findings about bilingual education (Greene, 1998; Willig, 1985).

Most important, Krashen (1996) shows that Rossell and Baker are content to compare programs by the labels they have been given, with little consideration of the actual pedagogies being used. They treat as equivalent all approaches called TBE, even though few program details are available in many of the studies under review. Researchers who take the time to visit real classrooms understand how dangerous such assumptions can be. According to Hopstock et al. (1993), bilingual education programs sometimes provide more instruction in English than ESL programs. Moreover, from a qualitative perspective, programs vary considerably in how (one or both) languages are integrated into the curriculum and into the social context of the school. Finally, simplistic labels are misleading because bilingual and English immersion techniques are not mutually exclusive; several studies have shown that successful programs make extensive use of both (see, e.g., Ramírez et al., 1991).

Even when program descriptions are available, Rossell and Baker sometimes ignore them. For example, they cite a bilingual immersion program in El Paso as a superior English-only (submersion) approach, although it includes 90 minutes of Spanish instruction each day in addition to sheltered English.

The researchers also include in their review several studies of French immersion in Canada, which they equate with all-English, structured immersion programs in the United States. As the Canadian program designers have repeatedly stressed, these models are bilingual in both methods and goals, and they serve students with needs that are quite distinct from those of English learners in this country.

Fallacy 10: Language-minority parents do not support bilingual education because they feel it is more important for their children to learn English than to maintain the native language.   Naturally, when pollsters place these

FIGURE 6.4   Dual Language Models of Education

Program	Goals	Students
Bilingual (dual, two-way) immersion	1. English and another language (bilingualism/biliteracy) 2. High academic achievement 3. Positive cross-cultural relations	Language majority and minority populations
French Canadian immersion	1. English and another language (bilingualism/biliteracy) 2. High academic achievement	Language majority population
Maintenance/ enrichment bilingual education	1. English and a second language (bilingualism/biliteracy) 2. High academic achievement 3. Positive cross-cultural relations	Language majority and minority populations
Content-based foreign language instruction	1. Full oral and academic proficiency in a second/foreign language 2. High academic achievement	Language majority population
Transitional bilingual education	English only	Language minority population
Structured and/or sheltered english immersion	English	Language minority population

goals in opposition, immigrant parents will opt for English by wide margins. Who knows better the need to learn English than those who struggle with language barriers on a daily basis? But the premise of such surveys is false. Truly bilingual programs seek to cultivate proficiency in both tongues, and research has shown that students' native language can be maintained and developed at no cost to English. When polled on the principles underlying bilingual education—for example, that developing literacy in the first language facilitates literacy development in English or that bilingualism offers cognitive and career-related advantages—a majority of parents are strongly in favor of such approaches (Krashen, 1996).

FIGURE 6.4   Continued

Teacher Preparation	Role of L1/L2	Program Duration
Credential	L2 taught using second language methodology L1 and L2 used as a medium of instruction	K–6
Credential	L2 used as a medium of instruction in early grades L1 and L2 used as a medium of instruction in later grades	K–6
Credential	L2 taught using second language methodology in early grades L1 and L2 used as a medium of instruction	K–6
Credentialed foreign language teacher specialized in L2 as an academic subject	L2 used as a medium of instruction	6–12 and higher education toward international baccalaureate
Credential and/or support from an aide	L2 taught using second language methodology L1 used as a medium of instruction but phased out as L1 proficiency increases L2 becomes the exclusive medium of instruction	K–3 Usually 3–4 years in "early exit" programs
English dominant or English monolingual	L2 taught using second language methodology L2 used as the exclusive medium of instruction	9 months

FIGURE 6.5   Enrichment versus Compensatory Models of Language Education

Enrichment Model: French Canadian Immersion	Compensatory Model: Structured English Immersion (SEI)
Goals and Structure	
Is considered a form of bilingual education	Is considered a form of English-only education
Program objective is full bilingualism and biliteracy based on an additive model of bilingualism.	Program objective is proficiency in English based on a subtractive model. L1 literacy is not developed.
L1 and L2 are equally prestigious and recognized as valuable by the community as a resource.	L1 is a minority language. L2 is the majority language. L1 is denigrated and relegated to inferior status. The message is conveyed that only English is valid or important.
Minimum of four to six years to acquire "receptive" skills of listening and reading; higher levels of oral and literacy skills acquired gradually and reinforced through cross-linguistic instruction.	Students expected to gain proficiency enough to enter mainstream classes in one year.
Role of L1 and L2	
Uses L2 as the medium of instruction. Focuses on learning the target language through content teaching rather than on teaching the language.	Uses L2 as the medium of instruction. Focus depends on L2 proficiency, with L2 teaching the focus at the beginning levels and shifts to learning the target language through content teaching as students acquire L2 oral language proficiency.
The curriculum is designed to have coherence, balance, breadth, relevance, progression, and continuity. Students at all points receive a curriculum parallel to nonimmersion students. Initial focus is on understanding L2 and later on speaking L2 in a natural and gradual progression.	One year of immersion is seen as "normal." Students may be reenrolled for longer with parental consent. Students transfer into mainstream classes that may or may not be connected in terms of curriculum content. Students must be provided "appropriate services to overcome language barriers" until they attain academic achievement equivalent to average native English speakers.
Initial literacy developed in the second language. L1 language arts instruction often delayed but phased in over time until biliteracy is achieved.	Initial literacy developed in the second language. L1 literacy not developed as a part of the program.

FIGURE 6.5 Continued

Enrichment Model: **French Canadian Immersion**	**Compensatory Model:** **Structured English Immersion (SEI)**
Student Population and Grouping	
Approximately 6% of total school population enrolled in immersion.	Approximately 25% of total school population enrolled, unless students are granted "parental exception waivers."
Parents of students place them voluntarily. Programs are promoted and supported by parents. Parents are generally middle class or upper class.	Sheltered immersion is the "default mode" for limited-English-proficient students. Under special circumstances, parents may opt out of the program; otherwise, it is mandatory. Parents are generally lower socioeconomic class and are non-to-beginning English speakers themselves.
Students are all at the same academic level—usually they progress as a cohort group beginning with no L2 proficiency.	Students grouped by English proficiency levels, but multigrade level grouping permitted.
Presumes a homogeneous language classroom—most students are native speakers of the same L1.	Encourages heterogeneous classrooms—students are expected to speak a variety of native languages.
Teacher Qualifications	
Teachers are highly skilled bilinguals with a strong commitment to bilingualism and multiculturalism as educational aims. Teachers serve as linguistic role models. Teachers use L2 methodology systematically. Teachers are trained to provide comprehensible input through the use of their L1 skills and appropriate methodology.	Teachers may be monolingual English speakers with or without specialized training in L2 methodology (CLAD credential). Teachers may or may not value bilingualism. Bilingual teachers assigned to SEI are restricted by law in the use of L1 as a medium of instruction. Only noninstructional uses of L1 are permitted.
Historical and Expected Student Outcomes	
Students' expressive skills in L2 often lag behind the native-speaker norm, although listening and reading skills may be nearly equivalent.	There is no research evidence to demonstrate what levels of competency in the four language skills are attainable in a one-year program.
Predicted rates of L2 acquisition are based on the distinction between basic oral and conversational abilities, ranging from three to five years and cognitive academic proficiency, to meet the demands of higher-level thinking and literacy tasks, ranging from five to seven years average.	Assumptions are made that classroom language will be comprehensible when students acquire "a good working knowledge of English" so that students can transfer into a "mainstream English" program and out of remedial classes.

REFERENCES

California Department of Education (CDE). (1995). *Educational demographics unit. Language census report for California public schools.* Sacramento: Author.

Chambers, J., & Parrish, T. (1992). *Meeting the challenge of diversity: An evaluation of programs for pupils with limited proficiency in English. Vol. IV, cost of programs and services for LEP students.* Berkeley, CA: BW Associates.

Collier, V. P., & Thomas, W. P. (1989). How quickly can immigrants become proficient in school English? *Journal of Educational Issues of Language Minority Students, 5,* 26–39.

Cummins, J. (1992). Bilingual education and English immersion: The Ramírez Report in theoretical perspective. *Bilingual Research Journal, 16,* 91–104.

Dunkel, P. (1990). Implications of the CAI effectiveness research for limited-English-proficient learners. *Computers in the Schools, 7,* 31–52.

Greene, J. P. (1998). *A meta-analysis of the effectiveness of bilingual education.* Claremont, CA: Tomas Rivera Policy Institute.

Hopstock, P., Bucaro, B., Fleischman, H. L., Zehler, A. M., & Eu, H. (1993). *Descriptive study of services to limited English proficient students.* Arlington, VA: Development Associates.

Kloss, H. (1998). *The American Bilingual Tradition.* Washington, DC and McHenry, IL: ERIC Clearinghouse on Languages and Linguistics and Delta Systems Inc.

Krashen, S. D. (1996). *Under attack: The case against bilingual education.* Culver City, CA: Language Education Associates.

Lockwood, A. T. (1996). Caring, community, and personalization: Strategies to combat the Hispanic dropout problem. *Advances in Hispanic Education, 1.* Washington, DC: U.S. Department of Education.

Ramírez, J. D., Yuen, S. D., & Ramey, D. R. (1991). *Final report: Longitudinal study of structured immersion strategy, early-exit, and late-exit transitional bilingual education programs for language-minority children. Executive summary.* San Mateo, CA: Aguirre International.

Rossell, C., & Baker, K. (1996). The educational effectiveness of bilingual education. *Research in the Teaching of English, 30,* 7–74.

Veltman, C. (1988). *The future of the Spanish language in the United States.* Washington, DC: Hispanic Policy Development Project.

Waggoner, D. (1995, November). Are current home speakers of non-English languages learning English? *Numbers and Needs, 5.*

Willig, Ann C. 1985. A meta-analysis of selected studies on the effectiveness of bilingual education. *Review of Educational Research, 55,* 269–317.

7 Teaching Passionately—Spiritually

Authentic spiritual practice is not a naive experience. It does not lead us away from reality but allows us to accept the real more fully.

bell hooks, 1994, pp. 119–120

Spiritual exploration is fluid, dynamic, and constantly evolving, much like teaching and learning. Spiritual exploration requires receptivity, much like teaching and learning. Spiritual exploration follows a path laden with surprise and mystery. We never know what joys, sorrows, and unexpected events we will encounter. Exactly like teaching and learning.

This chapter explores the integration of heart and soul within the context of an academic curriculum. One does not mean the other must be sacrificed. We propose that more learning takes place when teachers' and students' spirits, their internal essence and innate goodness, are intimately involved in the classroom and the subject being studied. It is the awareness of a broader connection with a compassionate intelligence connecting us all that opens the door to learning.

Passionate spiritual pedagogy recognizes the sacredness of each and every child. Passionate spiritual pedagogy fosters an interactive relationship seeking truth between the student and what is being learned. Passionate spiritual pedagogy helps prepare students for the real world and the rest of their lives.

We assume that the readers of these pages will reflect diverse perspectives, paradigms, and prior experiences. For example, one elementary teacher, now working on her doctorate, wrote when we asked her how her spirituality affects her teaching, "I am not conscious of any spiritual traditions anywhere in my life, inside or outside of the classroom." When we asked a university professor the same question, the response was the opposite. "I cannot remember a time that I have not said a prayer before teaching a class. I have so much respect for the wide variety of experiences students bring to class that without calling on a source greater than myself, I simply am not enough. I pray students learn what they need to know." Another university professor surprised Joan one fall semester on the first day of class when he passed her on the sidewalk and quietly said, "Remember, when you look into the faces of the students tonight, you are looking into the face of God."

We recognize that the diversity of readers requires a diversity of truths. The English word "truth" comes from a Germanic root that also gives rise to our word "troth," as in the ancient vow "I pledge thee my troth." With this word, one person enters a covenant with another, a pledge to engage in a mutually accountable and transformative relationship, a relationship forged of trust and faith in the face of unknowable risks. To know something or someone in truth is to enter troth with the known. To know in truth is to become betrothed, to engage the known with one's whole self, an engagement one enters with attentiveness, care, and goodwill. (Palmer, 1993, p. 31)

A study (Astin & Astin, 1999) to explore the place of meaning and spirituality among college and university faculty found that many academics perceived "spirituality" to be a loaded word, as it carried a connotation of narrowly defined notions of sectarian religious indoctrination. This study also found a willingness of faculty to speak openly in the broader context of meaning, purpose, and spirituality. We, as did the principal investigators of this study, encourage a deeper meaning of spirituality in education, which includes finding our purpose in life and linking it to the whole of our life, be it professional or personal. The notion of the sense of self is grounded in spirituality.

The most beautiful and profound emotion we can experience is the sensation of the mystical. It is the sower of all true science.

ALBERT EINSTEIN

Bolman and Deal (2001) explore the place of soul in leadership and conclude that leaders with soul bring spirit to organizations. Building on this idea, we say that teachers with soul bring spirit to the classroom. The spirit is centered in life, livelihood, learning, and love. We welcome its place in the classroom.

Thus, spirituality in education is founded on an interactive and mutual relationship in search of the truth. Traditionally, the teacher holds the sanctioned truth in the classroom. Spiritual pedagogy recognizes there is never any one truth but a full spectrum of truths, unique to each individual.

For the diversity of truths to be found, the teacher remains open to unexpected discoveries in the learning. Therein lies the challenge for many teachers of a true betrothal with truth. It requires that teachers reflect on their own assumptions about control in the classroom. Instead of seeking restrictive control, the teacher leads students to seek guidance from within and gain an awareness of their innate power, inspiration, and wisdom.

This chapter will be divided into the same subheadings as the other chapters; however, as the contents fall outside the norm, we, too, have had to adapt the chapter format. The Voice of Schools section will focus on *what* spirituality in education is. The Voice of Life section will focus on the *why,* or the rationale. The Praxis section will focus on the *how.*

The Voice of Schools

Spirituality in education carries unique and subtle connotations for each person. One person's definition of spirituality may be in complete opposition to another's. It is an emotionally laden word, no doubt. To facilitate full communication while reading, this chapter is founded on the understanding of spirituality as *the awareness we each carry within us of an internal essence, a soul.* It is specific to no single belief system or organized religion but is rather an inherent sense of goodness and connection accessible to all.

Meeks and Austin (2003) see cultural and spiritual beliefs in education as providing a fundamental lens through which a person "sees" and knows the world. For example, each of us enters a classroom with a unique cultural lens that refracts our ways of knowing, the texts we read, and the people we encounter. The cultural lens includes our spiritual perspective, age, gender, race, social class, education, political beliefs, marital status, sexual experience and orientation, work experience, and home language. These multiple lenses are the sum total of our vision.

We are spiritual beings: body, mind, and soul. Each of us has unique ways of learning and of contributing to the greater good. The arts provide for some a golden slice of time and space to find their center, their humanity. The aesthetics of art, music, literature, and dance have the potential to elicit the soul of each of us. For some children, it may be the only opportunity they get for this centering type of educational and spiritual experience.

A curriculum and classroom infused with spirit and soul is a dynamic place constantly in change. Some days the air cracks and pops with the energy of ideas being discussed, whereas on other days the air is tranquil and still as students quietly look within. Vitality bursts out of this classroom no matter the mood. *Magical Encounters* happen when teaching and learning with spirit as noted by Ada (2003). We suggest that the magical encounters she creates are a result of her spiritual beliefs, which enter every classroom with her. The Ford Foundation found that peoples' spiritual practices significantly influence and encourage their commitment toward social change (Dart, 2002).

In this chapter we focus on spirituality in education. The emerging body of literature on this topic uses three different terms: *spirituality in education, spiritual education,* and *soulful education.* For our purposes, we use the terms interchangeably.

The Soul

The soul cannot be limited by religious beliefs. We refer to the sense of connection, compassion, and guidance necessary to live a contented, fulfilled life. We shared our understanding of the soul earlier as "an internal essence within us all." The soul has also been described as "a deep and vital energy that gives meaning and direction to our lives" (Miller, 2000, p. 9) and a "call for attention in schools to the inner life; to the depth dimension of human experience; to students' longings for something more than an ordinary, material, and fragmented existence" (Kessler, 2000, p. x).

Some find soul and spirit to be very much the same. Bolman and Deal (2001) see differences. They suggest that the soul grows from personal experience; it is unique in each of us. On the other hand, spirit is universal and transcendent. The soul and spirit join together to become more; it is the notion that the whole is greater than the sum of its parts.

We suggest schools will be immeasurably enhanced and peoples' lives expanded when honoring spirituality in education becomes a part of students' and teachers' experiences together. When we teach a *soulful education* (Miller, 2000), it is not the instillation of specific dogmas and teachings, but rather honoring the sacredness of each and every student. "Soul education requires imagination, not force" (p. viii).

Church and State

Often the question is how one balances the spiritual nurturance of students with our deeply held respect for the separation of church and state. Spirituality in the classroom does not refer to religious instruction as it has been commonly misunderstood, but rather a recognition and exploration of real-world issues through a spiritual lens. It is a spiritual lens that includes the ideas of compassion, honesty, and connection. The First Amendment of the Constitution of the United States safeguards students in public schools from the enforced imposition of specific religious beliefs. In our anxiousness not to infringe on this Amendment, spiritual issues are kept completely out of the classroom. "Young people have experiences that nourish their spiritual development and *yet are not directly related to worldview or religious dogma. We can* honor the First Amendment without abandoning our children's spiritual development" (Kessler, 2000, p. xiv).

Traditionally, the focus of schools in the United States has been on the promotion and interpretation of quantifiable academic achievements and results. Schools fail to recognize that students come to class crammed with unmanifested talent (Miller, 2000). However, we come from a long tradition in schools that often presumes students are empty vessels, simply needing to be filled by prescribed and sanctioned knowledge. This assumption does not often take into account the necessity of students' imagination and soul connection in learning.

It is a waste of precious energy and time to try and teach somebody something they are simply not interested in, *unless their soul becomes interested and curious.* It is excruciating to stand in front of an unengaged class, a frustrated class, or worse yet, a *bored* class. Langer (1997) states that rote memorization of facts leaves students at a loss as to how to apply the information in any other form than that presented. What is conspicuously absent in this curriculum is the key to unlocking the glorious mysteries of education.

When the hearts and souls of teachers and students in a classroom are interwoven with the curriculum, magic happens. The information takes life and students' learning takes flight. A curriculum that doesn't include and encourage the spiritual dimension of what is being taught leaves the student much like the untethered glider—ready to go, but with no other plane to lead its flight. A teacher and curriculum that include a spiritual lens provide the necessary lift to send the students soaring—and then let go of the rope allowing them to glide on their own.

The Voice of Life

> The separation between the spiritual and secular is false. To deny spirit is to deny an essential element of our being and thus diminish ourselves and our approach to education. By bringing soul more explicitly into the educational process we can have an education for the whole person rather than a fragmented self. (Miller, 2000, p. 9)

Life teaches us through experience that learning is unpredictable, rich, and heartfelt. The educational experience is a journey, with many unexpected and unforeseen twists and turns along the way. No teacher can, or should, assume to know exactly where the quest for knowledge will lead. It is the very capricious nature of learning that, when embraced, enriches the journey. Little room exists for the live quality of energy and ideas in a prescribed curriculum and a mandated, tightly scheduled day that uses external outcomes for motivation. The more a curriculum stresses tests and external rewards, the less students learn (Kohn, 2000).

Learning dwells in the sphere of the soul. The mind is not enough. Life recognizes that a "soulful education can help bring a *balance* to our education between such factors as inner and outer, the rational and intuitive, the qualitative and the quantitative" (Miller, 2000, p. 9). Memorization of facts rarely equates with genuine learning. For true learning, the creation of new ideas, the ability to reflect critically and draw independent conclusions, comes from within.

The brain does not account for what we are passionate about and what leaves us cold. Without genuine interest, inquiry, and *meaning*, the brain may memorize unrelated facts, but learning remains superficial and transitory. Traditionally the workings of the mind have been the primary focus in education. Life experiences teach us, however, that there is more at work here than solely the brain. Teaching and learning that ignore the spiritual component lack depth and dimension, as seen in Figure 7.1.

The Acorn Theory

Passionate spiritual pedagogy recognizes the sacredness of the students and opens the door to the possibility of new perspectives. Hillman (1996) provides an opportunity with his reflections on the acorn theory, which suggests each of us comes to life with a kernel of personal truth around which our life's path is destined to unfold. Each of us is born with inherent passions, strengths, and interests. Our call in life is to follow the path where these passions lead us, for that is their purpose. This is often not a conscious journey, but rather an organic path. We often do not know the destination or even the

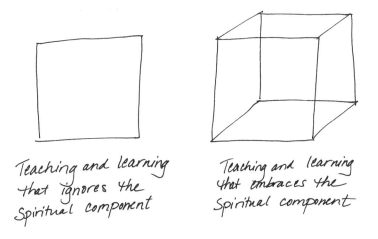

Teaching and learning
that ignores the
Spiritual component

Teaching and learning
that embraces the
Spiritual component

FIGURE 7.1   Teaching and Learning with Spirit

reason behind our personal truths. It is by trusting the inner voice that we honor the uniqueness of the acorn within.

The ramifications of the acorn theory in education are many. Traditionally, schools place value only on certain knowledge and skills and dismiss anything that does not fall within this narrow range. Because of this, many of the passions and strengths students bring to life and school are labeled invalid and squashed to the detriment of the students' overall growth. The acorn theory offers the idea that through the acknowledgment and fostering of students' passions, students are lead *toward* success. Inborn passions are life's road signs.

As teachers, we respect the rich diversity of the distinct life paths our students embody. To honor the sacredness of each student these unique paths are acknowledged and accepted within the overall context of the curriculum. We are brave enough to risk allowing students to view information and events through the glasses of their personal truth. Knowledge is never finite. Students bring an unlimited richness of experiences. Accepting the sacredness of students' intrinsic life paths, experiences, and perspectives encourages students to own their own knowledge.

A focus on the sacredness of each person fosters an awareness of individual hidden grace. "Looking for the acorn affects how we see each other and ourselves letting us find some beauty in what we see and so love what we see" (Hillman, 1996, p. 37). Frequently, the students in whom this beauty is most hidden have the most to teach us, as in the following experience.

"My first year of teaching I had one little boy who, for whatever reason, I just didn't like," the teacher confessed. "Now, looking back on it, he was just a squirmy, wiggly five-year-old acting his age. However, at the time, I just didn't like him."

In our experience it is the students who are hardest to love that need love the most. Nieto (1999) tells the story of a teacher, Mary, who believed in the absolute necessity of loving the students in her class. "Some, she confessed, were harder to love than others, but in all of her years of teaching, she had never failed to love any of her students" (p. 100).

Hidden Grace

By recognizing the unique acorn within every student, teachers gain new perspectives on negative behavior. The hidden grace within each connects us all within the classroom, as well as within life.

This hidden grace provides the deep sense of meaning that often defines the quality of a person's life. This sense of purpose often comes from a connection with a greater power and a focus on the broader perspective of life.

What would happen if a bit of grace manifested itself in schools? We believe that it would enrich us all and enhance the learning of all. We have entered many classrooms and campuses early in the day with only one thought in our mind or prayer in our hearts—that at the end of the day, we would leave with a bit of grace and goodwill left behind for others.

In the exhilarating but frequently exhaustive world of teaching, teachers' spiritual connection provides a well of strength to draw on as illustrated by these teachers' reflections. In the following three quotations, we hear the voices of bell hooks, Tove Skutnabb-Kangas, and Jane Goodall.

We begin with bell hooks (1999) as she describes her spirituality:

> I knew only that despite the troubles of my world, the suffering I witnessed around and within me, there was always a spiritual force that lifted me higher and gave me moments of transcendent bliss wherein I could surrender all thought of the world and know profound peace. . . . I was determined to live a life in the spirit. (p. 108)

Second, we hear some honest thoughts of Tove Skutnabb-Kangas, as she reflects: "I know every second that I am here to learn, and I have chosen myself before I entered this body, even if I do not remember it consciously, that I should have certain types of experience that allow me to learn and grow," and feels it is her duty to make the world a more equitable place by working tirelessly to prevent linguistic, cultural, and biodiversity genocide (in personal communication, September 25, 2002).

Third, it is the voice of Jane Goodall. "There are times before a lecture when I have been absolutely exhausted, or actually sick, and terrified that I am going to utterly fail the audience. And those lectures are often among the best. Because, I think, I have been able to tap into the spiritual power that is always there, providing strength and courage if only we reach out," she writes (1999, p. 267) regarding her travels around the world to bring awareness about the devastation taking place on our planet and to bring hope and positive action through her foundations. That strength is available to us all.

However, in order to have this strength in life and learning, we need to take care of ourselves. "Comfort, in my definition, means to strengthen," Jennifer Louden

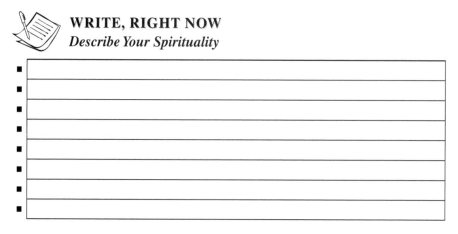

WRITE, RIGHT NOW
Describe Your Spirituality

FIGURE 7.2   Write, Right Now: Describe Your Spirituality

(2000, p. 41) wisely writes. In a profession that requires so much giving, a large part of nurturing the teacher's spirit is taking time for self-nurturance, which facilitates accessing the hidden grace within.

The inner meaning and strength described reflect the essential meaning of the acorn theory. These previously mentioned educators describe their deep sense of purpose and meaning intuitively felt and acted on. The acorn theory reminds us that each student comes to class with just such a purpose, often as yet not discovered. Passionate spiritual pedagogy respects these inherent kernels of hidden grace and encourages students to trust their inner guidance as they create their life's path. (See Figure 7.2.)

Praxis: Let the Magic Begin

If we are educating for wholeness, for citizenship, and for leadership in democracy, spiritual development belongs in schools.

RACHAEL KESSLER, 2000, p. 159

Spirituality in the classroom may appear as an amorphous idea, but in reality it can be made tangible. Spirituality in the curriculum focuses on connecting human spiritual responses to people and ideas. Inclusion of a spiritual perspective expands the potential for human and academic growth. Strength, wisdom, and resilience gained by the conscious exploration and development of connection and inner guidance will help students throughout life far more than the individual facts they learn.

A spiritual curriculum centers on the deeper questions and reflections students feel but are rarely in a comfortable position to voice, especially with peers and in the school setting. We ask you to imagine the possibilities if each student in class were provided a safe place to sit with a small group of peers and reflect on their lives, to share the questions that trouble or confuse or mystify them, to find support for their pain or joy, to discover the solace that comes in silence, and to be challenged to respect those who appear to be fundamentally different from them (Kessler, 2000). These are the life skills students need to survive and thrive throughout their lives.

In the following activities our purpose is to provide frameworks that can be adapted to help create those possibilities. Previously we said that methods are horizontal and theory is vertical. However, we now offer this perspective on methods that take students vertically. The subsequent pedagogical processes are designed to guide students to new depths of reflection and heights of action.

First, we offer seven main gateways to the soul in education: Deep Connection, Silence, Meaning and Purpose, Joy, Creativity, Transcendence, and Initiation (Kessler, 2000). In our academically focused world, these gateways traditionally garner little to no recognition. Posing questions based on these ideas regarding students' inner thoughts and feelings has a profound effect on curriculum. Examples of these questions include: "Please write about what you wonder about when you cannot sleep at night, when you're walking alone to the school bus, or when you're jogging on the track. What do you worry about? Or feel curious about? What are your questions about yourselves, about others, about life itself?" (Kessler, 2000, p. 11). Students' responses to such questions provide insight into their inner worlds. These insights focus and encourage reflection.

By structuring curriculum around these gateways, not only do students learn more, but they also develop crucial life skills in the process. Curriculum is elevated from knowledge based in facts to knowledge based in *meaning*.

Second, we offer guiding principles to foster personal happiness and success whose implementation enriches a classroom. Each day a different spiritual law, or principle, is addressed. These principles open students to their full potential by addressing the core experiences of living and learning on which the curriculum rests and work toward development of vital life skills. They need not take long, five minutes of discussion can be enough. The main idea for the day provides a framework within which the day's curriculum can be organized and understood or can stand on its own as a brief supplement. These laws are arranged for the seven-day week in the original text (Chopra, 1997). To make them applicable to the five-day school week, we have arranged the laws to meet this schedule, maintaining the essence of the lessons.

Monday is the day of Pure Potentiality. Students concentrate on the idea that everything is possible, no matter what. This principle highlights the reality of possibility and wisdom of looking within for guidance. To thine own heart be true. "Everything is inside ourselves; nothing in our nature can be created or destroyed by someone or something *out there*" (Chopra, 1997, p. 66).

Tuesday is the day of Giving. Today students are asked to concentrate on how it feels to give—a smile, a word of encouragement, help with schoolwork. Goodness and abundance are to be shared.

Wednesday is the day of Karma. Today students reflect on choices and actions. Ask students to think of one choice they made today. Then begin to explore the effects of that choice. "How did you feel about that? What do you think will happen?" The critical factor in making good choices is not only based on reason but also on how a choice feels. When you make a choice, you change the future. Our lives are directly determined by what we contribute and give to others.

Thursday is the day of Intention and Desire. Today we discuss with students, "What you wish plants a seed." Desire is what we want and intentions are the actions we take to get it. Human desire leads us down our life's true path. With conscious intention, we make choices and create situations to bring our desires into our lives. Intentions are not wishful thinking. Intentions are purposeful actions with full confidence in our purpose and ability to achieve our dreams.

Friday is the day of Detachment and Dharma. Detachment refers to passionate involvement and creativity, while surrendering control of the outcome. Dharma refers to an individual's innate duty and purpose. Both are necessary for happiness. Intense creative involvement fulfills us. In surrendering, we recognize that all outcomes depend on the universe. Today we tell students, "You have a life's purpose." A reason exists for every event, every action, and every thought. Our goal in life is to discover our purpose and build our life around its support.

Weaving these spiritual principles into the fabric of academia provides a curriculum designed to develop human wholeness. Many adults do not possess the knowledge and skills of giving, intention, and looking within for wisdom and guidance. Imagine if they did! Imagine the depression and suffering that would be alleviated. Let's teach these principles to students. Let's teach students to know there is a grand purpose to their life and to seek it. Let's teach them to examine facts through a whole spiritual lens. It is the ability to live life with compassion, wisdom, and a sense of purpose that will then enhance students' lives. (See Figure 7.3.)

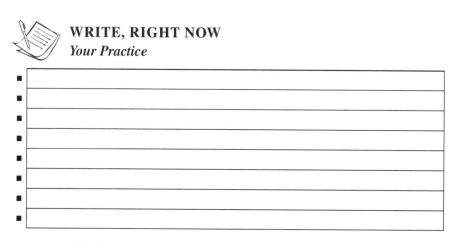

WRITE, RIGHT NOW
Your Practice

FIGURE 7.3   Write, Right Now: Your Practice

The Literacy Link

Everybody is talented, original, and has something important to say.
BRENDA EULAND, *1938*

Writing can be a spiritual experience. Writing connects the writer with his or her heart and dreams. Writing can make unbearable pain bearable. Through writing we relive exquisite joys that would otherwise fade away. Academia is so frequently focused on teaching the five-part essay and the mechanics of writing that the sheer magic and transcendence of writing are lost.

"The students hate writing," an English teacher complained one evening. "We have to teach there is only one correct way to write. The students have to follow a strict format and are allowed no creativity. Students never get to write for fun or learn why writing can be fun and meaningful. By the time I get them, their writing has been so controlled for so long, they despise putting pen to paper."

Students do need to learn what good writing is and how to write clear, concise, and well-organized pieces, but that need not be equated with dull, plodding, and forced mechanics. The heart of writing need not be sacrificed for the mechanics of it. Writing ideally communicates ideas, opinions, and stories. Let's teach writing in a manner that connects students with their own creativity. Let's teach the soul of writing as well as its form. (See Figure 7.4.)

First, we offer daily pages, which are, simply put, two pages of longhand, stream-of-consciousness writing done by the students every day (Cameron, 1992). No matter what. Even if it is two pages of "I don't know what to write today. I don't know what to write today. I don't know what to write today." Frequently, daily pages are full of the boring complaints and whining that crowd our heads. This is fine. Have students get it down on the paper, get it out of the way, so they can move on with learning. Frequently, though, in amongst the grime and sludge of complaining and boredom, glisten kernels of truths that would otherwise remain hidden from the writer. Suddenly, unsolvable problems have a solution, an artistic idea springs forth, the first steps of how to make a dream a reality shine forth. (See Figure 7.5.)

Daily pages bring to light inner thoughts, dreams, and ideas that would otherwise remain hidden. They connect students with the meaning and magic of writing—to

Creativity is an experience—to my eye, a spiritual experience. It does not matter which way you think of it: creativity leading to spirituality or spirituality leading to creativity. In fact, I do not make a distinction between the two.

Cameron, 1992, p. 2

FIGURE 7.4   A Spiritual Experience

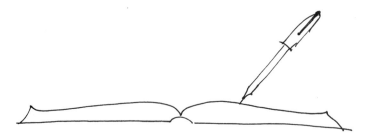

FIGURE 7.5 Pen and Notebook

uncover hidden understandings. Students write for the real purpose of writing—to express themselves. No grades, no "correct" or "incorrect," just writing from the heart. Students will discover these pages create a path for them to follow. Life becomes more manageable. The grammar and essay rules they must learn to present their thoughts coherently to others will take on a new meaning. Students realize it is the *ideas* that are important, and the grammar rules only work to support and clarify those.

"But, I don't have time," we hear. The time spent on daily pages makes the rest of the time students are with you that much more productive. Students become grounded and ready to learn.

Daily pages can be modeled for younger children and adapted to fit the level of students who are in the midst of developing literacy. Kindergarteners can "write" daily pages. This writing includes pictures and inventive spelling. It's the expression of thought that matters. To really see improvement, make a photocopy of the first day of every month in students' daily pages books and share them with the children and their parents at the end of the year. The teacher can write his or her daily pages across the chalkboard and read them aloud, pointing at each word as it is read. This not only models writing and critical thinking but develops literacy as well.

Try it. Commit one month to devoting time for students to write their daily pages in spiral-bound notebooks that are completely confidential. Nobody will ever see the contents. For this to work, the teacher commits to writing daily pages at the same time the students do. This is *not* time to prepare lessons or catch up on grading. At the end of the month ask students to write during their daily pages time what the consequences of those daily pages have been in the last four weeks. This they can share with the class and the teacher.

Second, we offer writing practice, which refers to timed writing exercises about specific topics. It involves picking a topic, *any* topic, and writing about it nonstop for the allotted amount of time. Writing practices, ". . . are the bottom line, the beginning of all writing, the foundation of learning to trust your mind. Trusting your own mind is essential for writing" (Goldberg, 1990, p. 1).

An underlying organization inevitably emerges at some point during the writing practice and differs from daily pages in that this free-flowing writing is centered on a specific topic. The topics are endless and can be designed to fit life topics or curriculum needs. Possible life topics: Write about your home. Write about a mountain. Write about the color pink. Possible curriculum topics: Write about invertebrates of the ocean. Write about Iraq. Write about nutrition.

Writing practice can take 10 minutes or two hours, and anywhere in between or beyond. It helps students get by the *great editor* we all carry around in our heads who criticizes everything we write. In an effort not to offend the editor, we play it safe. Usually the result is bland, boring, and safe writing. Who wants to read that? Who wants to write that? Let's guide students to connect with the raw power and energy that is writing.

As with daily pages, timed exercises can be customized to meet the needs of children of all ages. Younger children can draw their understandings for 10 minutes. Slightly older children can combine inventive spelling with drawing about the designated topic. The teacher can model writing practice in a spiral notebook or on the chalkboard and then read aloud to the children. The sky is the limit!

WHAT CAN BE LEARNED FROM THIS?

Teaching with spirit matters. Teaching and learning are intimately intertwined with matters of the heart and cannot be extricated from the spiritual dimension of the human experience. Our main goal as educators is to connect with students' spirits. Included in this charge is a challenge for us to encourage students to listen, to hear, and to respect the voice within. An unshakeable recognition of their inner spirit is a wondrous gift.

> To expect primary caretakers, for example, parents, to see through the child into the acorn, to know who is *in nuce,* and to tend to its concerns—is far too much. That is why teachers and mentors come into the world. He or she is another special person, often someone whom we fall in love with early, or who falls for us; we are two acorns on the same branch, echoing similar ideals. (Hillman, 2000, p. 163)

The spirit's call is frequently perceived as gut instincts. It is in strengthening students' spiritual connection with their inner strengths that true wisdom and resilience are born. Many students leave high school and college only to be disillusioned to discover that all of the information they've memorized that is supposed to prepare them adequately for life is often quite irrelevant to the real challenges of living. They feel cheated. It is the feeling of someone who sees the hefty, detailed front of an old-time western movie set, looking warm and inviting, only to discover when you enter, that it is a false front. It is empty behind the façade. The weakest wind can send it tumbling to the ground. (See Figure 7.6)

FIGURE 7.6   Old Western Movie Set

Sooner or later students will get their hearts broken by others and by the events of life. They often may be in the midst of these painful experiences now. Passionate spiritual pedagogy promotes the spiritual foundation and strength necessary to create a contented and fulfilled life.

8 Teaching Passionately— Politically

We cannot sit back and wait. It is not a cyclic thing, as in the past. We have to fight it right now. That is in the spirit of Dewey, which I am not quite hearing as strongly as I think I should.

LOUISE ROSENBLATT, age 96, AERA, 2001[1]

It turns out that we do not and cannot teach all we need to know in teacher education programs. Some things take time. For example, it takes time to rethink the assumption that education takes place on some purely apolitical pedagogical plateau.

In this chapter, we will explore the multifaceted relationships among pedagogical principles, practices, and politics. We come from a tradition of thought that assumed that pedagogy and politics were poles apart. However, our experiences teach us something very different. As we begin to think more critically about teaching and learning, we soon come to realize that politics is a part of education. How can it not be? Schools are filled with people, lots of people who bring a diversity of thought, perspectives, opinions, and experiences. Schools are social, schools are cultural, and schools are political environments that reflect the world around them. People and politics swirl through the same spiral of life and learning. Teaching is professional, public, personal, and political.

The Voice of Schools

In this section, we will focus on two educational paradigms, the official theory of learning and the classic theory of learning, as posited by Smith (1998). The purpose is to link pedagogical perspectives to politics and to policy. We will reach back to the voices of the antiquities to create a springboard to the future. This section will conclude with research that demonstrates why we tend to slip back into transmission, shedding light on the question: Why do we do what we do?

Pedagogical historical perspectives have profound political ramifications; indeed, even the various paradigms are grounded in the political. This was true in the past, is true today, and will continue to be true tomorrow. The only question is if we as educators will recognize and act on our political responsibilities in the same way we have with our pedagogical responsibilities. If we do not, our inaction is the greatest action of all. No one knows schools better than we do as educators—the moral mandate is ours. As the Chinese proverb states: We are blessed to be living in the most interesting of times.

Before reading Smith's dual models of education, please recall that at the turn of the 1900s, there were also two other models of education: scientific management and progressivism. These two schools of thought had very different perspectives on teaching and learning, and they competed for dominance in the schools.

The Official Theory of Learning

The official theory of learning has historical roots in behaviorism and positivism with the emphasis on teacher-centered and assessment-driven approaches, including memorization of facts and development of skills. The teacher is the manager and dispenser of knowledge. Students are considered passive learners, as it is their task to listen and learn. Extrinsic learning is valued, and motivation comes from external rewards in the sense of grades.

The official theory of learning extends beyond the last century to the mid- and late 1800s when the United States was focused on the literal building of the country. The construction of factories, buildings, and railroads was a key national goal. At that time, the concept of scientific management was central in measuring the efficiency of the factory workers. The dominant idea in running the factories was to get more production out of the workers in less time, making the factory as efficient as possible. It worked in steel factories. Eventually, people began to use this same model on the early schools. The historical and hidden assumption was that if it works with steel, then it certainly ought to work with kids.

In the early years of the 1900s, Frederick Taylor championed the scientific management movement, which was welcomed by many (Bracey, 2002b). A renowned educational leader of the time, Cubberley (1919), clearly stated the vision of the factory model of education (see Figure 8.1):

> Every manufacturing establishment that turns out a standard product or series of products of any kind maintains a force of efficiency experts to study methods of procedure and to measure and test the output of its works. . . . Our schools are, in a sense, factories in which the raw products (children) are to be shaped and fashioned into products to meet the various demands of life. The specifications for manufacturing come from the demands of the twentieth-century civilization, and it is the business of schools to build its pupils to the specifications laid down. (p. 338)

This is the reason that many today refer to the official theory of learning as the factory model. Those who promote this model of education often use the rationale that it is based on "hard science," so called because of the literal working with hard materials, such as steel. For many people, its contemporary usage merely promotes the continuation of imagery reaching back to the steel factories.

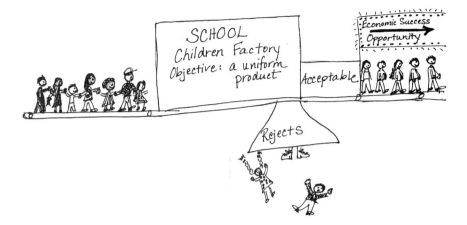

FIGURE 8.1   Schools as Factories

This model of education is also referred to as the "banking model of education," a Freirian term, meaning that the teacher has the capital and deposits it in the minds of the students, where it can accumulate interest and value (Freire & Macedo, 1987). The banking model is founded on the assumption that students are empty vessels.

The official theory of learning is also known as the transmission model of education. Its predominance in schools is verified by Goodlad (1984) and Sirotnik (1983). In addition, the Ramirez, Yuen, and Ramey (1991) report, which demonstrated that instruction in Spanish for part of the day results in no loss of English academic skills, also found that in both bilingual and English immersion classrooms, the *sage-on-stage* approach, with its heavy reliance on teachers talking and students listening, was the norm.

> Of major concern is that in over half of the interactions that teachers have with students, students do not produce any language as they are only listening or responding with non-verbal gestures or actions. . . . Of equal concern is that when students do respond, typically they provide only simple information recall statements. Rather than being provided with the opportunity to generate original statements, students are asked to provide simple discrete close-ended or patterned (i.e., expected) responses. This pattern of teacher/student interaction not only limits a student's opportunity to create and manipulate language freely, but also limits the student's ability to engage in more complex learning (i.e., higher order thinking skills). In sum . . . teachers in all three programs offer a passive language environment, limiting students' opportunities to produce language and develop more complex language and thinking skills. (Ramírez, Yuen, & Ramey, 1991, p. 8)

Today the official theory of learning is characterized by standards-based and outcome-based teaching and learning. Many consider this school of thought the status quo, the-way-it-has-always-been, the best way. This school of thought is not only pedagogical, but it is also political. It acutely affects the standards-driven policies roaring across the country today. Deborah Meier at age 71, founder of the small-schools movement, continues to speak out to encourage teachers that the only thing that will help schools today is if we will buck the nationwide trend for more and more standardized testing. She continues by saying that the current mania for account-ability with rewards and punishments for students, teachers, and administrators is borrowed from the corporate world. She likens it to Enron and points to the ways that educators can cook the books to make attendance, graduation rates, and test scores appear better than they are (retrieved from newyorktimes.com, September 30, 2002). When the only goal is a number on a form, data are easily distorted to fall in line with a policy and please a demanding and uninformed public. Pondering pedagogy can often be surprising, alarming, and revealing, but, ultimately, it is one way to see our-selves and our context more critically and to place ourselves in a larger historical perspective.

As can be seen in the time line in Figure 8.2, the official theory of learning has had an extreme effect on education for more than 100 years. Its influences continue to be felt.

The Classic Theory of Learning

The classic theory of learning emphasizes inquiry, discovery, and dialectical learning. It is often perceived that its historical roots reach back to Dewey's notion of progres-sivism with the emphasis on child-centered, meaning-centered, and experiential learn-ing. However, the roots actually go back to Socrates. The classic theory is just that: classical, in a historic sense. The teacher is a facilitator and the students are asked to engage actively with new knowledge. Intrinsic learning is valued. The reward for

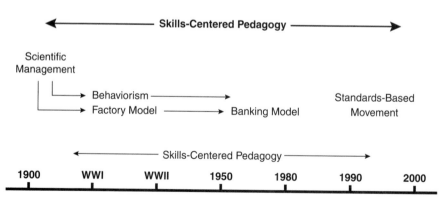

FIGURE 8.2   Roots of the Official Theory of Learning

(Adapted from Wink & Putney, 2002, p. 5)

learning is growth and development. Motivation is centered on competence. Growth is not dependent on control and testing but rather on the natural acquisition of knowledge. Learning is for learning's sake because it is meaningful.

> We learn "new things" from the company we keep by making them part of what we already know. They are not new bits to be added to a store of knowledge, but extensions or elaborations of the experiences and beliefs that make us what we are. (Smith, 1998, p. 13)

The classic theory of learning is characterized by the notions of active, interactive, and transactional learning. Meaning making is not only in the head, but it is also in the world and can be traced to the experiential learning of Dewey (Prawatt, 2002). Rosenblatt (1978) captured this construct by explaining that meaning comes into being through experience. The classic theory of learning evokes humanistic and holistic teaching and learning.

The Sages of the Ages. We are attracted to Smith (1998) for the following reasons. First, it would be safe to say that everyone reading this book has had personal experience with both models. Each of us can hook on to some prior knowledge of each of these paradigms. Second, by reflecting on the two approaches to education, it is fairly easy to see the dominance of the official over the classic, which caused Smith to opine that we backed the wrong horse.

We are attracted to the Smith model for a third reason also. By simply naming the second paradigm the classic theory of learning, he alludes to and connects this model to history, which extends well beyond the past 100 plus years. Although many perceive this model to be new and experimental, the truth is that it is rooted firmly in the classical teaching and learning of the antiquities.

As can be seen in the time line in Figure 8.3, the classic theory of learning includes the spirit and legacy of Socrates' ideas of teaching and learning. The Socratic method of dialectical or inquiry-based learning is central to the classic model of pedagogy. The classic theory of learning, historically grounded in Socrates' notions of justice and love of learning, recognizes and validates the experiences of the child and his or her interaction with the environment. The classic theory of learning also is grounded in the social and cultural context of constructionist learning.

Many who are opposed to the classic theory of learning think of it as "soft" and new. Some may not be aware that it has stood the test of time and reaches back into history to the sages of the ages. "To them, education was more about instilling a love of learning than about giving tests or making threats" (Good, 2002, p. 2). We concede that the official theory of learning has the momentum as we write this book. However, like Good, we can't shake this nagging feeling that the sages of the ages would not approve. However, if the presentation of classical wisdom does not ring clearly for you, we turn to a teenager who has a knack for direct-speak. "Some teachers teach from the point of view of the kid. They don't just come out and say, 'All right, do this, blah, blah, blah' " (Nieto, S., 1999, p. 110).

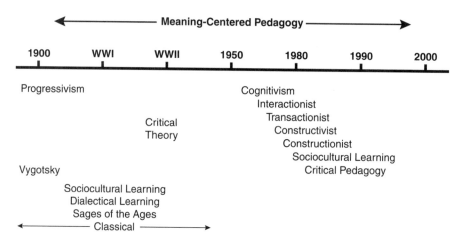

FIGURE 8.3   Roots of the Classic Theory of Learning

(Adapted from Wink & Putney, 2002, p. 5)

Simultaneous and Contradictory Perspectives on Education

The dueling dual models of education have a long history in education as simultaneous and contradictory perspectives, giving rise to the pendulum metaphor. As the nineteenth century gave way to the twentieth, scientific management and progressivism were hotly debated. As the twentieth century gave way to the twenty-first, the same debate continues.

However, this is the point: This time around, it is very different. The pendulum can no longer be used to rationalize what appears to be the ebb and flow of oppositional ideas. Wolfe and Poynor (2001) challenge the metaphor of the pendulum and offer an alternative understanding that captures the complexities of the human and educational processes that ground all of education. Wolfe and Poynor posit that the pendulum idea is in actuality a sociopolitical movement inextricably linked to conflicts over hegemonic control. In addition, they argue that metaphors are used to mask the inherent and inevitable political nature of all educational processes. (See Figure 8.4.)

We encourage you to describe an experience you had as a student with each of these two approaches. (See Figure 8.5.)

After charting your memories, please answer this question: Which theory worked better for you? Which content do you still remember?

Why We Slip Back to Transmission

So, if it is not the swing of a pendulum, why do we slip back to transmission? In order to answer this question, we need once again need to look below the surface of what is readily visible. First, we will look at the role of control and how it is buried within ped-

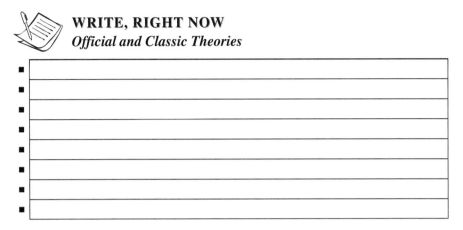

WRITE, RIGHT NOW
Official and Classic Theories

-
-
-
-
-
-
-
-

FIGURE 8.4   Write, Right Now: Official and Classic Theories

	Official Theory	**Classic Theory**
Your age		
The teacher		
The grade		
The content		
Role of the teacher		
Role of the student (you)		
What did you learn?		
How did you learn it?		

FIGURE 8.5   Chart Your Experiences

agogy, politics, and policies. This will be followed with a discussion of the deficit perspective and how it undergirds the transmission model of education. This section will conclude with responses that shed light on why we slip back to transmission, which is similar to Dewey's (1916) question of years ago.

> Why is it, in spite of the fact that teaching by pouring in, learning by a passive absorption, are universally condemned, that they are still so entrenched in practice? That education is not an affair of "telling" and being told but an active and constructive process is a principle almost as generally violated in practice as conceded in theory. (p. 38)

First, we need to stare the demon, *control,* in the face. Gerry Coles (in personal communication, September 25, 2002) illuminates our understanding of control. The transmission school of thought becomes practice in the form of controlled, mandated, scripted teacher-directed programs. Coles writes that those who impose such programs become transmitters of an ideology whose ideas are selected for use by those in power to maintain that power rather than as leaders of a movement that emerged because of the strength of its ideas created as an alternative to that ideology. At this moment, ideologues are using their power to impose the transmission model of education because it has the power to control the language of teachers and students. If language is controlled, thought is controlled. "Power, after all, is what it is all about" (Skutnabb-Kangas & Cummins, 1988, p. 390).

But it's essential to link this control to the continuous fight over resources for education. Skills-emphasis, sequential DI instruction, fosters education on the cheap. It reduces the need for a trained teaching force. It's always benefited from sexism by using women as replaceable, low-paying cogs. It allows for larger classes. It requires fewer materials. It enables minimal resources to be used for education, especially for the education of working-class and poor children. To paraphrase the great line of Her Majesty, Marie Antoinette, "Let them eat skills" (Coles, September 25, 2002, in personal communication).

Second, to find answers as to why we have a tendency to slip back into transmission, we must also understand the assumptions behind the deficit model. The deficit model is an assumption that some students and their families "are riddled with deficiencies" (Nieto, 1999, p. 175). The deficiencies are rationalized by students' social class, race, gender, or ethnicity. Taking issue with the deficit model is as difficult as tackling the issues of control because those with deficit model assumptions often do not recognize it; and, if they do, may deny it. However, ask any of the students who are assumed to be "deficient." They can easily see and feel the deficit model at work daily in their lives. Remember the Mexican American student who told us, "It's as if the teachers think we're dirty." The deficit model assumes that one group of students can do less. If educators or policy makers assume that one group of students cannot do something, conditions of learning will be consciously or unconsciously created that ensure that the assumption is valid.

In the writing of this chapter, we kept asking ourselves: Why do we constantly slip back into transmission? Evans (2002) offers a response that resonates with us. She notes that teachers often slip back into transmission when they feel their control over students is threatened. Obviously, this can happen for many reasons, including the fact that transmission models may be appropriate at times. However, Evans found that teachers who had a deficit model of students were more apt to slip back into transmission. For her, the deficit model refers to the assumption that students' failure to meet expectations stems from a personal deficiency. In order words, teachers slip into transmission and blame the students, exactly as Professor JS revealed about himself. Even more striking in her data analysis is that she found that transmission models and deficit models seemed to be mutually enabling.

Evans points to the direct linkages from transmission to deficit assumptions and, eventually, to teachers' need for control. From this vantage point, it is only a short jump from control to power, which is often just below the surface of the educational iceberg. Our assumptions go deep, even if we do not see them; even if we deny them.

> We have long seen as problematic reliance on transmission models of communication—models which do not recognize the role of context in shaping interpretation and which assume that stable, fixed meanings can be neatly transmitted from person to person. Then, suggesting that transmission models are both pervasive and resilient, I account for this resilience on a macro-social level. I conclude by recognizing that transmission models are sometimes appropriate and by discussing implications for research, theory-building, and teacher training. (Evans, 2002, p. 1)

We find the dual model of education posited by Smith (1988) provides a vehicle for demonstrating the linkages from pedagogy to politics to policy. Often we find the dual model, the either/or approach, to anything very limiting. The irony of this model is that it does not restrict thinking; rather it enhances our understandings of what is often unseen and unsaid. In this particular case, philosophical perspective has become a mandated political policy.

In our work in public schools, we are constantly amazed at the level of discouragement of teachers. On multiple occasions, we have asked teachers about how democracy is taught in their schools. We have heard marvelous methodologies about ways of teaching democracy. However, when we follow up this activity with the following question, we are always shocked and saddened to watch as pride of methodology falls immediately into despair of theoretical foundations. We ask: Do you teach in a democratic institution? It has been years since we have heard a positive response.

"The context is my having said that we need education *for* democracy because no matter the rhetoric and the wishes, we don't have a democracy now when democracy is defined as a system in which people participate meaningfully in decisions that affect their lives" (Edelsky, 1994, p. 253).

The Voice of Life

A Letter to First-Year Teachers from Joan

In what follows, we will provide examples of the linkages among pedagogy, politics, and policies. The advent of the twenty-first century brought the skills-centric, standards-based movement to schools across the nation. The changes mandated by the $5 billion Reading First, No Child Left Behind program have dramatically changed reading and writing activities. Math will be next ("Reading First," 2002), with the first grant already having been awarded to three back-to-the-basic math professionals. Although standards years ago might have been perceived to be laudable, mainstream goals, for many who are actually in schools daily, the voices of discontent are

Dear Beginning Teachers,

As you begin your teaching career, it makes me reflect on my own. Maybe some of my experiences might provide a hint of what's to come for you, too.

I began teaching in 1966. I came from the rural northern prairies and started teaching in a school on the Mainline of Philadelphia. This area was very upscale, very sophisticated, and very urban. It was everything I was not.

This school believed in life-long learning. I had just finished a four-year degree program and thought I knew all there was to know. I was the only teacher without an advanced degree; and I knew that I would never, ever want one of those.

The school was new and huge. Every wall was entirely made of glass windows, floor to ceiling. I could stand in my room and see over the heads of students in many other classes.

When the principal was coming down the hall, we knew well in advance. And I always watched for him. I can remember exactly what he looked like: He was impeccably dressed and very rigid—physically and philosophically. I remember thinking that one of his suits probably cost more than my entire wardrobe for teaching.

I would like to say that I was a day ahead of each class all year long, but the truth is that I was rarely more than 5 minutes ahead of each class. In 1966 when I began teaching, I thought: I will teach; they will learn. Turns out I was wrong. I remember that I taught—oh, did I teach. The question is: Did the students learn?

My most vivid memory of my first year of teaching is a continual headache. I remember taking aspirin every day. Sunday nights were the worst time of the week. I swore I would never teach again. I have been teaching and learning ever since.

Before I finished my first year, I was able to articulate one concept that had impressed me more than any others: Teachers who teach in glass schools should not throw stones.

If your first year of teaching should be anything like mine, don't do what I did. Instead, I would advise you to laugh often, exercise a lot, enjoy your friends and family, read good books, and drink lots of water.

In my first year of teaching, it seemed like everything I had learned in college didn't fit—an experience I have had several times since. In this open letter to you, I plan to share with you several things you will need to know that you can only learn by teaching.

The very first thing you will unfortunately learn in your first year of teaching is that we didn't teach you everything in your teacher preparation program. It's true: There will be a whole bunch of things that you didn't learn in the teacher preparation classes.

When you first start to notice this, it will be very annoying. Some of you will even start to blame some of us. You might even be tempted to mutter: if they had only told me about Program A, B, or C or Method D, E, or F. Now, here is what will happen: In your tenth year of teaching, this will all make you laugh.

With any luck at all, and if you are receptive to new ideas, you will learn more in your first year of teaching than we ever taught you.

Second, you are going to have days when you come to class excited and thrilled about your new lesson or your new idea, and you will have worked hard preparing it. And, not long after you begin your lesson, you will notice that it is not as exciting to the

FIGURE 8.6 A Letter to First-Year Teachers from Joan

students as it was to you. In fact, it's not even very exciting to you anymore. The lesson falls flat. This doesn't mean you are a bad teacher. This doesn't even mean it is bad lesson. Do not panic. When this happens, and it will, I suggest you fix it, try it again, or just toss it. Above all, do not beat a dead horse. Better you grab a book and read a good story with the kids.

Third, and some of you aren't going to like learning this, but when you teach, politics will be a part of it. How can it not be? Schools are filled with people, lots of people who all bring a diversity of thought, perspectives, opinions, and experiences. Schools are social, schools are cultural, and schools are political environments that reflect the world around them.

When you choose curriculum, it is a political act. When you make decisions about who will learn what and how, you are taking political action. And even if you choose not to act, your passivity is also a political action.

The thing about pondering our pedagogy politically is that it makes us look at the whole thing. Does a piece of a puzzle make any sense to you? Do you need to look at the whole puzzle to make some sense? If you are someone who likes to see the whole thing before putting the puzzle together, you are like most others. I learned this when I started teaching (Wink, 2001).

FIGURE 8.6   Continued

emerging. In what follows, our goal is to demonstrate the reality we have experienced far too often in recent years.

Freedom to Teach, Learn, and Live

Once we had as much freedom as we wanted. Teachers used books by a wide variety of thinkers and writers. Rigor and joy were central to classes. Classes made books, read books, and reflected on books. Teachers and students loved each other, loved their class, and loved learning. Teachers and students loved the freedom to teach and learn. However, that has changed drastically on a global scale. Micromanagement, mandates, and military metaphors are eroding academic and intellectual freedoms. In addition, we use the word *rigor* in a strictly Freirian sense of academic develoment that challenges and enriches us. When we say rigor, we do not mean rigidity or inflexibility. We use rigor to mean teaching and learning that is intellectually demanding, but never demeaning.

Martin Luther King, Jr. once gave a speech on creative maladjustment. He talked about how we all eventually have to adjust to many things. However, there were some things he could never adjust to, for example, racism. Today we would add sexism, classicism, and xenophobia. In today's political climate in education, teachers have to find creative forms of maladjustment to survive and thrive. Incidentally, you will find that a sense of humor is very handy. It also helps to be a bit nimble (Wink, 2001).

Mandated Minutia and That Darned Democracy

Presently, teachers feel so mandated with minutia that they do not have time for the bigger picture—much less their place in it. Although the number of hours in their workday has not changed, teachers are now required and are often monitored by various state laws to do more and to do it with less money. The mandated minutia have multiplied to a level where teachers have to focus for little pieces of time on little pieces of curriculum. It is no wonder that students leave at the end of the day with little pieces of learning. Nor is it any wonder that teachers feel resistant to stop, collect their little pieces of breath, and ponder their own pedagogy in the larger picture of educational ideas moving forward on a continuum of free thought that cannot be denied in a democracy.

To varying degrees, at different times and places, there always has been resistance and always will be. If we surround ourselves with the legacy of educators and ideas that preceded us, we see that we are in good company and doing important work. We are not the first group of educators, nor the last, who will be called on to have the courage to promote teaching and learning that lead to self and social transformation. Each of us is informed by the theory and practice of colleagues who have gone before us. Each of us is called on to contribute to those who come after us.

A second challenge teachers face centers around democracy. Schools pride themselves on transmitting democratic ideals. Ask any group of teachers if their school teaches democracy, and the answer will be in the affirmative. Ask the same group of teachers if they are teaching and learning in a democratic school, and the answer is often very different. It appears that it is good in theory but not in practice.

This question, more than any other we ask, consistently triggers an alarming display of cynicism, often followed by honest dialogue. This is a good place to begin a discussion of how we are influenced by the world around us. The purpose of the following story is to provide an example of connections from pedagogy to principles to politics. It tells of Joan's experiences this past year trying to adapt her teaching to meet the new one-size-fits-all state-mandated approach to literacy.

> Out with Freire; in with phonemes. Out with schema; in with the schwa. Out with meaning; in with minutia. Out with the whole, in with the parts. This is how I felt when I sat down to update my bilingual reading/language arts syllabus to reflect the new, state-mandated, one-size-fits-all approach to literacy. With the guidelines from the state, dictating that I must prepare credential students with a knowledge of fricatives, phonemes, and phonology, I find myself feeling philosophically frustrated. This would be funny, if it weren't fact. (Wink, 2001, p. 211)

Absurdities of the Twenty-First Century

When I began this award I said that this period would be known in the not to distant future as the period of the Pedagogy of the Absurd. The year 2002 has produced increasingly absurd examples all centered around the absurd claim that the science of reading can be reduced to a small number of phonics-based reading programs. The campaign to impose this on teachers and students is leaving no aspect of education untouched. Foremost is the way the Reading First aspect of No Child Left Behind (NCLB) law is being enforced (Goodman, personal correspondence, November 9, 2002). Ohanian (2003) continues to maintain a log of absurdities, which she refers to as atrocities.

The present political climate in education begs a section focused entirely on the academic absurdities taking place in the twenty-first century. In what follows we describe a few acts that represent the current state of education.

Susan Neuman (2001b), assistant secretary of education, said the new federal No Child Left Behind Act, if implemented the right way, will put an end to creative and experimental teaching methods in the nation's classrooms. "It will stifle, and hopefully it will kill [them]," said Neuman (retrieved www.CATEnet.net, November 9, 2002). Although killing creative teaching methods in the classroom, current decision makers in education have implemented some of the following absurdities instead.

Absurdity 1.   The AFT (American Federation of Teachers) came out with the following statement endorsing the current emphasis on "scientific research."

> The AFT believes that there is a tremendous need for core pedagogy curricula, an agreement within the education profession about what prospective teachers should know about teaching subject matter such as reading and mathematics. *There is no consensus on core pedagogy and the AFT believes that the federal government could play a major role in correcting this impediment* [emphasis added]. We urge the [Congress] to fund an effort by the National Academy of Sciences to develop such curricula and promote their adoption by colleges of education. The recommendations should be based on the best research into how students learn and on the content-specific teaching methods shown to be effective with students. (Fraas, 2003)

Response 1.   No consensus on core pedagogy about how people learn and effective teaching methods? Ladies and gentlemen, you know the past 2,000 years of pedagogical inquiry and discovery—it apparently didn't happen after all.

Absurdity 2.   Ohanian (2002) cites consistent instances of students and teachers being essentially bribed for good test scores. In one school, teachers throw a party for kids who score well on the SAT-9 test. Invitations are passed out in class. Two hundred students were invited: 40 were left out. Superintendents and teachers cite these exercises in ostracization and humiliation as student motivators. Other schools offer bicycles and cash prizes. Ask the students intentionally alienated how motivated they feel to attend and enjoy school now. Adding insult to injury, the tests contain questions such as the following for second graders:

> A very important person came to our class yesterday. He was a firefighter. He told us how to be safe at school and at home. We liked listening to him because he was very friendly. Which of these would go best after the last sentence?
> After he talked to us, we asked him many questions.

He spoke to us after we had finished reading a story.
This important person was someone from our town. (Ohanian, 2002, p. 89)

Response 2.   Care to venture a guess as to which the "correct" answer might be? Some second grader somewhere may not pass on to the next grade if this is incorrectly marked.

Absurdity 3.   Ohanian (2002) reveals students are not the only people being bribed. Approximately 250 Florida teachers destroyed "incentive" checks from the state, citing as their reason that accepting them would make them culpable of supporting a flawed school-ranking system. She goes on to describe how teachers are coached how to handle children becoming so upset they vomit on the test. It happens enough so that teachers actually receive instruction on this matter.

Response 3.   It is not only students who suffer under the enforcements of a standards-driven curriculum. The effect on teachers is devastating also as we see in the following Letter to the Editor from the *San Francisco Chronicle* (November 24, 2002):

Editorial: Frustration in the Classroom

In recent years, teachers have been pummeled, shamed, cajoled, even humiliated, under the relentless pressures to conform to the profusion of dictates emerging from Sacramento and Washington.

Conversations we've had with teachers reveal that many are frustrated, worn out, and, increasingly, angry. Experienced teachers are marking time until they are eligible for retirement benefits—and then plan to bolt the profession. And this at a time when the state needs every experienced teacher it can get—and thousands more.

One fifth-grade teacher, an 18-year-veteran of the classroom, described "stress beyond belief" to meet new reporting requirements which take five times longer than in the past. What used to make teaching fun, challenging, and creative has instead become a tedious, boring exercise. And, they say, children are increasingly reacting the same way. A first-grade teacher told us that for the first time in the 10 years on the job students ask, "Is it time to go home yet?"

Even the financial rewards doled out by Sacramento to motivate teachers to find ways to improve their students' test scores may have had just the opposite effect. Many teachers find the rewards insulting, because a reward implies that teachers will be more effective if a government handout is dangled in front of them.

You'd think teachers would rise up in protest. What has kept teachers from outright revolt, they say, is the prevailing ethic not to make waves, and to "be professionals."

"Every time we say something in a meeting, we have higher-ups who stand up and say, 'We are professionals, we will respect one another, we are not here to argue.' " Even tenured teachers fear the dreaded "involuntary transfer"— assignment to another grade or a more distant or less desirable school—if they challenge the reform orthodoxy.

"Our jobs are on the line. Teachers are afraid to do anything."

So far teacher frustrations have been largely hidden from public view. The reason they're staying, however, has more to do with economic realities than because they love their jobs. "If this testing thing keeps up, and the economy picks up, you'll see a lot of people leaving the profession," said Peter Farrugio, who taught elementary school for 18 years, and now trains new bilingual teachers.

One second-grade teacher told us that after 27 years he'll stay only until he qualifies for retirement benefits. "If I could afford to leave financially, I would leave now," he said. "I'll try to do three more years, but then I'm walking away from California. I don't want to be a part of it. I have sold my soul."

Clearly any serious reform program must include boosting teacher salaries. Parents want their children taught by an energized teacher, not by one who feels trapped in the classroom. Teachers need to feel free to express their views without retaliation.

Sadly, these absurdities have become the norm. They are, in fact, absurdly dangerous.

Deleting History

As students are being forced to memorize more and more facts and bits of information, the U.S. Department of Education proceeds to take public information off its Web site. The American Educational Research Association (AERA) and the American Library Association (ALA), along with 12 other national organizations, are working in concert to petition the Department of Education that research be left accessible.

This effort was initiated in the fall of 2002 after the library, educational research, and related social science communities learned of an internal memo, "Criteria and Process for Removing Old Content from www.ed.gov," that the Education Department issued to staff members on May 31, 2002. According to the internal government memo, the federal initiative strives to remove from public access information that either is outdated or "does not reflect the priorities, philosophies, or goals of the present administration" (American Educational Research Association, 2002).

Back to Democracy

"Today democracy is threatened from within," 96-year-old Louise Rosenblatt spoke of the current threat to democracy at the American Educational Research Association Conference (AERA, 2001) as she received the John Dewey Award. She noted that in her life, she has experienced a number of crises in education, but none as dangerous as the present. Previous battles waged against opponents to democracy were fought against an outside threat. Democracy is now being challenged from within the field of education itself, a much more insidious threat. Rosenblatt emphasized Dewey's willingness to fight, pointing out Dewey's willingness to defend even those with whom he didn't agree in the spirit of fighting injustice.

Praxis: Let the Magic Begin

The following two activities are designed for teacher preparation candidates to integrate the curriculum with social foundations, social studies, and reading/language arts classes. In addition, the two activities create processes that introduce the university students to marginalized groups within the school communities where they will be student teaching and/or teaching.

Class Inquiry Project[2]

Overview of Project: Students will engage in a learning experience that is integrated across the curriculum and is inquiry based. In small groups the teacher education candidates will collaboratively choose a topic of choice. In researching the chosen topic, students will think and work as geographers, anthropologists, sociologists, political scientists, historians, and economists. It will be the students' responsibility to identify what they want to know. The groups' questions will drive the groups' action research plans. Students must pose their questions, how and where they will find the answers, how they will analyze and organize the knowledge they generate, and how the information will be presented to the whole class.

Students' Roles and Responsibilities: Students will actively engage with material and collaborate to pose and investigate within local communities, answer questions, and develop interpretations to be presented in class. Students will acquire the methods of social scientists as they conduct their fieldwork. Initial research will be kept in individual field notebooks; individual learning will be shared in small groups. Each group will collaborate as they present in oral and written form to the class.

Instructor's Roles and Responsibilities: The instructor serves as a facilitator, providing resource materials, guiding instruction, and most importantly, learning with the students.

Oral History Project

Overview: The purpose of this process is to write an oral history based on taped interviews to provide primary source data of a target population in the community near where teachers are teaching.

Students' Roles and Responsibilities: Students will focus on interviews from one family. Students will explain the purpose of the project to the interviewee and assure each family member that the anonymity of all is protected in the written report. Students must prepare questions before interviewing. The questions serve as a guide, and flexibility during the interview is required. There are no right or wrong responses; oral histories are based on personal perspectives of experiences. Students will ask for permission to tape record the interview. Family members can choose to participate or not; they can choose to answer questions or not. The written report will be shared with participants. Students will take notes during the interview and write their narrative after the interviews.

Instructor's Roles and Responsibilities: The instructor serves as a human connection between the students and the target families within the community. The instructor facilitates the connections with participants and with other resources. Most importantly, the instructor learns with the teacher preparation students.

The previous two activities are prepared for university-level students; however, they could easily be adapted for different contexts. The following section focuses directly on an urban public school teacher (Codell, 2001), whose fifth graders' math and reading scores jumped dramatically on the annual achievement test. The supervisor asked her to explain why the students' scores had improved. The teacher explained.

Esmé Educates

I feel like we did a lot of interesting things this year. Some of my favorites: When learning about electricity, we made light-up quiz games. When learning about light, we put on shadow-puppet shows. When learning medieval history, we built an accurate castle, then decorated it with colored marshmallows and put it in our fairy tale book display. When we learned about air, we had a bubble festival. When learning about Asia, we made sushi. We made video commercials to promote our favorite books. We had a book character masquerade party. We went to an outdoor Beethoven concert and visited Buckingham Fountain downtown. The kids had checking accounts in a classroom economy. We had a cereal box supermarket, and the kids learned to make change. We had formal debates. We made a book of fables. My kids write the best descriptive compositions. They have international pen pals. They illustrated poetry anthologies. They read and wrote treasure maps. They know all the dances from the 1960s. (Codell, 2001, pp. 177–178)

Her answer tells us much about passionate pedagogy, political action (even though it didn't look like it), and methods that are effective in raising academic scores. Sadly, in this age of controlled curriculum and high-stakes testing, far too many teachers, we know, are reduced to teaching the tests; and the students are reduced to memorizing the answers and repeating them back.

The Literacy Link

In this section, we will share more theoretically grounded activities that are linked to literacy experiences.

The Creative Reading Methodology/Creative Dialogue

The following four phases are a part of what Alma Flor Ada (2003) refers to as the creative reading methodology. Do not be fooled: It is much more than that. Although many perceive it to be a process for teaching reading, and indeed it is that, it also serves in other contexts. The creative reading process always reminds us of the four pedagogical principles (meaningful, purposeful, relevant, and respectful) that we learned from the Goodmans: We never leave home without them.

In our experiences with elementary, secondary, higher education, and graduate students and many varieties of in-services and professional development programs, Alma Flor Ada's method and the Goodmans' principles will function extremely well with diverse groups of learners of all ages. The curriculum is any content area, and the methodology is applicable for any age group—even for professors reading this who are intrigued. Try it. Focusing on the creative dialogue with these four phases invites a newer and deeper level of reflection and, thus, learning. Each phase of the process is linked through interaction that leads to critical reflection and, finally, to action. If you add passion, it is even better. (See Figure 8.7.)

When using this method, Ada encourages teachers to recognize that the phases appear to be very separate; however, the reality is that they often are interwoven and happen concurrently.

The creative reading methodology is well grounded in the critical theory of Freire (1974) who taught us, not only about the place of love in teaching and learn-

---

Descriptive Phase: During this phase of reading/learning, the content or information is shared by teacher, text, media, and so on. This is the initial phase that focuses on the content to be learned. Comprehension of new knowledge is the goal. This phase serves only as a springboard to students' interaction with new knowledge.

Personal Interpretation Phase: Students grapple with new information based on their lived experiences. This phase moves us beyond what, where, when, how, and who questions to questions that invite reflection of the new knowledge. For example, students are asked: Have you ever experienced this? Does this relate to your family? How do you feel about your new understandings? During this phase the new knowledge is linked to the lives of the students.

Critical Analysis Phase: After comprehension of knowledge and the creation of linkages to the students' lives, the students are now encouraged to reflect critically, draw inferences, seek implications, and analyze. Is the knowledge valid? For whom? Always? Why? Is it applicable for all cultures, classes, and ethnicities? Is it gender free?

Creative Action Phase: This is the action phase of learning. How can students take the theory or new knowledge and use it to improve the life of the community? How can learning move from the classroom to the real world of the students?

FIGURE 8.7   Creative Reading Methodology

ing, but also about reading the word on the page, and reading the world, or the social, cultural, political, and historical influences and implications of our own pedagogy. Within critical theory, teachers and learners are asked to connect the learning of school with the learning of life. Freire's legacy includes a challenge that calls us to name, to reflect critically, and to act. Alma Flor Ada's theoretically and critically grounded methods do exactly that, culminating in creative action, whether it be as in the Codell (2001) methods, writing letters to the editor, or, as in the case that follows, creating something from our own learning.

Who I Am and Who I Want To Be.   Dee, an impassioned middle school teacher we know and love, shared one of her lessons, which demonstrates how she applies Alma Flor Ada's work. In this process, Dee and the eighth-grade students begin with a poem about Spiderman by James Hall and end with students creating their own scrapbook that chronicles their learning and developing during their eighth-grade year.

Dee opens the process by sharing a poem, "Maybe Dats Youwr Pwoblem Too." In this poem, Spiderman complains that he can never burn his suit, and he's tired of doing the same old thing. He would like to race cars, but no, that's not an option. After sharing this poem, Dee and the class discuss how people see us, and how we would like to be seen, and that we're not really stuck in our suits, as is Spiderman. Dee guides the discussion to questions regarding each person's "suit," with all of its flaws and strengths. The students then write two paragraphs about who they are now and who they would like to be. After responding to, revising, and editing their paragraphs in groups, they use these paragraphs to create scrapbook pages that commemorate the start of their eighth-grade year. The pages are eventually put away and are updated midyear and near the end of the school year.

Linking this activity to the creative reading methodology of Alma Flor Ada, Dee works with the students so they understand that the *descriptive phase* is the poem. The *personal interpretive and critical phases,* in which the class dialogues and reflects in writing, individually, in small groups, and eventually in oral sharing with the whole group follow the poem. The *creative phase* is the journal/scrapbook, an autobiographical and pictorial account, of each personal eighth-grade year.

A Critical Literacy Framework

We began this book with a discussion of the spiral and how it relates to literacy development. Obviously, the spiral also symbolizes our ways of learning in schools and in life. It reflects the individual path we each take in our development, whether it be literacy development, pedagogical development, human development, and so on. Now we return to the spiral to use it again, as a cognitive coathook for personal reflection of literacy and critical literacy. If literacy is learning to read, critical literacy is learning to read the world (Freire & Macedo, 1987). (See Figure 8.8.)

When we first began to think seriously about literacies and critical literacies, our spiral of development led us to understand that literacy is grounded in politics. For us, our understandings of literacy eventually led us to connect literacy to democracy. This

---

Reading the Word Means

■ to decode/encode those words;

■ to bring ourselves to those pages;

■ to make meaning of those pages as they relate to our experiences, our possibilities, our cultures, and our knowledges.

Reading the World Means

■ to decode/encode the people around us;

■ to decode/encode the community that surrounds us;

■ to decode/encode the visible and invisible messages of the world.

FIGURE 8.8   Reading the Word and the World

is why we have included many literacy processes throughout this book. Theoretically grounded literacy experiences lead each of us further up our own spiral of development.

Our understanding of the linkages between critical literacy and passionate pedagogy is shown in Figure 8.9, where it can be seen that the grounding rod states that "human relations are at the heart of school." This is where we begin. From there, the

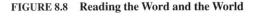

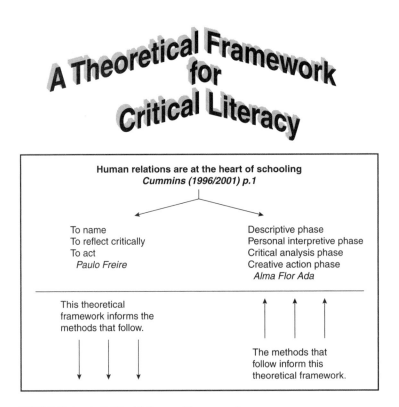

FIGURE 8.9   A Critical Literacy Framework

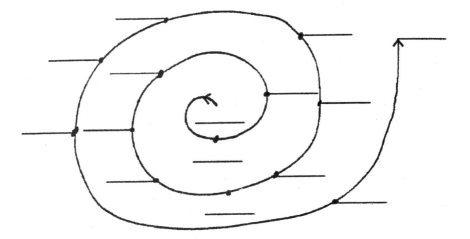

FIGURE 8.10   The Spiral of Your Theoretical and Methodological Development

connections flow to Freire's legacy of problem posing (to name, to reflect critically, and to act) and Alma Flor Ada's methodology that takes it all to the classroom and the community.

We said in the beginning of this book that some of us come to methods via theory, and some of us come to theory via methods. It doesn't matter, as each person's spiral of development is unique. However, theory and methods are mutually informative, which is why we have interspersed them in this book.

In the spiral in Figure 8.10, plot your own theoretical and methodological development.

WHAT CAN BE LEARNED FROM THIS?

People and politics matter. People have primacy in school, and where people gather, a multitude of political views will exist. Experience is a great teacher also. Sometimes it takes years of teaching and learning to internalize that politics and pedagogy are linked passionately. The words of Herbert (2003) ring all too true for us when he questions why the richest, most powerful nation in history cannot (or will not) provide a sound education for all of its children. He likens education to the food that nourishes the nation's soul. We join with him in spirit by asking: Why are we starving our kids?

"Teaching is so public, so personal, so dangerous" (Burke, 2002, p. 13). Yes, and it is so political.

CHAPTER NOTES

1. Audio can be purchased at Audio Archives, 3043 Foothill Blvd., Suite 2, La Crescenta, CA 91214.

2. We appreciate the contributions of Ana Floriani, who shared both the Oral History Project and the Class Inquiry Project. The purpose of the original projects was to introduce the teacher preparation students to the families of the local Mexican American migrant communities. We have adapted the original activities so that readers can use these activities with other target groups. If you would like more information on the original projects, please contact Ana Floriani at aflorian@iwu.edu.

9 Teaching Passionately with Action

Look, my friends, there is no possibility for greater achievement without running risk. Without freedom you cannot risk. When you are not free, you have to risk in order to get freedom. Education is a game like this. Constantly teaching is not to spend a weekend on a tropical beach. It is to be committed to the process of teaching and committed to the adventure and creation, both teachers as teachers and students as students.

PAULO FREIRE, 1993

Personal and professional excitement and energy strengthen one another. Personal passion and professional passion cannot be separated. Each is intimately interwoven to the support or detriment of the other. Excitement is contagious. Students are drawn into its wake despite themselves when the teacher brings genuine curiosity and enthusiasm into the classroom. We, as teachers, know there are two main ways to do this: be genuinely excited or fake it. We've all experienced both. We also know that pretending to be excited, especially for extended periods of time, is exhausting. Feigned enthusiasm ranks as a significant component in teacher burnout.

This chapter is a guide to infuse passion and energy into life and teaching, making teaching and learning a dynamic and meaningful process for both teacher and learner. This can sound quite abstract and unattainable. This process is broken down into pragmatic and practical exercises and insightful reflections that can be implemented in life and in the classroom *tomorrow.*

The Plan for Practical Passion

. . . Passion is not just a personality trait that some people have and others lack, but rather something discoverable, teachable, and reproducible, even when the regularities of school life gang up against it.

ROBERT FRIED, 1995, p. 6

This section covers two complimentary approaches to bringing joy and passion into teaching and learning. First are the four quests, which are individual, reflective processes designed to guide teachers in energizing curriculum by infusing the classroom with joy and passion. Second, the creation of passionate pedagogue circles, collaborative processes, designed to help teachers and learners discover and/or recover those powerful human connections that are at the heart of schooling. All activities connect to the spiral of learning and link to concepts presented previously in the book.

A word of caution before beginning: To teach with passion, it is necessary to have a desire for this change in life and in teaching. To risk is essential: to risk the joy and heartbreak that come with creating a life and teaching career full of passion, in all of its gorgeous messiness. On the following pages, theory becomes action as we turn passion into a concrete pedagogical plan.

If the will is not there the quests and the circles are a waste of time. If the aspiration is there, though, the quests and the circles provide a way to tap passion and use it as a vehicle for a deeper and more joyful approach to pedagogy.

Work is love made visible.

KAHLIL GIBRAN

A Life Transformed

Sally came to one of our workshops in a funk. Life wasn't bad, teaching wasn't bad, but she felt she was going through the motions instead of *living* life. We saw this in her, though she didn't seem that aware of her situation herself. She had experienced this state of uninspired living for so long that she didn't appear to even be aware of how flat her life had become. Slowly, throughout the course of the day, we witnessed her dawning realization that life could be more and better than she had understood.

As Sally worked through the exercises and heard other teachers' stories of passion, she blossomed before our eyes. At the workshop's beginning, she entered the room very politely and smiling, but subdued. As the day progressed, her eyes lit up and began to twinkle, her polite smile became an infectious laugh, and she radiated an energy of excitement and hope. We watched the shift take place as she began to think with her heart instead of her mind. The mind does have a place in our quest, ". . . but as the servant of your heart, not as its master" (Beck, 2001, p. 112).

Sally drew the whole class into her excitement as she held her action plan in hand, animatedly describing her curriculum plans for the upcoming year. By the end of the day she stood straighter, looked people directly in the eye more, and carried herself with a confident and upbeat ease. She glowed with an inner joy.

The object of this chapter is to create a personal plan toward passionate pedagogy. Far from being a gift some people are lucky enough to be born with while others are not, to teach passionately is available to all.

Goals

To teach with passion, our life must be grounded in passion. Individual passions are the axis around which the spokes of the rest of our life turns. This is not to say we base life on what we feel we *should* be passionate about or we're *supposed* to be passionate about. Here we are going to explore genuine passions, be it comic books, impractical shoes, fishing, or funny-faced dogs. While this plan is very practical, passions frequently are not. Here we will not only respect that but also encourage it and have some fun. Teaching infused with passion makes learning more stimulating and fun for both teacher and learner.

Passionate teaching encourages relationships within the classroom to thrive. Teacher–student, parent–teacher, and student–student relationships grow to be grounded in mutual respect in the pursuit of learning and discovery. Teaching and learning turn out to be journeys to be explored.

Returning to the metaphor of the spiral, another loop of the journey winds through this section. This loop is divided into four main segments for further exploration: first, *identification* of personal goals for teaching and learning; second, *prioritization* of actions working toward the goals deemed most important; third, *application* of these ideas in the classroom; and fourth, a *completion* of the original goal set. The following pragmatic exercises lead from goal identification to how concise actions can accomplish these ideals. (See Figure 9.1.)

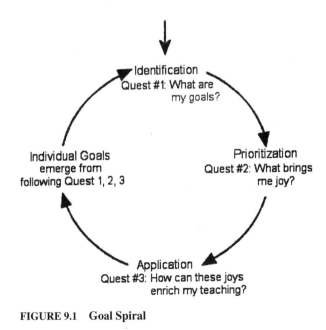

FIGURE 9.1   Goal Spiral

Quests

> First Quest—Identification: What are my goals? How do I envision the teaching and learning environment for my classroom?

First, we'll first focus on the teaching and learning experience you would like to create in the classroom. We're going to do some dreaming here. Imagine yourself in your ideal world where you have absolute control over your teaching environment. You control class size, you control the curriculum, and you control the literature—we're dreaming here! Don't hold yourself back from dreaming because a little voice says in your head, "Oh, my principal would never allow that" or "Well, maybe in my dream world, but there's no way this could ever happen in the real world." Push those voices aside just for now. Goal and dream making are the first step in creating our world. Use your imagination. What would you create?

Cluster Exercise: On a blank sheet of paper write "teaching and learning experience" in the middle of the page and then draw a circle around it (see Figure 9.2). The key to this exercise is not to overthink but to write and get ideas down on paper as quickly as possible. Think of your own expectations of the ideal atmosphere surrounding teaching and learning experiences for you and your students. Be wild, be crazy, dream! Whatever you do, don't edit yourself at this stage. Don't trip the baby who's trying to walk! Let those dreams out. Let them fly!

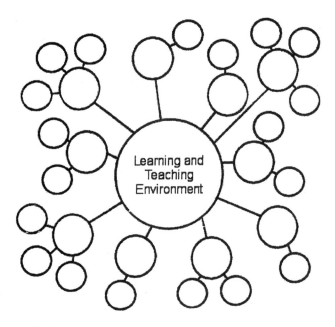

FIGURE 9.2 Teaching and Learning Cluster Exercise

As ideas come into your head of what you would like to create in your classroom, write these ideas down as quickly as you can, drawing a circle around each and then connecting it to the whole with a line. Keep your pen moving. Don't allow yourself to edit your thoughts or kill off your dreams as they're taking shape. Don't stop writing until you have added at least 10 clusters of ideas surrounding the main idea.

After you've finished writing, and you have at least 10 secondary idea clusters, review your clusters briefly. An organic organization will begin to take form in your mind as you muse on what you wrote. As this inherent organization begins to form, with the cluster in sight, begin to write these thoughts down essay style in the order they come. Again, write quickly without putting too much thought into the organization or what you write. If you slow down or begin to overthink the content or organization, the flow of ideas slows. Write quickly and easily.

Congratulations! You now have tangible goals of the teaching and learning environment you would like to create. The act of recognizing, writing, and organizing these goals has already alerted your mind to be aware of actions and possibilities that will bring these goals about. Goethe reminds us, "Whatever you think you can do, begin it, because action has magic, grace, and power in it."

Second Quest—Prioritization: What brings me joy? What am I passionate about?

To pursue pedagogical passion is to articulate its importance in life. Many of us consistently block out inner joy from our lives because "we don't have time." We ignore our inner joys for so long that when the time finally comes to identify what brings passion to life, we are left with a blank stare, literally unable to remember. We do not allow ourselves these joys because we falsely deem them unproductive. We successfully callous ourselves from our own feelings, indeed, from our souls' life directions. This illusion of a lack of productivity could not be more false. It is in the act of listening and pursuing our passions that we are most productive.

Treasure Map Exercise: Write down in a list as many things as you can think of that make you happy. Anything, *anything!* Don't hold back. Don't think. For heaven's sake, don't be practical! Go for it, let your mind go where it will and don't censor, just write. What brought you joy as a child? Close your eyes and let your mind wander—what activities, what colors, what experiences, what textures, sounds, and smells make you feel peaceful?

If it has been a while since you've let yourself entertain these thoughts, you may only come up with one or two—as each of us did when we first did this. Now, that's a sobering thought, isn't it? The harder it is for you to think of things in life that bring you joy, the more you need to do them. Two years ago when Dawn did this for the first time, the only joyous thing she could think of was reading. Clearly, it had been a while since she'd focused on basing her profession on what brings her joy. After three years of centering her life on joy, here is a tiny portion of her current list: bright, vibrant colors, the desert, sunsets, books, running, good friends, family, textures, sunlight, jelly beans, Mexican food, Celtic music, travel books, wildflowers, words, fabric, laughter, sunshine yellow, blue doors, good coffee, and saguaro cacti. It is no coincidence that during these same three years, her professional life bloomed.

Ready? Write. (See Figure 9.3).

Look at your completed list. Before you lies your own personal treasure map. From here we will salvage those passions ignored due to the busyness of life, studies, families, and jobs. Think of your list as a trove of treasure full of clues that we shall sift through in the next exercise.

Third Quest—Application: How can these joys enrich my teaching?

Infusing your days with passion enriches life. Colors become brighter, textures become richer, and life is expanded. The little nuances and subtleties of life that make up our days gain significance that might otherwise have been missed. In today's current exhausting political climate in education, as teachers we need to find our grounding, our center to strengthen ourselves personally, as well as professionally. The strength and wisdom gathered from this sense of center, of strength, bring a steadiness to the day. We gain strength from within and go forth into the hectic giving of our days.

How do we do this in a pragmatic way? There are two main ways: (a) to make time, and (b) to bring joyful activities into the class.

First, we need to commit to make time for our personal passions outside of the school. Their inclusion in our life *outside* of school energizes and fortifies us *inside*

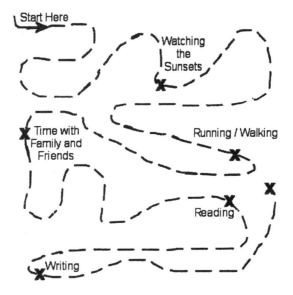

FIGURE 9.3   Treasure Map

of school. One teacher we know rises at 4:00 A.M. to write in her journal, another to work on his current watercolor painting. It is about making time to go for a good run even if the house is a disaster, getting out on the mountain bike sitting dusty in the garage, or getting together with friends you have been too busy to see. Even if it is only 15 minutes a day, the time is well spent. To consistently deny yourself the passions that bring you joy and energy is the surest road to fatigue and burnout. In simpler terms, as far as productivity, you're shooting yourself in the foot.

"What is the difference between an obsession and passion?" Norton (1996) asked the class in a recent writing workshop. People voiced a variety of thoughts. Our own interpretation is that a passion enriches life and an obsession detracts from it. There are those activities that walk a fine line, however. For Dawn and Joan, writing would be one—not that it detracts from our lives but because it so dominates our thoughts and actions. But it clearly makes our lives better. Perhaps for those activities that walk a fine line, instead of saying "We're obsessed!" we might change our terminology and say, "We're impassioned!"

Remember the teacher in the beginning of this book who missed watching the sunsets? By taking time each day to watch the sunsets, to revel in the joy and peace that it brings, she directly influences her teaching. If we are fulfilled, our teaching is better. Beck (2001) applies two rules to charting a course for the passionate life intended for us.

> Rule 1: If it brings you joy, do it.

> Rule 2: No really, if it brings you joy, do it. (p. 208)

Try it. We think you will be amazed. Since reorganizing our thoughts and actions around our passions and joys, both professional and personal magic has come tumbling into our lives in ways it never did before.

Commitment Exercise (Part One): Bring out your treasure map. Quickly, scrolling down with your eyes, pick out three passions you have that you have not been including in your life lately. Three passions that are out of doors, quiet and reflective, artistic, whatever calls to you. Now fill in these three passions in Figure 9.4.

The second way to energize teaching is to bring elements of joyful activities into the classroom. When we bring our passions into the classroom, our enthusiasm is infectious. Students intuit this.

Commitment Exercise (Part Two): Now, we expand on bringing your passions into the classroom to enrich teaching and learning. At the end of this quest you will have a pragmatic and surprisingly concise blueprint how to energize yourself, your teaching, and your students. We love what we teach when we teach what we love.

Refer to your treasure map. Read it quickly through once more. Certain words inherently carry an extra charge of energy for you. Circle those words quickly and move on until you have read to the bottom of the list. Write those words in the column on the left hand side of the page under *Passions.*

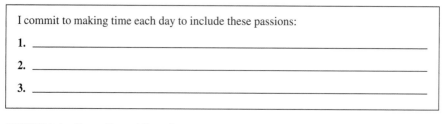

I commit to making time each day to include these passions:

1. _____

2. _____

3. _____

FIGURE 9.4 Commitment Exercise

Now, think through the curriculum you're going to cover in the next week, month, or semester. Not the details, rather the main themes you've planned. Write those down on the right side of the page under *Curriculum.* For example, some of Dawn's passions include colors, textures, wildflowers, and blue doors. The curriculum she needs to cover includes social studies (the history of California), language arts, and spelling. (See Figure 9.5.)

Now, complete a cluster exercise for each curriculum theme. Place the curriculum topic in the center circle. Surround this circle with connecting circles with one of your chosen passions in each circle. Then let your mind fly. What ideas come to you as you link your curriculum and passions in your mind? As these ideas start flowing, continue to cluster around each of the passion circles. Soon, you'll have to add other passion circles to complete your ideas, and you will have ideas about how you'll impassion your curriculum clustered all over the page. Complete each curriculum/passion cluster in one sitting. At the end of this exercise, you will have specific ideas linking your passions to each curricular area. (See Figure 9.6.)

You can also reverse this process to stimulate ideas of connecting curriculum to passions. Place your passion in the center circle and your curriculum in the sur-

Passions	**Curriculum**
Colors	Social Studies (History of California)
Textures	Language Arts
Wildflowers	Spelling
Blue Doors	_____
_____	_____
_____	_____
_____	_____
_____	_____

FIGURE 9.5 Commitment Exercise

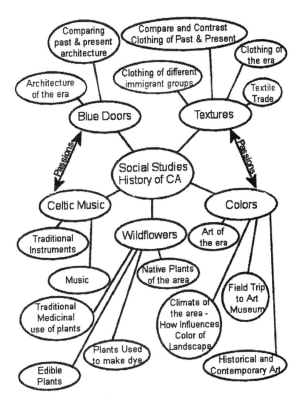

FIGURE 9.6   Cluster Exercise, Dawn's Example

rounding circles and start clustering. Soon, you will have pages filled with ideas. (See Figure 9.7.)

> Fourth Quest—Return to Goals: How can I implement more change toward my vision of teaching and learning?

Plans and dreams remain useless until we incorporate them into our lives in practical ways. What good are all of these wonderful ideas on how to infuse your teaching with passion if they stay clustered on the piece of paper, tucked in some dark drawer somewhere? Not one bit of good at all. In the fourth quest, you will focus on turning those great ideas into reality.

Scheduling Exercise: In the following exercise, you will create a practical and usable schedule of how to implement your passions into current curriculum plans. Lay out all of your clusters before you. Now, using the outline of the weekly and monthly schedule in Figure 9.8, schedule your upcoming academic topics and corresponding curriculum from the cluster exercise.

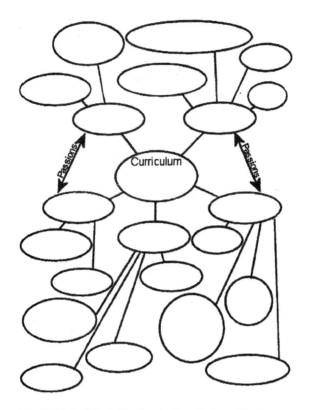

FIGURE 9.7   Blank Passion to Curriculum Cluster

Congratulations! You have just created your own action plan for passionate ped-agogy. Hopefully, we never fully attain our goals, because as we move along the spiral our hopes, dreams, and goals continue to shift and grow as we do. As one goal is being accomplished, another goal is in its early stages. Optimistically, the clusters and cur-riculum schedule will be constantly in motion, being revised, changed, and expanded.

Passionate Pedagogue Circles

A passionate teacher is a teacher who breaks out of the isolation of a
classroom, who refuses to submit to apathy or cynicism.

ROBERT FRIED, 1995, p. 1

In addition to the individual quests, collaborative passionate pedagogue circles call us into a community where we draw strength, courage, and love from other teachers and learners. Now, more than ever, we need this. Whereas graduate classes, credentialing

	Month	Month	Month	Month	Month	Month
Week						
Week						
Week						
Week						
Week						

FIGURE 9.8   Blank Curriculum Schedule

processes, and inservicing used to be a place of continuing the cycle of learning about pedagogy, today, in our experiences, professional development has become a place of anxious administrators and tired, frantic teachers. We marvel at how it has affected our own professional work in the last few years. Now, when educators come together, we need each other. We need a safe haven. The quests and passionate pedagogue circles are designed to heal and strengthen, as we continue to challenge injustice.

Passionate pedagogue circles are collaborative groups of pedagogues (teachers and/or learners) who come together to infuse passion into the teaching and learning processes. These are groups of educators and community members who have made that initial, challenging decision: They want to find their passion and bring that joy to the classroom. These groups are founded on the assumption that we cannot always control the outside forces in our environment, but we can individually and collaboratively influence how we live, learn, and teach. As the whole is greater than the sum of its parts, the goal is to tap into the combined inner strength of each person to enhance each member and the group.

Guidelines for Passionate Pedagogue Circles

- The primary purpose is to mutually support one another in pursuit of passionate living and teaching.
- How to begin: Form a group of people interested in impassioning their lives and teaching. Although any size works, a group of eight people seems to work well.

The group is small enough to be intimate and large enough to stimulate discussion. A wide variety of life experiences among the group works well. The most positive and powerful groups are those full of people who are independently passionate and interested in being around others who have a love of ideas. When forming the group, look for positive people interested in life, ideas, and teaching. Stay away from those people who ooze bitterness.

- We cannot stress enough: This is *not* the appropriate place to invite the teachers on your staff who rarely have a good word to say about anything. Although you might want them to be inspired, chances are they'll just poison the atmosphere for the rest of the group.
- Initial decisions to be made by the group: where and when to meet. In addition, during the formation of the group, we recommend that the group discuss options for the group's discussion format.
- Possible format and discussion ideas: Members share their own experiences with passion in life and in schools, discuss ideas how to enrich curriculum, discuss current frustrations and possible ways of handling them, encourage and strengthen one another in individual pursuits and academic life, or talk about relevant books and their ideas.

As you begin your own individual quests and join with others in passionate pedagogue circles, you create and control your own future in the classroom.

Praxis: Let the Magic Begin

> *We love because it is the only true adventure.*
>
> NIKKI GIOVANNI

When we take the steps toward impassioning our teaching and our lives, magic follows. Frequently this magic comes in forms we could not have imagined. Sometimes we are inspired to take drastic actions to spur the magic forward, as in the case of the next teacher who has taught for 23 years:

> Teaching is fascinating, but it can also get to you. One year, not too long ago, I felt my enthusiasm withering. Everything seemed all right, but I felt myself getting stale. So I did something absolutely crazy—I opened up the file cabinet and threw out all my files! All of them—the old lesson plans, the lectures, the course materials. I made myself start over. (Fried, 1995, p. 34)

The teacher goes on to describe how scary and invigorating this action was for her and how it enriched and energized her teaching enormously.

We pass this magic on to students in often unimagined ways. Zack, a teacher we know, learned how his passionate teaching influenced one student. Zack taught ninth-grade English in a small town, in an albeit misguided state close to our hearts. As part of the curriculum, his class was reading George Orwell's *Animal Farm* and *1984*. The subject of existentialism was raised in class one day.

"Existentialists believe that much of life is unfathomable, not real, including God. To existentialists, God is kind of like the whole Santa Claus thing. People are telling you all along that he's real, and then you find out he's not."

Students asked questions and explored the concept of existentialism in a stimulating discussion throughout the rest of class. That night, Zack received a call that an emergency school board meeting had been convened, and he was to go the meeting immediately. There it was announced to him that he had been teaching the class that God did not exist. He was then prohibited from teaching anything else from *Animal Farm* and *1984*. The principal greeted him the next day by taking away all copies of those books and replacing them with a standardized text, telling him explicitly not to deviate from that text.

After school, Zack drove 90 miles to buy copies of *Animal Farm* and *1984*. The class continued to read and discuss the books for the next two weeks, until the administration discovered what he had done. He was asked to resign immediately. He resigned that day and never saw any of those students again.

Ten years passed. One day Zack received a call out of the blue from one of his previous students' siblings, requesting his address. A college graduation announcement arrived in the mail. Zack attended his former student's college graduation. This student bounded up to him after the ceremony and greeted him, "You are the reason I went to college and I am graduating!" He produced his master's thesis, written on *Animal Farm*. As teachers, we seldom know when or how magical moments happen in class. Teaching with passion increases their occurrence exponentially.

We can govern or we can lead. Right now the national trend is an imposed governing of teachers, curriculum, and students. Through the logistic governing of curriculum, the intention is not only to govern people but to govern thought as well. We suggest that rather than governing we *lead*.

We hoped to include Maya Angelou's reflection, "The future was plump with promise," but we sadly couldn't put it as a header. We don't know what the future will bring. Presently, we think of Tove Skutnabb-Kangas's words in her championship of linguistic human rights and ecological health, "I'm a pessimist who works optimistically."

The truth: We don't know the future. However, we do have a vision of how we see the future of education, based on our present and past experience. To ground the conversation in reality, we will focus the discussion on the type of teaching and learning we envision for Dawn's three children and Joan's four grandchildren. Our vision explores an early ideal for education and a sobering modern reflection. First, a quotation from Ralph Waldo Emerson (1884), reminding us of the possibilities in education.

> Education is so cold, so hopeless a sound. A treatise on education, a convention for education, a lecture, a system, affects us with slight paralysis and a certain yawning of the jaws . . . Education should be as broad as a [sic] person. Whatever elements are in him/her that should foster and demonstrate. If he be dexterous, his tuition should make it appear; if he/she be capable of dividing [people] by the trenchant sword of his/her

thought, education should unsheathe and sharpen it; if he/she is one to cement society by his/her all-reconciling affinities, oh! Hasten their action! If he/she is jovial, he he/she is mercurial, he, she is great hearted, a cunning artificer, a strong commander, a potent ally, ingenious, useful, elegant, witty, prophet, diviner—society has need of all these. The imagination must be addressed. (p. 133)

Over a century ago, one of the main philosophical thinkers of the day promoted the notion that education should ideally bring out individual strengths and foster student imagination. Presently, our national educational policy demands students stay within the confines of the limited academic scope. Teachers are also being required to walk a narrow predetermined path, which has sent teacher morale plummeting throughout the United States.

Emerson guides our search for answers to the questions: "So, how do we last in education and maintain our passion?" and "What do we visualize for the future?" Emerson's words illustrate the vital role in education of recognizing and encouraging students' natural strengths through the curriculum. Emerson wrote, "The imagination of each is addressed." One teacher described to us an example of what addressing the imagination of each looks like in the present:

I had just started teaching in a tough inner-city school in Dallas. Sam's Club donated a computer to our school in 1992. This was just the beginning of the big computer boom. This was the first and only computer on our campus. The principal called us to his office and asked who wanted the computer. Forty teachers all excitedly raised their hands, calling, "I do! I do!" The principal then asked who knew how to turn on and use a computer. I was the only person on the staff who did, and so I got the computer.

The next day a kid I had never seen before walked into my room and sat down. It was the eighth week of school, and this was the first time I'd seen him.

"May I help you?" I asked.

"I am Paul," he replied. He sat down without making eye contact.

Fifteen minutes later he got up to leave.

"You'll need a hall pass, Paul."

"Up yours," he replied and he walked out.

The next day Paul showed up again and sat down in his seat, still not making eye contact or acknowledging anyone around him.

"What's that?" he interrupted my lesson halfway through class.

"It's a computer, Paul."

"I know what it is. Can I play on it?"

"Sure," I said. Paul played on the computer for the rest of the day.

The next day Paul showed up again and went directly to the computer.

"Paul, you can use that computer, but you've got to finish your work first." Paul looked at the assignment written on the board, sat down, and completed it in 10 minutes. I thought for sure it would be a mess, but it was perfect, absolutely perfect. This became our routine. Paul came, finished what took the other students hours in a matter of minutes and spent the rest of the day on the computer. By now, he was teaching other kids how to use it.

One day I got called into the principal's office.

"I understand Paul has been in your classroom all day these past weeks."

"Well, yes, he's actually completing his work and teaching the other students all about the computer." The principal reached down and picked up a stack of textbooks from under his desk.

"Here are the texts and assignments for all his other classes. See that he does his work."

The rest of the school year Paul came to my class. Every morning he finished his work for the day in all of the subjects. It was always perfect. He was brilliant. Then he spent the rest of the day on the computer in my class.

Are we advocating anarchy in the classroom? Of course not. What we do advocate is the acknowledgment that human beings are unique! Human beings learn in endlessly different ways. Because this teacher understood that, Paul not only attended school every day and completed all of his work, but he also interacted in a positive manner with other students in an area in which he was the expert. U.S. schools increasingly acknowledge fewer and fewer of the variety of ways people learn.

Cole (2002) writes of ways of addressing students' individual imaginations and the amazing results when teachers celebrate little things and look for the "good stuff." She posits that the mere holding of a teaching certificate implies a level of caring and kindness.

Why not invite the kids into the kindness circle, as well? Take five minutes now and then to invite students to trade papers with someone and then find every good thing they can about that person's response. They can jot these brief compliments on a sticky note that can be placed atop the paper. I model it first and call it "Lookin' for the good stuff." Wouldn't it be great if this perspective carried over into other facets of life as well? Famous authors and artists tell of teachers they had who saw the good stuff in them when they could not see it in themselves (Cole, 2002, p. 69).

Addressing each individual's imagination, as Cole describes, is becoming more and more difficult in today's schools. Students are increasingly viewed from a deterministic, one-size-fits-all perspective. This philosophy is the foundation for contemporary curriculum and standards, addressing the imaginations of very few. It is becoming harder and harder for stories like the previous one to happen.

So how do we draw from Emerson's envisioned education and maintain our passion? Passion resides within. It is something so personal and internal that nobody can take it away without our consent. It is possible to feel passion and teach passionately amidst oppression and discouragement. Despite external oppression, we can maintain our passion in our area of knowledge. We can still be gripped by a dedication to linguistic human rights, fascinated by Shakespeare's prose and Mark Twain's insights, thrilled with geometry and algebraic equations, intrigued by world history and government, and captured with scientific experimentation and discoveries. In short, we look within to our own personal passions and parlay those into our teaching even in the most discouraging of atmospheres. It is possible.

Paulo Freire continued to teach Brazilian peasants to read until he was exiled from his country by the ruling elite, who did not want those peasants becoming literate and empowered. He continued to work toward literacy for all from other parts of the world, including the United States, before returning years later to become the minister of education for Brazil.

We draw strength from Emerson's vision about what education *can* be to create this reality as much as possible for students and ourselves. We maintain this vision of the possibilities in an effort to transform.

The present leads us to the future. As stated earlier, we ground our discussion for the future in our hopes of what we visualize for Dawn's three children and Joan's four grandchildren. We hark back to Emerson's words, as we hear his words of years ago calling us to action today: Hasten, he tells us. If she is jovial, if he is mercurial, if he is great hearted, if she is a cunning artificer, if they be strong commanders, potent allies, ingenious, useful, elegant, witty, prophet, diviner—society has need of all these. The imagination must be addressed.

This is what we wish for these four children we love, each unique and very different from the others. We envision a future where their natural strengths are recognized and encouraged, not left to decay unacknowledged because they are too busy studying for standardized tests.

To think all students learn in the same way is patently absurd! To treat all students the same is to provide *in*equality in education. This one-size-fits-all approach denies the learning styles, the histories, and the experiences of young people.

We envision a future in education where teachers have the deserved freedom and responsibility to treat each student as the individual he or she is, tailoring instruction to each one's needs. We envision a future where teachers and students still dream, reach for the clouds, and let their imagination carry them further along their educational paths. We envision a future where this dreaming and learning need not be covert but an honored aspect of education. We envision students being excited about their daily learning and discoveries. We want their inherent strengths and interests to be fostered and honored. We want them to be treated with the kindness, respect, and high expectations they deserve: to interact with teachers who are passionate about their fields of expertise, who are constantly seeking to enrich their own lives and knowledge themselves, to feel as passionately about learning as we do, to feel comfortable and at ease in the classroom, to feel they belong, to discuss issues of social justice in real contexts, to learn to think, analyze, and feel, not merely memorize and regurgitate information. We want them to be loved.

Going with the Spiral

So how do these words of wisdom inform our understanding of how teachers last in education and maintain passion?

We draw courage and passion from those who have gone before us. In the big picture of education, we are just a tiny speck. We try to see the big picture. At our computers, surrounded by our books, we think of all the work that others have done and how our lives are enriched because of their contributions. They have worked, and we have benefited.

Preparing to care (Noddings, 1992) can feel like the most vulnerable step of the process. In addition, teachers do not have the safety of caring from a distance. For teachers, the caring is up close and personal, minute by minute, day by day. Placing caring at the core of each day challenges us to great courage and great love. Love can be lived and expressed in a multitude of ways. It is often the most lasting legacy a teacher can share, and it is the greatest gift a student receives.

Love—that is it. Love is how educators last and stay connected to their own inner passion. We can never forget Paulo Freire speaking so openly of the place of love in learning. We remember that "human relations are at the heart of schooling" (Cummins, 2001, p. 1). Sonia Nieto so clearly writes of the political complexities of the world that discourage and defeat committed teachers. She acknowledges our experiences when she writes, "What happens in classrooms is first and foremost about personal and collective connections that exist among the individuals who inhabit those spaces" (Nieto, 1999, p. 130).

We finally make peace with the fact that we can each fight injustices in our own way and in our own context, if we are linked by love. Ask any adult who their favorite teacher was and then ask them why. Soon you will hear a story of pedagogical passion infusing teaching and learning with love. We also draw love and joy from the students we work with every day. They, too, live complex and demanding lives in their own way. How can we not be enriched? Cynicism is a luxury that we in education cannot afford.

Let's go back to the petroglyphs of spirals etched into cliffs in New Mexico (Figure 9.9). We stand again on the cliff overlooking a valley studded with junipers

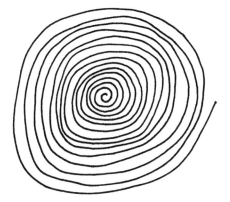

FIGURE 9.9   A Petroglyph Spiral

and piñon trees below. We look at the spirals carved into the cliffs thousands of years ago. We complete another loop of each of our individual spirals of life. We've explored various perspectives and ideas, each of us bringing our own experiences to our understandings. Our intention with this book is to bring new perspectives and paradigms to the field of education. We wish you the best in your continued journey.

Love in the classroom does not mean we learn less; rather, it opens each of us to our full potential. Love opens the door (even the classroom one) to more, not less. Love is the legacy that lasts.

BIBLIOGRAPHY

Ada, A. F. (2003). *A Magical Encounter: Latino Children's Literature in the Classroom.* Boston: Allyn and Bacon.

Ada, A. F., & Campoy, F. I. (2003). *Authors in the classroom: Transformative education for teachers, students, and families.* Boston: Allyn and Bacon.

American Educational Research Association. (2002). Societies raise concerns about document removal from U.S. Department of Education web site. Retrieved November 22, 2002, from www.aera.net/communications/news/021121.htm.

Astin, A. W., & Astin, H. S. (1999, November). *Meaning and spirituality in the lives of college faculty: A study of values, authenticity, and stress.* Los Angeles: Higher Education Research Institute University of California, Los Angeles.

Bartolomé, L. (2000). Effective transition strategies: Are we asking the right questions. In J. V. a. R. A. DeVillar (Ed.), *The power of two languages 2000: Effective dual-language use across the curriculum* (pp. 142–154). New York: McGraw-Hill School Division.

Bartolomé, L. I. (1994). Beyond the methods fetish: Toward a humanizing pedagogy. *Harvard Educational Review, 64,* 173–194.

Beck, M. (2001). *Finding your own north star: Claiming the life you were meant to live.* New York: Three Rivers Press.

Berends, P. (1983). *Whole child/whole parent.* New York: Harper & Row.

Betances, S. (1986, Winter). My people made it without bilingual education: What's wrong with your people? *The Journal of California School Boards, 44*(7), 14–16.

Bolman, L. G., & Deal, T. E. (2001). *Leading with soul: An uncommon journey of spirit.* San Francisco: Jossey-Bass.

Bracey, G. (2002a). The 12th Bracey report on the condition of education. *Phi Delta Kappan,* 135–150.

Bracey, G. (2002b). *The war against America's public schools: Privatizing schools, commercializing education.* Boston: Allyn and Bacon.

Burke, J. (2002). This is where teaching gets read. In S. Intrator (Ed.), *Stories of the courage to teach: Honoring the treacher's heart* (pp. 13–16). San Francisco: Jossey-Bass.

California Department of Education (CDE). (1995). *Educational demographics unit. Language census report for California public schools.* Sacramento: Author.

Calkins, L., & Bellino, L. (1997). *Raising lifelong learners: A parent's guide.* Cambridge, MA: Perseus Books.

Cambourne, B., & Turbill, J. (1999). Teaching reading. In J. Turbill, A. Butler, B. Cambourne, & G. Langston (Eds.), *Literacy and learning: Readings* (pp. 99–103). Newark, NY: Wayne Finger Lakes Board of Cooperative Education Services.

Cameron, J. (1992). *The artist's way: A spiritual path to higher creativity.* New York: Jeremy P. Tarcher/Putnum.

Chambers, J., & Perrish, T. (1992). *Meeting the challenge of diversity: An evaluation of programs for pupils with limited proficiency in English. Vol. IV, cost of programs and services for LEP students.* Berkley, CA: BW Associates.

Cho, G., & Krashen, S. (2000). The role of voluntary factors in heritage language development: How speakers can develop the heritage language on their own. *ITL: Review of Applied Linguistics,* 127–128, 127–140.

Chomsky, H. (1965). *Aspects of the theory of syntax.* Cambridge, MA: MIT Press.

Chopra, D. (1997). *The seven spiritual laws for parenting.* New York: Harmony Books.

Codell, E. R. (2001). *Educating Esmé: Diary of a teacher's first year.* Chapel Hill, NC: Algonquin Books of Chapel Hill.

Cole, A. D. (2002). *Better answers: Written performance that looks good and sounds smart.* Portland, ME: Stenhouse Publishers.

Coles, G. (2000). *Misreading reading: The bad science that hurts children.* Portsmouth, NH: Heinemann.

Coles, R. (1990). *The spiritual life of children.* Boston: Houghton Mifflin.

Collier, V. P., & Thomas, W. P. (1989). How quickly can immigrants become proficient in school English? *Journal of Education Issues of Language Minority Students, 5,* 26–39.

Colvin, R. L. (2002, May 10). *The nation; U.S. history barely passed; Education: High school seniors can't say what happened when. Earlier grades fare a little better. Los Angeles Times.* Retrieved October 3, 2002, from www.rohan.sdsu.edu/~rgibson/ushistorytests.html.

Cooper, H., Nye, B., Charlton, K., Lindsay, J., & Greathouse, S. (1996). The effects of summer vacation on achievement test scores: A narrative and meta-analytic review. *Review of Educational Research, 66*(3), 227–268.

Crawford, J. (1997). *Ten common fallacies about bilingual education.* Retrieved February 26, 2003, from www.cal.org/ericc11/digest/crawford01.html.

Cuban, L. (1993). *How teachers taught: Constancy and change in American classrooms,1880–1990* (2nd ed.). New York: Teachers College Press.

Cubberley, J. (1919). *Public school administration in United States.* Boston: Houghton Mifflin.

Cummins, J. (1992). Bilingual education and English immersion: The Ramírez Report in theoretical perspective. *Bilingual Research Journal, 16,* 91–104.

Cummins, J. (2000a). Biliteracy, empowerment, and transformative pedagogy. In J. V. Tinajero & R. A. DeVillar (Eds.), *The power of two languages 2000: Effective dual-language use across the curriculum* (pp. 9–19). New York: McGraw-Hill School Division.

Cummins, J. (2000b). *Language, power, and pedagogy: Bilingual children in the crossfire* (Vol. 23). Tonawanda, NY: Multilingual Matters Ltd.

Cummins, J. (2001). *Negotiating identities: Education for empowerment in a diverse society* (2nd ed.). Ontario, CA: California Association for Bilingual Education (CABE).

Cummins, J., & Sayers, D. (1995). *Brave new schools: Challenging cultural illiteracy.* New York: St. Martin's Press.

Dart, J. (2002, October 23–November 5). *Christian Century,* 15.

Dewey, J. (1916). *Democracy and education.* New York: Macmillan.

Dillard, A. (1989). *The writing life.* New York: Harper Perennial.

Draper, S. M. (2001). *Not quite burned out: But, crispy around the edges.* Portsmouth, NH: Heinemann.

Dunham, L. (2001). *Graceful living: Your faith, values, and money in changing times.* Indianapolis: Ecumenical Stewardship Center (ESC).

Dunkel, P. (1990). Implications of the CAI effectiveness research for limited-English-proficient learners. *Computers in the Schools, 7,* 31–52.

Dyson, A. (1993). *Social worlds of children learning to write in an urban primary school.* New York: Teachers College Press.

Edelsky, C. (1994). Education for democracy. *Language Arts, 71,* 252–257.

Edelsky, C., Altwerger, B., & Flores, B. (1991). *Whole language: What's the difference?* Portsmouth, NH: Heinemann.

Emerson, R. W. (1884). *Lectures and biographical sketches.* Cambridge, MA: Riverside.

Enright, D. S., & McClosky, M. L. (1998). *Integrating English reading.* Boston: Addision-Wesley.

Evans, K. (2002). *Accounting for conflicting mental models of communication in student–teacher interaction: An activity theory analysis,* unpublished dissertation.

Evans, K. (2003). Accounting for conflicting mental models of communication in student-teacher Interaction: An activity theory Analysis. In C. Bazerman and D. Russell (Eds.), *Writing selves/Writing societies: Research from activity perspectives. Perspectives on writing.* Fort Collins, CO: The WAC Clearinghouse and Mind, Culture, and Activity, http://wac.colostate.edu/books/selves_societies.

Fox, M. (2001). *Reading magic: Why reading aloud to our children will change their lives forever.* New York: Harvest Original.

Fraas, C. (2003). *AFT letter to Capitol Hill regarding the Higher Education Act.* Retrieved January 7, 2003, from http://cateweb.org.

Freeman, Y., & Freeman, D. (1994). *Between worlds: Access to second language acquisition.* Portsmouth, NH: Heinamann.

Freire, P. (1974). *Pedagogy of the oppressed.* New York: The Continuum Publishing Corporation.

Freire, P. (1987). Letter to North-American teachers. In I. Shor (Ed.), *Freire for the classroom* (pp. 211–214). Portsmouth, NH: Boynton/Cook.

Freire, P. (1993). Teaching and learning. Paper presented at the annual convention of California Association of Bilingual Education (CABE), Los Angeles, CA.

Freire, P., & Macedo, D. (1987). *Literacy: Reading the word and the world.* South Hadley, MA: Bergin & Garvey Publishers, Inc.

Fried, R. L. (1995). *The Passionate teacher: A practical guide.* Boston: Beacon Press.

Fuchs, N. (1996). *Our share of night, our share of morning: Parenting as a spiritual journey.* San Francisco: HarperCollins.

Goldberg, N. (1990). *Wild mind: Living the writer's life.* New York: Bantam.

González, N. (2001). *I am my language: Discourse of women and children in the borderlands.* Tucson, AZ: The University of Arizona Press.

Good, H. (2002, May 8). *The age of impatience. Education Week.* Retrieved May 26, 2002, from www.edweek.org/edweek.org/ew/newstory.cfm?slug=34good.h21.

Goodall, J. (1999). *Reason for hope, a spiritual journey.* New York: Warner Books.

Goodlad, J. I. (1984). *A place called school: Prospects for the future.* New York: McGraw-Hill.

Goodman, K. S., Bridges Bird, L., & Goodman, Y. M. (1991). *The whole language catalog.* Santa Rosa, CA: American School Publishers.

Greene, J. (1998, March 2). *A meta-analysis of the effectiveness of bilingual education.* Retrieved July 26, 2001, from http://pespmcl.vub.ac.be/MENIN.html.

Gurian, M., Henley, P., & Trueman, T. (2001). *Boys and girls learn differently! A guide for teachers and parents.* San Francisco: Jossey-Bass/Wiley.

Herbert, B. (2003, March 6). The war on schools. *New York Times.*

Hillman, J. (1996). *The soul's code: In search of character and calling.* New York: Random House.

hooks, b. (1994). *Teaching to transgress: Education as the practice of freedom.* New York: Routledge.

hooks, b. (1999). Embracing freedom: Spirituality and liberation. In S. Glazer (Ed.), *The heart of learning: Spirituality in education* (pp. 113–130). New York: Jeremy P. Tarcher/Putnam.

Hopstock, P. Bucaro, B., Fleischman, H. L., Zehler, A. M., & Eu, H. (1993). Descriptive study of services to limited English proficient students. Arlington, VA: Development Associates.

Intrator, S. (2002). *Stories of the courage to teach: Honoring the teacher's heart.* San Francisco: Jossey-Bass.

Jalongo, M. R. (2003). *Early childhood: Language arts* (3rd ed.). Boston: Allyn and Bacon.

Johns, J. L. (December 2002/January 2003). Libraries: Powerful partners for reading, *Reading Today, 20,* 6–7.

Jukes, I., Dosaj, A., & Macdonald, B. (2000). *New savvy: Building information literacy in the classroom* (2nd ed.). Walnut Creek, CA: AltaMira.

Kagan, S. (1994). *Cooperative learning.* San Diego, CA: Moore Data Management Services.

Katz, S., & Kohl, H. (2002, December 9). Banish bilingual education policy in CA. *Nation, 275,* 6.

Kay, R. E. (2002, October 17). Children need less school, more playtime. Retrieved October 20, 2002, from the *Philadelphia Inquirer,* www.philly.com/mld/philly.

Kay, R. E. (2002, September 4). Helping poor readers. Retrieved September 6, 2002, from www.nytimes.com.

Kessler, R. (2000). *The Soul of education: Helping students find connection, compassion, and character at school.* Alexandria, VA: Association for Supervision and Curriculum Development.

Klassen-Endrizzi, C. (2000). Exploring our literacy beliefs with families. *Language Arts, 78*(1), 62–70.

Kloss, H. (1998). *The American bilingual tradition.* Washington, DC and McHenry, IL: ERIC Clearinghouse on Languages and Linguistics and Delta Systems.

Kohn, A. (2000). *The Case against standardized testing: Raising the scores, ruining the schools.* Portsmouth, NH: Heinemann.

Kohn, A. (2002). The 500-pound gorilla. *Phi Delta Kappan,* 113–119.

Krashen, S. (1993). *The power of reading.* Englewood, CO: Libraries Unlimited.

Krashen, S. (1996). *Under attack: The case against bilingual education.* Culver City, CA: Language Education Associates.

Krashen, S. (1999). *Condemned without a trial: Bogus arguments against bilingual education.* Portsmouth, NH: Heinemann.

Krashen, S. (2003). Bilingual is best. Retrieved February 26, 2003, from www.thedailyoklahoman.com.

Langer, E. J. (1997). *The power of mindful learning.* Cambridge, MA: Perseus Books.

L'Engle, M. (1972). *A circle of quiet.* Colorado Springs, CO: WaterBrook Press.

Letter to the Editor. (November 24, 2002). Retrieved November 26, 2002, from the *San Francisco Chronicle.*

Levine, M. (2002). *A mind at a time.* New York: Simon & Schuster.

Lockwood, A. T. (1996). Caring, community, and personalization: Strategies to combat the Hispanic dropout problem. *Advances in Hispanic Education, 1.* Washington, DC: U.S. Department of Education.

Louden, J. (2000). *The comfort queen's guide to life: Create all that you need with just what you've got.* New York: Harmony Books.

Macedo, D. (1997). An anti-method pedagogy. In J. W. Fraser, D. Macedo, T. McKinnon, & W. T. Stokes (Eds.), *Mentoring the mentor: A critical dialogue with Paulo Freire* (Vol. 60, pp. 1–9). New York: Peter Lang Publishing, Inc.

McIntyre, E., Kyle, D., Moore, G., Sweazy, R. A., & Greer, S. (2001). Linking home and school through family visits. *Language Arts, 78*(3), 264–272.

McNergney, R. F., & Herbert, J. M. (2001). *Foundations of education: The challenge of professional practice* (3rd ed.). Boston: Allyn and Bacon.

McQuillan, J. (1998). *The literacy crisis: False claims, real solutions.* Portsmouth, NH: Heinemann.

McQuillan, J., & Au, J. (2001). The effect of print access on reading frequency. *Reading Psychology, 22,* 225–248.

Meeks, L. L., & Austin, C. J. (2003). *Literacy in the secondary English classroom: Strategies for teaching the way kids learn.* Boston: Allyn and Bacon.

Mertens, D. (1998). *Research methods in education and psychology: Integrating diversity with quantitative and qualitative approaches.* Thousand Oaks, CA: Sage Publications, Inc.

Meyers, R. (1999). Spiders, rats, and transformation. *Primary Voices K–6, 8*(2).

Miller, J. P. (2000). *Education and the soul: Toward a spiritual curriculum.* Albany, NY: State University of New York Press.

Moll, L. C. (2000). Inspired by Vygotsky: Ethnographic experiments in education. In C. D. Lee & P. Smagorinsky (Eds.), *Vygotskian perspectives on literacy research: Constructing meaning through collaborative inquiry* (pp. 256–268). New York: Cambridge University Press.

Mora, J. K., Wink, J., & Wink, D. (2001, Fall). Dueling models of dual language instruction: A critical review of the literature and program implementation guide. *Bilingual Research Journal, 25*(4), 435–460.

Morgan, G. (1998). *Images of organization.* Thousand Oaks, CA: Sage Publications.

Morrison, T. G., Jacobs, J. S., & Swinyard, W. R. (1999). Do teachers who read personally use recommended literacy practices in their classrooms? *Reading Research and Instruction, 38,* 81–100.

Moustafa, M. (2002). Foundations for universal literacy. In C. Weaver (Ed.) *Reading Process and Practice* (3rd ed.). Portsmouth, NH: Heinemann.

Nash, G. (2002). Kids who read real books. Retrieved May 12, 2002 from www.latimes.com.

Neuman, S. (2001a). *Access to print: Problems, consequences, and day one instructional solutions.* Washington, DC: White House Summit on Early Childhood Cognitive Development Department of Education.

Neuman, S. (2001b). No Child Left Behind speech. Retrieved November 9, 2002, from www.susanohanian.org/atrocity_fetch.php?id=152.

Nieto, S. (1999). *The light in their eyes: Creating multicultural learning.* New York: Teachers College Press.

Nieto, S. (2000). *Affirming diversity: The sociopolitical context of multicultural education* (3rd ed.). White Plains, NY: Addison Wesley Longman, Inc.

Noddings, N. (1992). *The challenge to care in schools: An alternative approach to education.* New York: Teachers College Press.

Noddings, N. (1995). Teaching themes of care. *Phi Delta Kappan, 76*(9), 675–679.

Norton, L. D. (1996). *Hawk flies above: Journey to the heart of the sandhills.* New York: Picador.

Ohanian, S. (2002). *What happened to recess and why are our children struggling in kindergarten?* New York: McGraw-Hill.

Ohanian, S. (2003). Atrocities. Retrieved March 15, 2003, from www.susanohanian.org/atrocities.html.

Palmer, P. J. (1993). *To know as we are known: Education as a spiritual journey.* New York: HarperCollins.

Palmer, P. J. (1998). *The courage to teach: Exploring the inner landscape of a teacher's life.* San Francisco: Jossey-Bass Publisher.

Pataray-Ching, J., & Roberson, M. (2002, July). Misconceptions about a curriculum-as-inquiry framework. *Language Arts, 79*(6), 498–505.

Pipher, M. (1996). *The shelter of each other: Rebuilding our families.* New York: Ballantine Books.

Prawat, R. S. (2002, June/July). Dewey and Vygotsky viewed through the rearview mirror and dimly at that. *Educational Researcher, 31*(5), 16–20.

Putney, L. G., Green, J., Dixon, C., Durán, R., & Yeager, B. (2000). Consequential progressions: Exploring collective-individual development in a bilingual classroom. In C. D. Lee & P. Smagorinsky (Eds.), *Vygotskian perspectives on literacy research: Constructing meaning through collaborative inquiry* (pp. 86–126). New York: Cambridge University Press.

Quindlen, A. (1998). *How reading changed my life.* New York: The Ballantine Publishing Group.

Ramírez, J. D., Yuen, S. D., & Ramey, D. R. (1991). *Final report: Longitudinal study of structured English immersion strategy, early-exit and late-exit transitional bilingual education programs for language-minority children. Executive summary.* San Mateo, CA: Aquirre International.

Reading First, No Child Left Behind. (November 20, 2002). Retrieved November 22, 2002, from www.educationweek.org/ew/ewstory.cfm?slug=12math.h22.

Rosenblatt, L. M. (1978). *The reader, the text, and the poem: The transactional theory of the literary work.* Carbondale, IL: Southern Illinois University Press.

Rossell, C., & Baker, K. (1996). The educational effectiveness of bilingual education. *Research in the Teaching of English, 30,* 7–74.

Ruiz, R. (1984). Orientations in language planning. *NABE Journal, 7,* 15–34.

Scheurman, G. (1998, January). From behaviorist to constructivist teaching. *Social Education, 62*(1), 6–9, 31–34.

Seroussi, K. (2000). *Unraveling the mystery of autism and pervasive developmental disorder: A mother's story of research and recovery.* New York: Simon & Schuster.

Shin, F., & Krashen, S. (1999). Do people appreciate the benefits of advanced first language development? Attitudes towards continuing first language development after "transition." In S. Krashen, L. Tse, & J. McQuillan (Eds.), *Heritage language development* (pp. 89–94). Culver City, CA: Language Education Associates.

Sirotnik, K. A. (1983). What you see is what you get—consistency, persistency, and mediocrity in classroom. *Harvard Educational Review, 53,* 16–31.

Skutnabb-Kangas, T. (1988). Resource power and autonomy through discourse in conflict—a Finnish migrant school strike in Sweden. In T. Skutnabb-Kangas & J. Cummins (Eds.), *Minority education: From shame to struggle* (pp. 251–277). Clevedon, England: Multilingual Matters.

Skutnabb-Kangas, T. (1998). Human rights and language wrongs: The future for diversity. *Language Sciences, Special Issue, "Language Rights," 20*(1), 5–27.

Skutnabb-Kangas, T. (2000). *Linguistic genocide in education—or worldwide diversity and human rights?* Mahwah, NJ: Lawrence Erlbaum Associates.

Smith, F. (1998). *The book of learning and forgetting.* New York: Teacher College Press.

Smith, K., & Hudelson, S. (2001). The NCTE Reading Initiative: Politics, pedagogy, and possibilities. *Language Arts, 79*(1), 29–38.

Spencer, J. N. (2001–2002, Winter). Thought and action. *The NEA National Education Association Journal, XVII*(2), 93–100.

Tomlin, E. W. F. (1963). *The Western philosophers.* New York: Perennial Library.

Tse, L. (1997, December 17). A bilingual helping hand. *Los Angeles Times,* p. B7.

Tse, L. (2001). *Why don't they learn English? Separating fact from fallacy in the U.S. language debate.* New York: Teachers College Press.

Veltman, C. (1988). *The future of the Spanish language in the United States.* Washington, DC: Hispanic Policy Development Project.

Vygotsky, L. S. (1978). *Mind in society: The development of higher psychological processes.* Cambridge, MA: MIT Press.

Vygotsky, L. S. (1986). *Thought and language.* Cambridge, MA: MIT Press.

Waggoner, D. (1995, November). Are current home speakers of non-English languages learning English? *Numbers and Needs, 5.*

Willig, A. C. (1985). A meta-analysis of selected studies of the effectiveness of bilingual education. *Review of Educational Research, 55,* 269–317.

Wilson-Keenan, J., Solsken, J., & Willett, J. (2001). Troubling stories: Valuing productive tensions in collaborating with families. *Language Arts, 78*(6), 520–528.

Wink, D. (1998). *Bilingual immersion: Variables for language minority student success,* submitted in partial satisfaction of the requirements for the degree of Master of Arts in Education (Bilingual/Crosscultural) at California State University, Sacramento, Spring 1998.

Wink, J. (1991). Immersion Confusion. *TESOL Matters, 1*(6), 10.

Wink, J. (2000). *Critical pedagogy: Notes from the real world* (2nd ed.). New York: Addison Wesley Longman.

Wink, J. (2001). Finding the freedom to teach and learn, and live. In W. Goodman (Ed.), *Living (and teaching) in an unjust world: New perspectives on multicultural education.* Portsmouth, NH: Heinemann.

Wink, J., & Putney, L. (2000). Turning transformative principles into practice: Strategies for English-dominant teachers in a multilingual context. In J. V. and R. A. DeVillar (Ed.), *The power of two languages 2000: Effective dual-language use across the curriculum* (pp. 175–185). New York: McGraw-Hill School Division.

Wink, J., & Putney, L. (2002). *A vision of Vygotsky.* Boston: Allyn and Bacon.

Wink, J., & students. (1977, Fall). Those people: You know who they are. *Multicultural Education, 5*(1), 40–44.

Wolfe, P., & Poynor, L. (2001). Politics and the pendulum: An alternative understanding of the case of whole language as educational innovation. *Educational Researcher, 30*(1), 15–20.

Wong Fillmore, L. (1991). When learning a second language means losing the first. *Early Childhood Research Quarterly, 6,* 323–346.

INDEX